(NOT) KEEPING UP WITH OUR PARENTS

(NOT) KEEPING UP WITH OUR PARENTS

The Decline of the Professional Middle Class

Nan Mooney

BEACON PRESS, BOSTON

Beacon Press
25 Beacon Street
Boston, Massachusetts 02108–2892
www.beacon.org

Beacon Press books
are published under the auspices of
the Unitarian Universalist Association of Congregations.

11 10 09 08   8 7 6 5 4 3 2 1

This book is printed on acid-free paper that meets the uncoated paper
ANSI/NISO specifications for permanence as revised in 1992.

Composition by Wilsted & Taylor Publishing Services

Library of Congress Cataloging-in-Publication Data

Mooney, Nan
  (Not) keeping up with our parents : the decline of the professional
middle class / Nan Mooney.
    p. cm.
  Includes bibliographical references and index.
  ISBN 978-0-8070-1138-6 (alk. paper)
  1. Professional employees—United States. 2. Middle class—United
States—Economic conditions. 3. College graduates—United States—
Economic conditions—21st century. I. Title.

HD8038.U5M66 2008
330.9730086'22—dc22   2007038364

CONTENTS

PREFACE

These days, when my college-educated, gainfully employed thirty-something friends and I get together, we talk about money. Not how much we paid for that new Jetta or Prius, not the house we're thinking of buying or where we're going to spend our end-of-the-year bonuses. We talk about our inadequate health insurance and whether we can afford it, about how to juggle credit card payments and crushing student loans, how to both work and pay for child care or whether we feel we can afford to have children at all.

I'll be honest: this wasn't the life I'd expected. I grew up as the only child in a dual-income, middle-class household in the 1970s. My father was a sales representative for a textbook publishing company and my mother was a third-grade teacher. Even at the height of their careers, even with investments taken into account, their combined income never crossed over into the six figures. Yet we lived in a comfortable four-bedroom house in a comfortable residential neighborhood in Seattle. I attended private schools from kindergarten on and most years we took at least one family vacation.

We weren't rolling in it but we weren't scrambling either. Most of the families I knew were the same. They ranged from middle to upper class, though as a child I had only the vaguest sense which was which. There seemed little outward difference between those families headed by doctors or architects, stockbrokers or college professors. Everyone owned a house and a car. Some of my peers went to private colleges, others went to the University of Washington, some vacationed in Hawaii, others on the Oregon Coast.

My parents worked hard and spent sensibly, fleshing out their incomes with conservative investments in the stock market and conscientiously saving for retirement. Both received generous health benefits through their employers. They carried mortgage debt but nothing else, and paid my college tuition in full with the help of a small scholarship. Beyond stressing that I should get the best possible education, they encouraged me to choose a career that I loved above one that would be financially lucrative. I always assumed that, if I followed their model, I wouldn't have to worry about money. That my life would unfold along the same "not wealthy but comfortable" lines as my parents' had.

But the sort of family I grew up in seems near extinction these days, a middle-class family who can support themselves on a pair of middle-class jobs. Not only do many of today's educated middle-class professionals worry that they won't exceed their parents when it comes to financial success, they fear they can't even keep up with the middle-class, and often the working-class, lifestyles their parents modeled for them just decades ago. These days, the middle class faces a new and newly challenging set of financial choices, choices that inform not just our current economic lives but also the kind of value systems we will embody and pass down to our own children. The old standards still apply—buy a house and two cars and take your kids to Disneyland—but now there are new rules our generation hadn't anticipated. You also have to pay your own health insurance, save for your own retirement, navigate spiraling housing costs, and worry about losing your job to outsourcing or downsizing. It can quickly become too much for anyone—individual or family—to withstand on their own.

As members of the educated professional middle class, we've always fallen into categories like "full of potential" and "capable of changing the world," not broke or strapped or scared out of our minds. But somehow in the course of doing everything right—and by that I mean embodying the American dream, from having the privilege of going to college to getting what would widely be considered a good job—something seems to have gone awry.

Take me, for instance. I'm not disenfranchised, nor am I underprivileged in any way. I have a private school education and split my college time between two fancy liberal arts colleges. I've written three books and work as a teacher and freelance writer. Yet I live month to month, cent to cent, in a rented room in New York with nothing more valuable than my laptop to call my own. I'm thirty-seven years old and only recently managed to stash a few hundred dollars in a savings account—most of which I've already tapped to pay my health insurance—never mind opening an IRA or 401(k). I would like to think about moving to a more affordable city than Manhattan and having a child in the next year, things I consider less extravagant dreams than standard life choices. But the cost of either is almost too daunting to consider.

I've tried consulting the mass of financial-planning books for help, and they all tell me to forgo my daily latte or trip to the mall and tuck away a few dollars for my future instead. But I don't have a daily latte habit. I am spending more than I make not because I'm immature and frivolous but because just living has become prohibitively expensive and I flat out don't earn enough money to support myself.

I know via the thrum of hushed conversations that my position is far from unique. Who are the inhabitants of this new educated professional economic limbo? We are those people who exited college or graduate school two, five, ten, twenty years ago and didn't hop on the corporate fast track or join the high end of one of the professions—law, medicine, finance. We're the educators, the journalists, the publishers, the artists, the therapists, the architects, the environmental scientists, the television reporters, the legal aid attorneys, the graphic designers, the social workers, and the nonprofit employees. We range from people like me who have trouble paying the bills to those who can meet basic expenses but still feel shut out of middle-class expectations like owning homes or providing college educations for their children.

We are meant to be the poster boys and girls for the American success story. But in recent years, that story has changed. The financially strapped have a new face, one that's popping up in places we aren't accustomed to seeing it. That face has a diploma on the wall and a "good job" or "serious accomplishments" in its back pocket.

In this book, you'll share in the intimate financial lives of scores of the professional middle class, and I believe their stories will resonate for you as deeply as they did for me. We will trace how and why today's educated professionals are experiencing a "middle-class squeeze" more profound and paralyzing than the struggles experienced by preceding generations and discuss how—as individuals and as a community—we can work to combat it.

1

THE NEW REALITY

Since the 1950s, what we've considered the American experience —be it sock hopping, suburban living, or SUV buying—has been largely dictated by the professional middle class. In her 1989 social critique, *Fear of Falling: The Inner Life of the Middle Class,* Barbara Ehrenreich defined this mainstream population in terms of education, occupation, lifestyle, and tastes, but also in terms of income. "Middle class couples," she wrote, "earn enough for home ownership in a neighborhood inhabited by other members of their class; college educations for the children; and such enriching experiences as vacation trips, psychotherapy, fitness training, summer camp and the consumption of 'culture' in various forms."[1]

This thriving middle class didn't develop by accident. It emerged with the introduction of government and social policies designed to lift the country out of the Great Depression and sustain economic health in the postwar era. By the 1950s, a combination of social programs including Social Security, unemployment insurance, the GI Bill, and federal housing loans helped middle-class salaries stretch. Employers supplied health insurance and pensions. A surge in suburban building made housing widely accessible. You no longer had to be a doctor or a businessman to afford a two-story colonial with a dishwasher and a color TV. For a white male supporting a family— the typical middle-class profile at the time—it was possible to work in an array of professions whereby you didn't necessarily get rich, but you could count on being fairly comfortable. A house, a job, a car or two in the garage, a fun summer vacation, these were absolute indicators of middle-class success.

Economic realities have undergone seismic shifts since our parents' and grandparents' generations. Education and housing cost more. Incomes have leveled off for all but a small minority. Employers and the government supply few social safety nets, cutting health insurance and pensions and replacing them with new "benefits" like 401(k)s and health savings plans that benefit only those with income to set aside. But many of those middle-class expectations set in place back in the '50s still hold.

Alongside our schooling in philosophy and economics, today's college-educated professionals have been conditioned to see ourselves as among the financially stable, mainstream haves. Many of us attended what are considered strong academic institutions. Others come from families with comfortable financial backgrounds. Our childhood friends, our college roommates, the couple we met at that holiday party are those same lawyers and financiers who've hit the financial jackpot, driving multiple Mercedeses and buying $2 million starter homes. We know we aren't like them. We've aspired to different career and financial goals, those more rooted in education, the arts, or public service. But, given our often-similar backgrounds and educations, it's clear we aren't entirely unlike them either. This rising and dramatic economic inequality among college-educated professionals, leaving so many of us to struggle while a select few enter the strata of the "superrich," was not supposed to be part of the package.

When we read about the middle-class squeeze, we tend to think blue collar—the machinist who used to make $25 an hour now making $15, the vocationally trained worker whose job just got cut. But what about the social worker who makes $30,000 a year, the environmental scientist who makes $40,000, the college professor who makes $50,000? The rules of the game have changed. The educated professional middle-class experience no longer guarantees two cars in every driveway, or even the driveway itself. Instead we face relatively low-paying jobs in fields requiring a high-cost education, increasing mortgages, student-loan and credit card debt, less employer or government help with health care, retirement, education, and child care, and an overall higher cost of living. As the gap between the rich and the middle-class widens, a huge segment of that once comfortable center section is finding that reality means plummeting financial and emotional security and lack of control over our lives.

DIFFICULT TIMES

Diana, thirty-six, is a licensed psychologist with a PhD in clinical psychology. She splits her four-day workweek between two jobs: maintaining her own private practice and working as an assessment director for a nonprofit where she supervises and helps place school counselors. Though her income varies, she typically earns about $35,000 a year. Her husband, Byron, who has a BA in engineering, makes $40,000 as a technical writer for a patent attorney. They're both contract workers, getting paid on a per-project or per-client basis, so the size of their paychecks fluctuates from month to month. On months when the money coming in doesn't stretch quite far enough, they turn to credit cards to pay bills and buy groceries. They're currently carrying $17,000 in credit card debt.

Before the birth of their son five years ago, Diana worked eighty-hour weeks as a clinician at a major research hospital in Cincinnati. "I was making $38,000 a year and working nonstop," she recalls. "The administration promised me raises and promotions, but they never came through. Instead, they demoted me when I came back from maternity leave. So I cut back to part-time work and opened my own practice."

The couple now has two children, a five-year-old son and a five-month-old daughter, plus a third on the way in the spring.

"This child was unplanned," Diana admits. "And I'm terrified how we're going to afford her. We haven't even recovered from the financial hit we took on my last maternity leave."

Both Diana's previous pregnancies were difficult and she anticipates having to cut back her work hours as this one advances. In addition, her son suffers from a kidney disease that requires occasional hospital stays. The family has health insurance through Byron's job but any days her son spends in the hospital are days Diana has to take off work.

Up until a month ago, the family paid $1,200 a month for child care, which included preschool for her son and day care for the baby. But when the day care shut down—the family who owned it sold the building to real estate developers—Diana and Byron decided the most economically feasible choice was to keep the kids home, hopefully until her son starts kindergarten in the fall.

"I'm only in the office two days a week and my husband works at home, so it's the best option right now," she explains. "We're saving on the child care bill, but we're also getting less work done, which means less money coming in. Until I had kids, I had no idea how insanely expensive child care would be. We'll see how long we can keep this up."

Though they own their house in a Cincinnati suburb—a fixer-upper they bought six years ago and "put back together piece by piece all by ourselves"—it currently contains very little equity. They pay $1,150 a month on a thirty-year fixed-rate mortgage and two years ago they maxed out their home equity line of credit to purchase the condominium that houses Diana's office space, plus two offices she rents out to other therapists. The fifteen-year mortgage on that property plus condo fees come to $750 a month. Diana also still pays $450 a month in student loans, a graduated plan that will go up to $550 next year, when their new baby is six months old.

"We're definitely not doing as well as my working-class parents did," Diana tells me. "My father owned his own garage for thirty years and my mother worked for him. They raised seven kids on what he made, and though we didn't live extravagantly, we never wanted for anything. I was the first one in my family to go to college."

Diana and Byron have no savings left to raid and no equity, except for the $10,000 invested in Diana's office space. Though she had a 401(k) from her hospital job, Diana cashed it out last year to float them through her maternity leave. Neither she nor Byron have room for raises or promotion in their current jobs, save an annual cost-of-living increase, so the only way to boost their income is for Diana to add hours in her private practice.

"I feel like we've cut every corner we can cut," she says. "We don't take vacations. We never go out. Right now, I just keep my fingers crossed that nothing breaks. We need a new roof and new tires for the car. And we're going to get hit hard by taxes this year, because we haven't been able to set anything aside."

She wonders if she and Byron made some sort of crucial mistake along the way. If they should have sought out more lucrative and less personally rewarding careers, moved to a bigger or smaller city, invested less of their money in real estate or more. She sees neighbors buying a third car and remodeling their kitchens and worries what it will be like for her children growing up among kids who have everything, when they're struggling each week just to pay their bills.

"I'm scared," she tells me, her voice cracking. "I'm scared we'll never be able to retire. I'm scared we won't be covered for health care. I'm scared we won't be able to send our kids to college. We've never had much, but before I always felt like we were doing our time. We were working our way toward a more comfortable future. That doesn't seem true anymore. At this point, I see no way out at all."

In the past few decades, this country has seen a dramatic economic polarization between educated professionals, dividing them into the very few very rich, and the many like Diana and Byron whose financial lives are chronically unstable and insecure. We're discovering that college or even graduate school is no longer enough. Having a full-time job is no longer enough. You can do everything you're supposed to do to "make it" in America and still wind up scrambling and scared.

The financial insecurity that's come to haunt so many educated professional middle-class lives provides a powerful wake-up call about the extent of compromised choices in America today. It's pushing us away from many of the lower-paying public service professions that are essential to a well-functioning society like teaching, social work, and careers in the nonprofit sector, it's making us question whether we can afford to have families, and it's increasing the number of economic crises—like bankruptcies and home foreclosures—striking the middle-class population. Such insecurity obliterates the standard fallback that if only every worker had access to an education and a job they too could achieve the American dream. And it speaks to a shift that runs far deeper than just our financial state.

THE ECONOMICS

Why this dramatic change? The economics are simple and well documented. We're earning less and having to pay for more. Earnings for college graduates have remained stagnant for the past five years, but the costs of housing, health care, and education have all risen faster than inflation. The share of family income devoted to "fixed costs" like housing, child care, health insurance, and taxes has climbed from 53 percent to 75 percent in the past two decades.[2]

Though a college degree still earns you a bigger paycheck than a high school one, the price of a four-year education has grown increasingly dear. Between 2000 and 2004, tuition rose 32 percent at four-year public colleges and 21 percent at private colleges, requiring the majority of students to take out loans to fund their education.[3]

Once we hit the workforce, those rising numbers do an about-face. Real earnings for those with four-year college degrees have flattened out since 2003, not even rising to keep pace with inflation.[4] Graduates quickly discover that many careers requiring a high level of education don't come with equally high-level salaries. Even the money we do make tends to arrive under tenuous circumstances, with middle-class incomes subject to the dramatic peaks and dives economists refer to as income volatility. A typical annual drop has gone from 25 percent to as high as 40 percent. That means a couple like Byron and Diana, earning $75,000, could dip to just $45,000. In a single year. To add discomfort to discomfort, long-term unemployment is also booming and the long-term unemployed are older, better educated, and more likely to be professionals than the general unemployed population.[5]

When it comes to supporting a family, those numbers start climbing once again. Raising one child through age eighteen costs a middle-income family roughly $237,000. Child care alone runs, on average, between $3,803 and $13,480 a year per child, with accredited care facilities charging as much as $5,000 more per child than their nonaccredited counterparts. And despite the surge in dual-income households since the 1970s, there's been no accompanying double up on discretionary income. Once we cover all the major fixed-cost expenses, we're now relying on two incomes to support a lifestyle that used to require one.[6]

Even owning your own home, once the cornerstone of the middle-class existence, has become a shaky proposition. Housing prices have shot up—in 2005 they rose six times as fast as household incomes in most major metropolitan areas.[7] And though more of us may own homes than we used to, we own a whole lot less of them. We're buying with the help of steep mortgages—fixed rate, adjustable rate, interest only—then pulling out the money as fast as we poured it in, refinancing to the tune of $900 billion in 2006 alone, almost triple the $333 billion we took out between 2001 and 2003.[8]

Given the increased cost of just about everything, it's no shock we're sliding deeper into debt. Only 18 percent of middle-class families report having at least three months of their income in savings to ride out an economic downturn.[9] Such bare-bones living means we have no choice but to borrow to bridge any unforeseen gaps, turning to credits cards to cover everything from home repairs to medical expenses to college tuition. The level of U.S. household debt has risen consistently over the course of the century, climbing from just 33.2 percent of disposable income in 1949 to 102.2 percent in 2000, and to 131.8 percent in 2005, making it the highest ever measured in our national history.[10]

To top it off, government and businesses have stepped aside and decided we should be "personally responsible" for covering the rising costs of health care and retirement. Health care premiums for families have increased 87 percent since 2000. (Remember that wages for college-educated workers remained stagnant for that same period.) As of 2005, only 60 percent of the population had employer-provided health insurance, down from 69 percent in 2000.[11]

As for retirement, employee-contribution plans like 401(k)s are replacing employer-provided defined-benefit plans at warp speed. With scarcely enough money to manage our current finances, we're having a hard time raiding our personal pockets to put away for the future. The median 401(k) holdings—among the 60 percent of workers who even have access and contribute to a retirement account—is just under $20,000. A sobering figure when you consider that, after factoring in longer lives and rising health care costs, experts say most people will need 75 to 100 percent of their annual incomes in order to comfortably retire.[12]

THE VALUES

Alarming as these numbers may be, they only tell a fraction of the story. Such persistent, collective economic stress has profound psychological effects. Worrying about money keeps us up nights, it rips holes in our relationships, and becomes our greatest source of uncertainty, tension, and fear. We can begin to doubt our career choices and even our value systems. We grow confused about how to walk that increasingly tricky line between wanting to have enough money without making the pursuit of money our ultimate goal. In a country whose motto has become "The more you make, the more you're worth," for those adhering to an alternative value system, it's a tough road.

It hasn't always been like this. The United States was founded as a nation of iconoclasts and pioneers. Even when there were no more literal trails to blaze, "the land of opportunity" still made room for a different sort of expansion. One could choose to keep up with the Jones's, but one could also chart a less lucrative alternative route—such as being a social worker or a high school chemistry teacher—and still raise a family, count on reliable health care, and comfortably retire.

Ironically, over the past several decades our society, so proudly grounded in individuality, has crushed this notion of a personal frontier. We've gone corporate, meaning that the institutional good supersedes the good of individual members. Meaning that it's acceptable for the rich to get richer and the poor to get poorer as long as the gross income keeps climbing. In the process, we've generated a state of income inequality unseen in this country since the gilded excesses of the Roaring Twenties. And we show no sign of slowing down. In order for our current market-driven economy to thrive, those who partake must spend, not save, even if it means spending beyond their means. If Americans today began saving only 5 percent more of their incomes, their annual spending would drop by $500 billion.[13] Both government and corporations have every reason to urge us to buy, buy, buy—whether it's cars, houses, clothing, or health insurance—and none to facilitate our storing up for the future. Responsibility, moderation, and thrift may be old-fashioned watchwords, but they don't grind the gears that run the machine.

A society can't help but disintegrate under such a one-sided value system. If fortune trickles down, misfortune trickles down even faster. Time and energy focused on money, especially the lack of it, takes time and energy away from healthy families and communities. A struggling educated professional middle class doesn't just impact the middle. We are the teachers, the social workers, the environmentalists, the writers and reporters who weave together much of the social fabric of this country. Yet we're already seeing disturbing trends in young people shying away from public interest and service careers because of legitimate fears about how they will manage financially. A 2006 study by the U.S. Public Interest Research Group found that 23 percent of public college graduates and 38 percent of private college graduates attempting to live on a starting teacher's salary would have an unmanageable level of debt. For social workers, such debt would be unmanageable for 37 percent of public college and 55 percent of private college graduates.[14] Political activism, taking an interest in the even littler guy, an abiding sense of financial and societal generosity—all of these suffer when money becomes our guiding star.

Of course, financial hardship is nothing new in our society. The poor, the working class, and what sociologists Katherine Newman and Victor Tan Chen call "the missing class"—those people sandwiched between the poor and middle classes—are in a truly precarious position, as they don't have even the few safety nets many in the middle class possess.[15] But the struggles of today's educated professional middle class can and should serve as a bellwether. In exploring the educated professional middle-class experience, we're addressing that segment of society that did everything we were supposed to do in order to "make it" in America. We have the college, even graduate, degrees. We have jobs—good jobs—and make salaries that on the surface look like solid middle-class salaries. There is already serious cause for alarm in an affluent nation with a poverty rate as high as America has today. But when even we, the ones who had every opportunity, are struggling for financial security, you have a society that can't possibly sustain itself over the long run.

WHO ARE WE?

There's no pre-coined term to describe that financial limbo where so many members of the educated professional middle class now reside.

I have one friend who refers to us as nuppies—non–upwardly mobile urban professionals—a category that encompasses all those members of the educated professional middle class who aren't solely financially driven but still have an enormous amount to contribute. The description seems apt, but the label is a bit ungainly. So, for simplicity's sake, I've decided to stick with calling us the educated professional middle class.

Of course, real people don't fit into neat sociological compartments. Their incomes and expenses rise and fall. They have varying goals, demands, desires, and definitions of success throughout the course of their lives. Nevertheless, it is possible to loosely define this segment of society in terms of education, occupation, income, and lifestyle and tastes, categories Barbara Ehrenreich set out to describe the professional middle class nearly thirty years ago.

Education—The middle class is unique in that it creates, rather than inheriting, its success. If you're born poor and do nothing, you stay poor. If you're born rich and do nothing, you usually stay rich. But if you're born middle class, you have to start pedaling if you want to stay in place. The first step toward the promised land of middle-class opportunity and prosperity is to get an education. For the purposes of this book, those in the educated professional middle class have at least a four-year college degree.

Occupation—Members of the educated professional middle class work in white-collar or creative professions, jobs that require an education but fall outside the scope of big-money careers in fields like finance, medicine, or law. This group is highly concentrated in, but by no means confined to, creative, intellectual, educational, and service or nurturing fields—a vast array of professions that tend to provide more prestige or moral sustenance than financial reward.

Income—This one is particularly tricky. A dollar stretches differently depending on where you live. Making $60,000 in Manhattan barely gets you a rental apartment while in rural Iowa it would have you sitting pretty. And what do we do about those households whose incomes can swing dramatically from year to year? If you made $70,000 last year in a job with high income volatility, are you more or less secure than someone with a guaranteed $50,000 a year?

According to the 2005 Census, those households that fall into the middle three quintiles of earnings make between $19,179 and $91,705. In their examination of middle-class bankruptcy, *The Two-Income Trap,* Harvard law professor Elizabeth Warren and coauthor Amelia Warren Tyagi widen the field to include households earning $20,000–$100,000. Because there are many factors beyond income that can contribute to our sense of economic stability, I'm inclined to keep the boundaries here particularly loose. Most individuals mentioned in this book earn between $30,000 and $70,000 a year, with couples earning as much as a combined $100,000.[16]

Lifestyle and tastes—What are our expectations as members of the educated professional middle class? What's a fair definition of financial security and how has it changed since our parents' generation? Most members of the educated professional middle class aspire to certain indicators of prosperity—to be able to afford a house and a car, to take modest vacations, to educate their children, and to know their health care and retirement are covered. We're hardly immune to the consumer society surrounding us and its efforts to blur the line between want and need, but second homes in St. Bart's and multiple BMWs have never been part of the middle-class package. Though we may fantasize about a luxury lifestyle, most members of the educated professional middle class aim toward something far more grounded—a degree of comfort, stability, and financial freedom in our lives.

Of course, few members of the educated professional middle class balance in the actual middle, that sweet and secure fulcrum on an economist's line graph. On the one hand, we're grappling with a number of the issues traditionally assigned to the working poor—inadequate or nonexistent health insurance, rising debt, difficulty paying for child care and education, lack of savings, and the need for government or organizational support to make ends meet. Many of us live in a constant state of economic vulnerability, meaning we could be ruined by one unforeseen financial blow like job loss, divorce, or illness. These are the sorts of blows that have long proved devastating to the working poor, but now they've become incredibly damaging to those residing in the supposedly safe zone of the middle class as well.

On the other hand, we're still very much aligned with the educated well-to-do. We have college degrees, white-collar professions, and aspirations to middle-class comforts like houses, cars, and travel. We share similar tastes and backgrounds. It's not upbringing or education but career choices and value systems that tend to distinguish us from our wealthier peers. Though we're neither rich nor poor, at any given time we can brush up against either boundary. Understanding this tug-of-war is critical to understanding the chronic uncertainty that characterizes the educated middle-class experience.

OUR STORIES

If you want a true understanding of how a society operates, you don't just chart its economic statistics. You walk right up and ask people about their lives. The stories included here are based on over a hundred interviews I conducted with members of today's educated professional middle class. We discussed intimate financial details, from their monthly rent or mortgage payments to the money fights they have with their spouses, to the realization that, despite an education, a job, and "unlimited potential," they still foresee a lifetime worrying about whether they'll be able to provide for themselves and their families.

Interviews ranged in length from a half hour to two to three hours. Some were conducted over the phone, others over kitchen counters or coffee shop tables. Though I wish there wasn't such a sense of shame attached to our money struggles, I respect that most people I spoke to didn't want their private financial details shared with the world. To that end, I've changed names and identifying characteristics of all those mentioned here, but all are actual individuals, there are no "composites."

There's no such thing as a typical member of the educated professional middle class. We cover a wide range of professions, backgrounds, family set-ups, and goals for the future. I recruited anyone with a college education who went into a white-collar profession (though some supplemented with blue-collar jobs like construction or waiting tables). Interview subjects came through friends and acquaintances, online bulletin boards, groups I addressed in other contexts, and the Web sites for my previous books.

I made no effort to confine my sample by age—as long as they were old enough to have graduated college and young enough to remain in the workforce—and interviewees ranged from early twenties to mid-sixties, though most fell in the twenty-five to fifty range. Too often, rising financial pressures are considered a problem for the eighteen to thirty-four set, as if once you're thirty-five, the issue has been permanently resolved one way or the other. But, especially as we're going to college and graduate school later, marrying later, and having kids later, often for financial reasons, financial hardship is not a phenomenon exclusive to the twentysomething crowd. In fact, I found that money issues became more pressing to those in their thirties and forties whose financial needs are expanding to cover growing families and whose incomes have leveled off at a less than livable rate.

"As you get older it becomes less okay to admit you're struggling," explained Stella, forty-two, a Brooklyn-based graphic designer. "People just assume you must be doing okay. I've noticed that those who are still having trouble start to go underground about their financial lives. They secretly leave the city because they can't afford to stay. Now is the time you really begin to question your choices. You worry that this is the pinnacle of your life. There will be no more rapid expansion from here. Or, even worse, that you've passed your prime and you didn't even notice it. Life actually won't get any better than it is right now, so you'd better figure out how to make things work."

At twenty-five, being hard up can feel temporary and even a bit romantic. By thirty-five, we understand such financial insecurity as a permanent factor in our lives. This is not a youth problem. It's a life problem.

Those I spoke to came from a variety of family backgrounds, ranging from upper-middle to working class. But no matter what their roots, most people feared they wouldn't be as financially secure as their parents. They also felt tremendous pressure from and guilt toward this previous generation. Most hated the idea of being a financial burden to their families. At the same time, they resented their families' lack of appreciation for the changing economic times. Parents had often voiced the opinion that their grown children's financial troubles stemmed from carelessness or reckless spending. Again and again I heard, "They don't understand how I can be making so much money and still struggling so hard." I also spoke to baby boomers who have an all too real appreciation for today's mounting financial pressures—those grappling with late-career layoffs, rising health care costs, and inadequate retirement savings—making it clear that such struggles are far from just a generational blip.

I spoke mostly to people living in or around large cities and mid-size towns, including a number who'd downsized from the former to the latter for financial reasons. One could argue that moving to remote or rural areas could pare down the cost of living, though in most cases people would also take an accompanying salary cut. But there are numerous nonfinancial reasons why the bulk of the population is drawn to and deserves access to urban centers. They contain the most varied job markets, better schools, richer intellectual and artistic environments, and greater ethnic and cultural diversity.

I also heard from more women than men, I think for two important reasons. First of all, women are more likely to enter less lucrative middle-class professions like teaching, social work, or nonprofit careers, and more likely to be underpaid no matter what their career paths. But many of these women came with families attached: a husband existed out there, too, living the exact same economically stressful life but far less inclined to talk about it. Our society still places especially intense pressure on men to be financially successful and attaches an even bigger black mark to those for whom things are not going well. For men in particular, the message is that economic struggle equals personal failure.

Of course, my sample is, by definition, limited. I only could interview those willing to admit they fell into the struggling educated professional middle-class category. And that's not an easy thing for many who still harbor higher hopes.

"I'm a little concerned that for some of my peers, my proposing that they are having trouble making ends meet could come across as insulting," wrote one recruit about forwarding information on the book to friends. "Even though the situation you describe is clearly very common and would certainly apply to many of them."

Our financial struggles remain a taboo subject even among those doing the struggling. We do have a public voice—we're disproportionately well represented in the media, education, and the arts—but when it comes to airing our private financial details, most members of the educated professional middle class remain uncharacteristically zip-lipped. Perhaps we're ashamed to be so privileged yet not materially successful. After all, many in America define success as making money, and though having actual wealth to flaunt is best, maintaining the pretense of doing well beats admitting to anyone (even yourself) that you're not. Or maybe we keep convincing ourselves that next week, next month, next year things will improve. But things are not getting better. If anything they're getting worse. The income gap in the U.S. keeps widening, with the wealthiest 1 percent of the population receiving the largest share of our national income since 1928. The top 300,000 Americans now enjoy the same amount of income as the bottom 150 million. And as our incomes flounder, our collective debt keeps rising: 2005 was the first year since the Great Depression in which Americans spent more than they earned.[17]

A big part of the problem is that we have no models for how the financially strapped educated professional middle class can or should operate. On TV and in movies, people with our jobs and educations own houses and apartments with nary a mention of the word "mortgage." They wear chic outfits and go out to breakfast, lunch, and dinner. They never have trouble paying a bill. In literature, they're too caught up in internal middle-class angst to care about petty things like financial well-being. If money is addressed at all, it's usually in the form of a character's journey from broke to prosperous that symbolizes triumph, getting it together, mental health, and clarity. Rarely do such anxieties come across as merely a fact of existence. Most of the time, those fictional characters engaged in deeper problems—wrangling with self-doubt and questions of identity— never worry about money at all.

Financial planning and advice books promise that we can create our own financial destinies, that a positive and proactive attitude alone can generate a life of plenty. If we can just begin thinking like rich people, we too can have millionaire minds and bank accounts to match. The corollary is that if we are struggling, that must be our fault too. In essence, our strapped state is all in our minds. The upshot of this isolation is that we're all looking around and thinking—

but never saying—What am I doing wrong? How do other people do it? As one interviewee put it: "How does everyone else manage this, because I'm clearly too stupid to figure it out."

These were exactly the kind of questions bumping around in my own head that propelled me to write this book. But though the stories I heard revealed a great deal, not a single person came forward with a magical answer, that hoped- and prayed-for financial silver bullet. If anything's to improve, we first have to understand that the problems of the educated professional middle class are far more complicated than our individual ignorance or mistakes. This isn't a question of poor financial planning, though that certainly can factor in. It's a widespread sociological phenomenon. Nobody feels comfortable or secure. Everyone has doubts about the choices they've made and the futures they may have sacrificed. And if we're going to start altering our realities, the first thing we have to admit is that something far more powerful than just our individual choices needs to change.

This educated middle-class struggle is embodied in an ongoing clash between our expectations and our actual lives. It begins early, when our ideas about what a college education should provide—opportunity, opportunity, opportunity—bump up against high student debt shouldered so we can enter low-paying careers that require an expensive education. The typical college graduate enters the workplace with a five-figure student loan debt.

This shaky financial start is exacerbated by our career choices, saddling those who enter socially essential fields like teaching, social work, nonprofit work, psychology, journalism, and the arts with a lifetime of being overworked and underpaid. We discover that, far from facilitating the freedom to chart our own exciting, self-defined career paths, today's workplace is replete with layoffs, salary freezes, long hours, and an absence of employer loyalty.

Struggling to provide for a family under such conditions has become a major source of stress for the educated professional middle class. Many find that—far from embracing the full middle-class package—we are being forced to choose between career and children, house and children, retirement and children. Some of us are seriously questioning the wisdom of having children at all. Many of the social freedoms we've won in the past few decades, including the wider acceptance of divorce, single parenthood, and living in blended families, are now being chipped away by tightening financial constraints.

Even as we're juggling higher education costs and lower-paying jobs, both the government and our employers are demanding that individuals pay more for social benefits like health care and retirement. We're floundering under a system designed for a different time, a time when workers stayed with a single employer, when a spouse went into the workplace only in periods of financial duress, and when unemployment was largely, though not always, a temporary state. Many members of today's educated professional middle class assume they will never retire, because they can't foresee saving enough money to cover living expenses and medical costs in their waning years.

Owning your own home has long been the foundation of any middle-class, and most certainly the educated professional middle-class, dream. But skyrocketing housing markets and tighter finances mean many of us struggle to buy, pay off, and maintain what is supposed to be our major financial asset. This housing crisis is changing not just our individual financial situations but the entire shape of our cities as educated professionals flee urban centers in search of a lifestyle they can afford.

Given these escalating financial demands, a complex dance has developed between spending, saving, and debt. Credit has replaced savings as our default safety net. So much of our spending is caught up in fixed expenses that going debt-free would include sacrificing housing, education, child care, or even having children. The credit card industry has learned to exploit our dependence on credit, pushing up interest rates and fees and penalties to make it as difficult as possible to pull ourselves out of the hole once we've tumbled in. And though we increasingly rely upon credit cards and family gifts and loans to keep our heads above water, we're also finding there's a finite limit to the amount of help either can provide.

Of course, money struggles aren't simply a financial issue. They speak volumes about social character and social values. It's part of the American myth that anyone with enough moxie can make it to the big time, that a lack of material success reflects nothing so much as a lack of self-discipline. Members of today's educated professional middle class look around and assume everyone else is somehow making it. They're afraid to let friends and families know their true financial stories for fear they'll be blamed or judged. As long as our economic insecurities remain hidden under this cloak of shame and isolation, we risk fragmenting our communities and ourselves.

One of the gravest mistakes any of us can make is to resign ourselves to our financially insecure state. Our stellar educations may have reneged on many promises, but they have endowed us with the skills and tools to fight back. To that end, I've filled these pages not just with questions about what is happening and why, but also with ideas for how to become proactive both as individuals and as a society. I propose steps we can all take to stop this downward spiral and reignite a sense of social responsibility—from improving government-backed education, health, and child care programs to initiating a shift in values so that our self-worth is no longer defined by our bank account. I've written this book not to blame or complain, but because I want to open up a sense of awareness and possibility, to promote a real dialogue about how we can all invest in a thriving, socially and creatively rich collective future.

2

FROM THE NEW DEAL TO THE NEW ECONOMY

A Short History of the American Middle Class

"We're hemorrhaging money and I don't know how to stop the leak."

"Dealing with finances was always like spinning plates. One unexpected thing thrown in the mix and suddenly it all goes tumbling."

"It's like we're living on the edge of a financial cliff and the tiniest thing could push us off."

"It always feels like I'm just this side of financial catastrophe."

No matter how colorfully they chose to phrase it, the individuals and families I spoke to expressed a level of panic and desperation that seems new to the middle-class experience, a sense of permanently careening out of control. When we first emerge from our college cocoons, many of us are determined to try and avoid financial hardship, but quickly learn that for most of us that attempt will be fruitless.

Perhaps the most striking aspect of this fear consuming so many of us is that it isn't one thing—one tangible, tackle-able thing—but the whole erratic picture, the combination of small problems and large stressors, that has us overwhelmed. One strand of financial stress—increased cost of housing, child care, or health care, or periodic dips in income—we might be able to handle. But being hit by all these economic blows simultaneously is too much, both financially and psychologically. You can't isolate and address them the way a social scientist or researcher would. Instead, one stumble causes another and then another—the mortgage, the credit card company, the biological clock that won't wait for you to pick yourself up and dust yourself off.

This sense of spinning out of control is not a product of our imaginations. Things are more perilous today. But for America's professional middle class, things have not always felt like this. Over the course of the twentieth century, the story of the middle class has traveled from one of comfort and even prosperity to one characterized by financial insecurity and fear.

The story of the middle class has long been the story of mainstream America. The majority of people identify themselves as middle class —according to a Greenberg poll in the mid-1990s, a full 90 percent of those with incomes ranging from $7,000 to $113,000.[1] The spectrum includes those with and without college educations, earning a wide range of salaries.[2]

What do we mean when we say middle class? The government has no official definition—perhaps in support of our guise as a classless society—but one commonly used reference is the median household income, $46,326 in 2005. The Center for American Progress describes the typical middle-class family as a dual-income couple earning between $18,500 and $88,030, those who sit squarely in the middle 60 percent of income distribution. In a 2005 *New York Times* poll on class, the middle three-fifths of respondents had a household income ranging from $30,000 to $100,000.[3] But for most people, membership in the middle class is far more mobile and indistinct than a number preceded by a dollar sign. It's a catchall category housing everyone who's not rich and not poor, the class into which you rise and out of which you can fall. Membership in the middle class is sustained by constant effort and, though it can open a vein of opportunity, that opportunity is by its very nature insecure. Middle-class success—if you do manage to obtain and sustain it—will be rewarded, for historically the middle has also been a leisure class, one providing enough financial comfort that its members can ask more of work than just a paycheck and more of life than just work. Membership buys you the freedom to care about something more meaningful and refined than the working-class daily grind.

To be a member of not just the middle class but the educated professional middle class wraps you in an additional layer of financial protection and social advantage. It's the reign of intellectuals, knowledge workers, and formulators of public opinion and trends. It's opportunity squared. Even Horatio Alger, whose dime-store novels have become synonymous with America's road from rags to riches, was a second-generation Harvard man and a Unitarian minister.[4] But if the educated professional middle class is an elite, it is—as Barbara Ehrenreich wrote in the late 1980s—"an insecure and deeply anxious one."[5] Its grasp on wealth and power is shaky, its susceptibility to personal misfortune and political and economic upheaval disconcertingly high.

As a country, America has long prided itself on sustaining a large and thriving middle class. And from the 1930s until the late 1970s, for the most part we succeeded. But over the past two decades, that middle-class story has undergone a dramatic change. Both traditional middle-class goals and the traditional routes to success have fluctuated, with aspirations growing more vaunted and opportunities taking a nosedive. Today's middle class is struggling to redefine itself in an era in which education and employment no longer guarantee you much of anything.

Nostalgia can be dangerous. Twentieth-century history comes too stained with discrimination based on race, gender, and sexual orientation to provide any template for the modern day. Nevertheless, analyzing the past can provide crucial insights into why things have evolved the way they have. As members of the educated professional middle class, we may not have the power to dictate the social agenda, but a closer examination of our history shows that—armed with enough knowledge and conviction—we do have the power to shape it.

A CENTURY OF THE AMERICAN MIDDLE CLASS

The initial decades of the twentieth century in America brought with them a massive wave of social, political, and economic change, much of which lay the groundwork for the middle-class experience as we know it today. By the 1920s, the country had witnessed rapid urbanization, the growth of giant industrial conglomerates like U.S. Steel and General Motors, large-scale immigration, new technologies like electrical power, automobiles, and radio and motion pictures, and the onset of mass-market advertising and consumer credit, all catering to a national population that nearly doubled in size between 1890 and 1920.[6]

The 1920s ushered in a period of national prosperity, but also economic decadence and abandon. Financial institutions were ruled by the principle of laissez-faire, the guiding hands a closed circle of extreme wealth with names like Rockefeller and Morgan. Economic inequality hit its highest point of the century, rising to a rate that wouldn't be revisited until the current day.[7] It was an era of robber barons, unregulated commerce, and a wildly soaring stock market.

On the opposite end of the spectrum, as the country shifted away from agriculture and toward manufacturing, scores of rural poor and recent immigrants flooded northern cities in search of jobs. For those who managed to find steady work, life did improve. With incomes for industrial workers rising 25 percent over the course of the decade, there was finally extra money to enjoy new luxuries like automobiles, telephones, canned food, and motion pictures. The educated business and professional classes were still small in number compared to the working class, but for both sectors there existed the tantalizing possibility of a financially stable future.

But as manufacturers amassed warehouses full of surplus product and the stock market's giddy rise lost all connection to the growth of industry itself, this greed-fueled economy was destined to self-destruct. The stock market crash of 1929 found bankers jumping off buildings and lauded financial institutions nailing boards over their doors. Though the stock market convulsion didn't cause the subsequent nationwide financial unraveling, the two shared a number of underlying causes—rampant overproduction, gross income inequality, and lack of government regulation or support to modulate the two. Over the next three years, unemployment rose to an astonishing 25 percent, more than five thousand banks failed, and the gross national product was cut in half. The nation succumbed to depression of every sort.[8]

As the country rounded into a new decade, it was clear that for the bulk of the population—rich or poor—the financial "survival of the fittest" that ruled the Jazz Age had proved disastrous. In 1932, the populace, restless for change, elected New York governor Franklin Delano Roosevelt to his first of four terms as president. Under FDR, and his economic New Deal, the 1930s ushered in scores of federal policies designed to bring some sense of balance and security to the masses. Between 1933 and 1938, a slew of new federal programs—referred to by acronyms like CWA, FDIC, FHA, FLSA, PWA, SSA, SEC, TVA, WPA—combined immediate economic relief with long-term financial recovery.[9]

Perhaps most significantly, the New Deal ushered in a shift in how the nation viewed the notion of social responsibility. It aimed for permanent changes in the standard of living for everyday Americans via improvements in the capital structure. Among its lasting legacies were Social Security, unemployment insurance, and minimum wage and child labor laws. It generated thousands of jobs, brought electricity to large swaths of the rural population, and built roads, bridges, and hospitals. The single theme underscoring this legislative reform was security. For individuals, for businesses, for farmers, home owners, bankers, and builders. An alternative system of values surfaced, one in which society as a whole pooled the shared risks of its individual members.[10]

The New Deal didn't engineer flawless social reform. It didn't end the Depression—it took the wartime economy of the 1940s to really cure the country of its economic ills—but it went a long way toward achieving FDR's goal of "a country in which no one is left out."[11] The middle class flourished under such aggressive social and economic change, which simultaneously created opportunity and diminished individual financial responsibility. In the two decades between 1929 and 1948, the middle class rose from just under 6 percent to nearly 18 percent of the population.[12]

Issuing from the social equities instilled by the New Deal and the financial windfalls of World War II, the 1950s was the quintessential middle-class decade. It was an age of blossoming consumerism and affluence that extended to ordinary folks who, by dint of hard work, became not rich but prosperous. Suddenly it seemed everyone could own a home and a car (though in truth far from everyone could.) Trends like buying on credit and keeping up with the suburban Joneses found their legs in the '50s. Debt became less frightening than it had been for those weaned on the Depression as Americans experienced a surging confidence in the stability of their economic future.

Consumerism came into its own during this period, feeding off a thriving new middle class that suddenly had the means to want and purchase and want even more. You no longer had to be a doctor or a businessman to afford a dishwasher or a color TV. Though middle-class comforts were still out of reach for most nonwhites, a white male supporting a family could work in an array of professions at which he could count on being comfortable enough to purchase his own home and stock it with all the modern appliances, take a yearly vacation, and have one car, maybe even two, in the garage. To drive the message home, advertising increased 400 percent between 1945 and 1960, with ads often linked to TV shows like *The Adventures of Ozzie and Harriet* and *Leave It to Beaver*, which depicted perfect middle-class American families.[13]

After two decades of first Depression-era and then wartime scarcity, the 1950s middle class—confronted with the prospect of such luxury living—initially experienced a conflict between pleasure and guilt. How many luxuries you deserved, how much debt was acceptable, was all up for negotiation. As the country edged further from those hard times, emphasis fell toward the pleasure principle. A whole sector of society began to be defined by what they could buy, and they began to buy more, buy newer, buy better. Consumerism elbowed out more old-fashioned values like thrift and saving, values that smacked of war and depression, of looking back instead of leaping ahead. This sense of economic tranquillity didn't last, but the consumerist idea that you are what you buy took its seat at the heart of the American zeitgeist.

The '50s was also an era of generous government subsidies, many of which aided individuals and families in supporting their middle-class lifestyles. The GI Bill, available to 40 percent of men twenty-four to thirty-four, helped a whole generation pay for college and saw to it that education was no longer the sole privilege of the wealthy elite. The Federal Housing Administration (FHA) and the Veterans Administration both supplied new low-interest housing loans. Government highway subsidies gave birth to the suburbs, creating affordable housing for a whole new sector of the population.

America's boom years, through the war and then two decades of postwar prosperity, were some of the most egalitarian in our history. The income gap narrowed, taxes on the wealthiest portion of the population rose, there was an unspoken faith that a loyal company man would be looked after by his employer, and the country on the whole thrived.[14] But the 1950s, though awash in relative affluence, was not an era of equal opportunity. Social programs and policies flagrantly favored white men. The FHA redlined entire inner-city and minority neighborhoods, making them ineligible for loans. Government lenders made it easy for banks to transfer money out of poor neighborhoods and into areas bubbling with new construction. Inner-city transportation received a fraction of the money that highways linking cities and suburbs did. Such government policies achieved precisely what they set out to. They built the foundation for two decades of a thriving lily-white American middle class.[15]

From the mid-'50s to the mid-'70s productivity and household incomes rose in lockstep. Incomes climbed faster than they had in any two decades since 1900. Employees craved job security and companies, hoping to bypass government or union interference, took the lead in providing health and pension plans, and generous raises and promotions.[16] As the whole country did well, so did its individual members.

The first cracks in this economy of abundance appeared in the early 1970s and by the end of the decade they had snowballed into a full-blown financial recession. The economic faltering was caused by a confluence of factors including rising energy prices, government outlays for the Vietnam War, market saturation for U.S. consumer products, and increased foreign trade competition, particularly from Japan, all giving rise to the twin evils of high inflation and high unemployment. Though times were tough, they were tough for everyone, with similar income drops hitting everybody right up to the top 1 percent of earners.[17]

Desperate for change—this time away from an ineffectual and bloated democratic regime—the nation elected Ronald Reagan to his first term in office in 1980 based on campaign promises of lower taxes and smaller government. Though he too took office at a time of national economic crisis, Reagan was the opposite of FDR. He preached minimal government, massive deregulation, tax breaks for corporations and the wealthy, slashing domestic welfare spending, and a return to the laissez-faire principles that had ruled the 1920s. The Reagan administration believed that a system of "trickle-down" economics was the most effective route toward generating financial gain. In short, they were convinced that the best way to prop the country back on its feet was to give the free market absolute and total free rein.

The lessons of the economic excesses of the Jazz Age were long forgotten as corporations, freed of government restrictions, began a mergers-and-acquisitions frenzy, dismantling existing businesses and disposing of excess employees with slash-and-burn abandon. Deregulation of the banking industry led to higher interest rates and the consolidation of financial institutions, merging banks, brokerage houses, and investment banks, and—again harking back to the 1920s—placing more money and financial power in the hands of a few. Progressive income tax structures established as part of the New Deal were abandoned in favor of more regressive measures catering to the wealthy.[18]

Over the course of the decade, the government also cut funding for social programs, resulting in a 7 percent drop in discretionary domestic spending.[19] Decreased federal support put added pressure on state and city governments, all but forcing them to slice education, health, and welfare funding on the local level too. With the onset of Reaganomics, the country shed the principle of a government whose duty is to look after the whole of its population rather than catering to a privileged elite. Along with it went that New Deal concept of a national shared social responsibility in which the wealthy bear a disproportionate amount of the burden for caring for the whole. Emphasis turned toward the market economy and away from community values and concerns, including public health, public schools and libraries, and public roads and transportation. Ozzie and Harriet were long gone, replaced by the hedonistic extremes of the oil-rich Ewings of *Dallas* and the oil-rich Carringtons of *Dynasty*. The needs of middle-class Americans, once celebrated as the heartbeat of the country, were cast aside.

Reaganomics was fantastic for a few people, but devastating to the many. In a major shift in corporate operations, profits were now redistributed upward to CEOs and other top executives instead of down to employees. As a result, median household income remained stagnant for the two decades between 1970 and 1990.[20] Corporate responsibility foundered and the notion of "personal responsibility" rose up to take its place. The 401(k), first introduced in 1981, began to crowd out traditional pension plans, introducing a setup that required workers to pay for their own retirements instead of saddling corporations with huge fixed-pension obligations.[21] Abandoned by their employers and subject to cuts in social programs and federal funding for health care and education, individuals were left to flourish or perish on the basis of luck, merit, or inherited wealth.

It was in the 1980s that sociologists and economists first began mentioning the disappearing middle class. At that point they were usually talking about blue-collar workers. With the rise of a lean and mean corporate culture characterized by rampant outsourcing and downsizing, that high-school-educated slice of the population that had been able to afford a home, a car, and a well-heeled wardrobe began a slippery slide toward food stamps and unemployment. But for the educated professional middle class, incomes held relatively steady or even perked up. This holding tight added to the sense of invulnerability promised by a job and a college degree. By and large, the educated professional middle class remained smug in their conviction that diminishing financial insecurity was a "them" issue, not an "us" one.

THE RISE AND FALLOUT OF THE NEW ECONOMY

That smugness was to prove short-lived. After weathering a late '80s and early '90s recession, the American economy resurged with the meteoric rise of the technology bubble. In 1995, *Newsweek* magazine revived the expression "the New Economy" to herald a major shift in our economic setup, the first such shift since the industrial revolution a century before. The country was moving away from its industrial and manufacturing roots and toward an economy fueled by knowledge and service workers. The New Economy became known not just for its profits but for the sense of boundless energy and possibility left in its wake. Sharper, sleeker assets like independence and creativity replaced the greed and ham-fistedness of the 1980s. Like many economic trends before it, the New Economy fed upon the glamorization of risk.

The explosion of information technology—faster computers, faster communication, a cheap and easy flow of information—facilitated a rapid rise in U.S. productivity, with rates more than doubling between the mid-1970s and the early years of the twenty-first century.[22] Some fantasized that an economy fueled by an entirely new technology could support steady growth, permanent low unemployment, and immunity from the boom-and-bust cycles of previous eras.

Initially, in the mid-'90s, the New Economy rose to such expectations, facilitating high employment rates and rising wages across the board. On the surface, it seemed to create never-ending opportunity for any middle-class worker with the proper education and drive. But though the era did revamp certain traditional corporate ways of thinking—ushering in the era of pool tables in the office and shorts and T-shirts as accepted business wear—overall it didn't venture far from that same "What's good for the rich is good for America" mantra that had driven the decade before.

Despite its tag as a business revolution, the New Economy did little to democratize wealth or opportunity. Two of its most persistent legacies were an increase in white-collar layoffs and a level of income inequality many thought had gone the way of robber barons and prohibition. Wealthy venture capitalists seemed to throw money at anybody with a computer and an idea—the rate of venture capital investment, largely in new industries like software and biotech, grew from under a billion dollars in 1990 to $100 billion in 2000.[23] But in truth the worlds of Silicon Valley and Silicon Alley remained rarefied. The tech boom didn't spread its wealth to college professors or social workers or book editors. Money was channeled into specific technology-based professions, and certain levels of those professions, and away from a great many others, ushering in an enormous redistribution and concentration of wealth.

Nor did the New Economy fuel that steady rise in employment many predicted. High employment rates dropped off late in the decade, as inflated tech stocks began to crumble. For larger organizations like IBM and AT&T, the massive layoffs that had become a prime source of profit making in the '80s now spread to management and other white-collar workers.[24] On the opposite end of the spectrum, overambitious start-ups flamed and died in record time, as many of those heralded knowledge workers found themselves hired by new or newly expanded companies, offered juicy salaries, then let go three, six, twelve months later. White-collar workers were laid off then hired back as "consultants" at reduced salaries with no benefits. And, with the rise in global technology, an increasing number of those same white-collar jobs began to move overseas. The final fraying strands of job security snapped.

In the past, if you needed more money you could always moonlight in a second job, or at the very least take comfort in getting to spend more quality time with your family. But the New Economy also ushered in the rise of the 24/7 work culture. Employers promoted round-the-clock hours as a form of freedom, away from rigid nine-to-five schedules of old and into anytime and anyplace, rolling back gains like overtime pay and the eight-hour workday. Instead of occupying different time, work just occupied more time, extending to fill every spare corner of our lives. With the onset of the Internet, cell phones, and smaller and smaller PCs, we entered an era where it was quite possible to be working at any moment and from any location, reawakening that puritanical scorn of wasted time. American household incomes have risen in the past thirty years not because we're making higher salaries but because wage earners—primarily women —are working more hours, an increase of five hundred hours a year between 1979 and 2000.[25] Even if the professional middle class began to suspect they were getting a raw deal, few had the time or the energy to object.

The New Economy left its psychological scars as well. Many members of today's educated middle class came of professional age during the dot-com boom. They often made more money at age twenty-five than they have since. This early brush with financial bounty set up expectations about the kind of money you can and should earn, the availability of lucrative jobs, and the possibilities in store for anyone smart and ambitious enough to seize them. Though the economy has changed, the afterimages of this heady time still linger. In tangible terms, like 401(k)s not touched in a decade, like the scars of multiple layoffs, like the measuring stick of six-figure starting salaries held against those now a decade older and earning half as much. But also in the intangibles, the strong message that you were lucky enough to graduate into an era of opportunity and that if you're struggling now it's not the system but you that has failed.

The New Economy also put the final nail in the coffin of company loyalty. This was the age of the free agent, knowledge workers liberated to move from job to job with no corporate strings tying them down. Organizations quickly seized upon the notion that nobody owed anything to anyone. Most individuals still relied on their employers for health and retirement benefits, not to mention a steady paycheck. But within corporate culture, the notion of job security was chucked to the curb. In the late '80s, 56 percent of major corporations still believed that "employees who are loyal to the company and further its business goals deserve an assurance of continued employment." By the late '90s, that number had dropped to just 6 percent.[26] As the overinflated tech boom began its nosedive, leaving many knowledge workers without work or negotiating serious salary cuts, the message from all fronts was crystal clear. From here out, you're on your own.

When the post-dot-com economy began to recover in 2001, most wage earners—blue or white collar—were not carried along with the rising tide. As America rolled into the twenty-first century, economic trends were set by a new administration, headed by President George W. Bush, bent on favoring the corporation over the worker and a wealthy few over the less privileged many. The Bush administration drove a crowbar into existing cracks in middle-class security, opening them up wide and deep.

Despite a robust economy and record corporate profits, incomes for all but the wealthiest 1 percent of the population have largely leveled off or even dropped in the twenty-first century.[27] And despite relatively high employment—unemployment has yet to rise above 6 percent since 2000, as opposed to the 25 percent it hit during the Depression or the current 8.7 percent in France and 8.1 percent in Spain—the sense of financial stability that results from a steady job has vanished. In an era characterized by stagnant wages, cutbacks in benefits, and higher housing, education, and child care costs, employment rates are no longer an accurate barometer of economic health. Middle-class Americans may be making money, but they're not making enough.[28]

How could low unemployment and a high gross domestic product (GDP) not equal prosperity? Since the 1970s, business productivity rates had been climbing faster than worker incomes, meaning that employees were getting an increasingly smaller portion of an increasingly larger economic pie. But with the start of the new century, this trend grew even more severe. From 2000 to 2005, worker productivity rose at over twice the rate of worker compensation. As corporations raked in the profits, salaries stayed low and individual employees reaped none of the benefits. Today, wages and salaries make up the smallest share of GDP since the 1940s.[29]

Where did all those corporate earnings go? Mostly into the pockets of CEOs and other top company executives. Between 1992 and 2005 CEO pay—including wages, bonuses, and stock options—rose a staggering 186 percent, while the average worker experienced an income gain of just 7 percent.[30] This rise in inequality was hardly an aberration likely to fade with the next economic boom or bust. It represented the high end of a growing income polarization dating back to the 1970s. Between 1979 and 2003, income for the middle fifth of the population grew just 9 percent, while that for the top 1 percent more than doubled, jetting up 111 percent. Compare that to the years between 1947 and 1973 when real wages rose 81 percent and income of the richest 1 percent rose just 38 percent.[31]

This redistribution of wealth hailed the arrival of a new strata of the upper class, the superrich, accompanied by a fierce cultural adulation of wealth and the rise—in terms of both money and power—of a new ruling elite. In 2005, for the first time the list of the Forbes 400 Richest Americans was composed entirely of billionaires, despite a period of relatively slow economic growth. Wealthier individuals but not more overall wealth means that what's gone into the bank accounts of the superrich has come out of the pockets of everyone else. While incomes for those in the bottom 90 percent failed to even keep pace with inflation, in 2006 the investment banking firm Goldman Sachs doled out $16.5 billion in salaries and bonuses, fueling the Manhattan luxury market for furs, jewelry, and multimillion-dollar starter apartments.[32]

Such economic inequality has been abetted by government policies like corporate subsidies, reduced taxes on dividends and capital gains, and individual tax cuts for the wealthy. Over half the tax cuts instituted by the Bush administration in 2003 go to people with incomes in the top 10 percent. The wealthiest 400 taxpayers in the country now pay the same percentage of their earnings in income, Social Security, and Medicare taxes as families earning $50,000 to $75,000 a year, those at the heart of the middle class.[33] The reigning philosophy these days seems to be that the more money you have, the more money you're entitled to.

The new century has also played host to a further expansion of the global economy. Nations, certainly powerful nations, can no longer operate in a financial trade bubble the way the United States did for much of the previous century. The world has become a global market in which everything is for sale. One of the most profound effects of globalization has been the continued outsourcing of jobs to less expensive markets. When outsourcing first became common in the '70s and '80s, the practice was largely confined to blue-collar manufacturing work as an increasing number of factory jobs were exported to Mexico and then Southeast Asia. But as other countries grew increasingly technologically sophisticated, U.S. companies also began to export jobs typically held by educated white-collar workers. Princeton economist Alan S. Blinder has estimated that as many as 30 to 40 million U.S. jobs are potentially exportable, many of them in fields requiring high levels of education, ranging from mathematics and microbiology to computer programming and graphic design.[34]

In many ways, perhaps the key ways, the legacy of the New Economy is not new at all. Despite the emphasis on individuality, we remain a corporate, big business, big government kind of nation. Megacompanies like Microsoft, Time Warner, General Motors, JPMorgan Chase, and Fannie Mae dictate prices, determine our health care, finance our educations, and manage our debt. The number of Americans without health insurance has jumped to an estimated 46 million, many of them educated, employed, and squarely middle class, even while drug companies and for-profit hospital chains rake in earnings.[35] Affluence—whether earned or inherited—is still lavishly celebrated through a cult of celebrity, even as financial stability eludes most of the American middle class no matter how hardworking or well educated.

We're working furiously, 24/7, to ignore the fact that America is no longer the wellspring of opportunity it was in the '40s, '50s, and '60s. Class mobility—the ability to move up or down the class spectrum given the proper amount of education, dedication, and ambition—has steadily declined with each decade since the 1970s. Economic mobility is actually lower in the United States than in many countries, including Canada, France, and even the United Kingdom, which supposedly feature rigid class structures that run counter to the American way of life.[36] Those streets paved in gold have been replaced by roads littered with mortgage payments, student loans, health care bills, and credit card debt.

HOW TIMES HAVE CHANGED

Of course, it's impossible to view the middle-class experience solely in its economic context. Opportunity may have shifted backward in some senses, but it's leapt forward in others. The American middle class is no longer a population dominated by heterosexual white men supporting their families on a single income. With broadening social views on race, gender, and sexuality, the terrain of Ozzie and Harriet has indeed broken out of the box.

Women aren't new to the middle class, but they do play an entirely different role today than they did in the '50s or even '70s. As late as 1970, 78 percent of married women under forty-five still felt it was preferable for women to be homemakers and men to do the breadwinning.[37] But such thinking was upended in the following decades as feminism's second wave took hold and the number of women in the workforce more than doubled from 32 million in 1971 to 70 million today. This influx of career women shifted our entire economic structure, flooding the workplace with twice as many workers when there weren't twice as many jobs. Working women boosted family incomes, increased competition for positions and salaries, shifted the balance of power in many a marriage, and even began to shift the balance of society as a whole. Today women comprise 46 percent of the labor force, and the higher a woman's education level, the more likely she is to hold a job.[38]

Those women flooding the workforce in the '60s and '70s came largely from the middle and upper middle classes. Their working-class peers had always held down jobs to help support their families. They didn't have a choice. But at first, this fresh surge of educated middle-class women was driven less by financial need than a change in ideology, the burgeoning belief—fueled by the publication of Betty Friedan's *The Feminine Mystique* and other feminist works—that women were ready to put their mark on the male-dominated public sphere. College-educated minds weren't sufficiently stimulated by a lifetime of baking birthday cakes, folding laundry, or retiring into discreet spinsterhood with a houseful of cats. It wasn't until the rising inflation of the late '70s then continuing through the '80s and '90s as expenses rose and government and employer support disintegrated, that what began as a political and social movement morphed into an economic necessity.[39]

Today, the prototype of the American family with a single male breadwinner has become not only sociologically but also financially obsolete. Of all the contemporary families I spoke to, none had a traditional stay-at-home wife or mom setup, though one unmarried couple was temporarily experimenting with a stay-at-home dad. Only a handful of women worked less than part-time, under twenty hours a week, while essentially living on their husband's paycheck—two of whom did so because the child care costs ran higher than the money they would've earned in their low-paying educated professional careers.

Most middle-class families today need two members in the workforce, not to allow for luxuries like vacations and flat-screen TVs, but to cover fixed expenses. Higher housing, education, health care, transportation, and child care costs can easily swallow up an entire second income. The salaries of college-educated women have risen much faster than those of male graduates, up 34.4 percent since 1979 versus 21.7 percent for men. While women still earn less than men, these second incomes are often the only thing that allows to-day's educated professional households to cling to their slippery class status.[40]

The women of today's dual-income families face the added stress of balancing career and family. Though, theoretically, part-time work might sound good, in reality most women—75 percent—opt for full-time jobs in order to contribute enough to the family income.[41] This means struggling to find affordable and reliable child care, not to mention adequate time to spend with children, particularly in today's demanding round-the-clock work culture. These are stresses for which our antiquated government child care and family leave policies—largely formulated at a time when there was still likely to be one parent in the home—offer scant relief.

Women's growing financial independence has also reshaped the middle-class household, giving women access to social freedoms only few could afford in the '40s, '50s, and '60s. Today, middle-class women have the choice to stay single, marry later, leave a failing marriage, or have children on their own. In over 25 percent of families, women now bring home more money than their husbands do.[42] These new social models have necessitated new financial models that also challenge conventional gender roles—male as provider, female as nurturer—and are forcing us to reexamine the definition of marriage, family, and independence.

But despite awesome gains, women still haven't reached equal economic footing with men. Middle-class women are still more likely to be single parents, to suffer sharper financial blows in face of divorce or death of a spouse, and to ride the roller coaster of economic volatility. College-educated women still make lower salaries than college-educated men do and women remain more likely than men to take time off work to care for children or other relatives, a choice that can easily hamper their career advancement. Women also face higher likelihood of bankruptcy, debt, and home foreclosure. What's precarious for the educated professional middle class as a whole is even more precarious for its female members.[43]

The mainstream American middle class of the 1950s may not have been as clean-cut and white-bread as Ward, June, Wally, and the

Beaver, but it wasn't too far off. Segregation in the South meant people of color couldn't live in the same neighborhoods, eat in the same restaurants, or send their children to the same schools as white families. In the North, discriminatory housing and employment policies were nearly as effective in shutting minority families out of the mainstream middle-class experience. The proportion of blacks who were middle class did not reach even 10 percent until the 1960s, while more than 20 percent of whites were middle class as early as 1910. Meanwhile, the poverty rate for black families in the 1950s ran as high as 80 percent.[44]

Today's educated professional middle class looks nothing like its counterpart fifty years ago. It's Hispanic, African American, Asian, Caribbean, and Native American. As of 2005, the middle class was 72 percent white, 11.6 percent black, 3.3 percent Asian, and 11.3 percent Hispanic, numbers that come close to reflecting the population as a whole.[45] But though they may share careers, neighborhoods, and financial anxieties with their white counterparts, it's impossible to discount race as a factor in the current class struggle. In addition to shouldering the everyday financial stresses—the stagnant wages and escalating fixed expenses, the struggle to balance work and family, the conflict between finding meaningful work and paying the bills—people of color must contend with what it means to be black or Hispanic or Asian in what was once an almost purely white enclave. Despite the education, despite the respected career, the screen of race still very much exists.

Americans like to presume a society that's achieved racial equality, just as they like to presume one free of class boundaries. This is a nation where a black man can run for president and your doctor's last name might just as easily be Smith, Singh, or Perez. But it also continues to be a country where minorities scramble harder than their white counterparts to hold on to their middle-class status. It's a country where the net worth of black and Hispanic college graduates is similar to the net worth of white high school graduates. And it's a nation where the median wealth of Hispanic households is $11,450, and of black households is $19,010, while—in a stunning disparity—the median wealth of white households is $86,100.[46] Today, being a minority member of the educated middle class still means fighting a very different fight.

People of color—particularly those coming from immigrant families—are more likely to be the first generation of their family to get a four-year college degree. Friends and family can exert more pressure on them to succeed financially and can be less sympathetic when, despite a job and a college education, they continue to struggle. Oftentimes, there can be additional pressure to pass the presumed wealth around, helping out friends and family members in poverty, in trouble, and in need.

White members of the middle class are more likely than minorities to come from middle- or upper-middle-class families; there are often parents, grandparents, or other relatives who can help with major expenses like buying homes or paying for school. They don't have to take out as many early loans—student loans, car loans, mortgage loans—or acquire as much debt in an attempt to cement their middle-class status. White middle-class families are also more likely to have connections to other middle-class or upper-middle-class families—dad's old fraternity brother, the bank vice president who used to live down the street, Aunt Susan who's in real estate—the sort of inside line that can facilitate anything from better jobs to deals on more affordable cars and homes.

Even when educations and incomes are equal, other discriminatory practices continue to play out. It's still harder for people of color to access middle-class privileges—decent mortgages and auto loans, homes in affluent areas, or a wide range of employment opportunities. Research has shown that upper-income black and Hispanic borrowers are up to three times more likely than upper-income white families to be offered sub-prime mortgages, with significantly higher interest rates, fees, and penalties, even when they clearly qualify for prime loans.[47]

When the middle class as a whole receives a blow, its minority members, like its female members, still absorb a disproportionate share of the impact. The small gains in the racial income divide that occurred with the tight labor market of the mid-'90s were largely rolled back with the recession and jobless recovery that followed. Between 2000 and 2003, income growth for black and Hispanic families declined nearly three to five times as much as the losses suffered by white families.[48] When it comes to lower wages, higher mortgages, lack of health insurance, heavier student debt, fewer retirement savings, and higher level of income volatility, African American and Hispanic families consistently fare worse than white ones.[49]

For people of color, who are shouldering a long history of being denied and disfranchised, access to material goods can also have a deeper and more complex social significance than it may to educated professional white families. To choose a lower-paying but more intellectually or emotionally rewarding job may hold a sort of prestige for a member of the educated white middle class to whom intellectualism still bears some social clout. But if your heritage is one for which access to "the good things in life," in material terms, signifies overcoming long-standing abuse and discrimination, the choice to pursue meaningful work over a high salary career can just read like another strand of failure.

THE GREAT AMERICAN MIDDLE-CLASS SHIFT

There's no question that the definition of what it means to be middle class, the expectations it sets up and how fully those expectations can be met, have all shifted over time. The 1950s gave rise to the classic, largely white, comfortable but not luxurious middle-class existence—house, car, two kids, housewife mom, and commuter dad. For a while in the '60s and '70s cultural values swung away from financial pursuits and toward more spiritual and intellectual ideals, but that trend quickly reversed itself as we dove into the Reagan-era '80s.

Today, successful members of the educated professional middle class are meant to pursue their passions, find work that they love, and make a comfortable living in the process. They may be women or men, they may come from diverse racial and ethnic backgrounds, but they're largely being diverted into one narrow, and largely unattainable, corporate-style model for success and happiness. Those who fall outside that model, no matter how well they are educated and how hard they work, too often find themselves in a situation remarkably different from their parents, not only financially but also emotionally. This shift, and its profound impact on our current middle-class lives, involves a complicated tale of changing financial circumstances, changing values, and the inability of our middle-class expectations to keep apace with the economic realities of the new century. That story begins where so many of these expectations are first engendered, with the promise, the privilege, and the price of a college education.

3

COLLEGE PROMISES

Real Debt and False Expectations

When Charles, forty, graduated with his PhD in clinical psychology seven years ago, he dreamed of getting the sort of job he has now— working as a faculty member at one of New York's top medical schools doing research on the human brain. The position, though high in prestige, pays a more modest $60,000 a year, an income he supplements by teaching as an adjunct professor and seeing private patients, though his contract with the medical school limits him to patients referred by the school at its discounted rates.

Charles's wife, Jessie, has an equally impressive educational slate, having earned her master's in social work from a top-notch West Coast university. Though Charles won a 50 percent tuition remission and both of them worked—restaurant jobs, teaching, temping— throughout their schooling, the couple had to take out $130,000 in loans to pay for his PhD and her undergraduate and graduate degrees.

Jessie spent three years working as a full-time psychotherapist for a company that provided government agencies with in-house thera- pists. She took ten months off when their daughter, Teresa, was born three years ago, then went back to work, placing Teresa in full-time day care. But when their son, Nat, arrived two years later, combining work and parenting seemed a practical impossibility.

"We paid about $1,300 to have Teresa in good child care we felt comfortable with" Charles explains. "Even working full-time, Jessie's income as a clinical social worker would barely be able to cover that sort of cost for two kids."

Though Jessie likes being able stay home with the kids, the couple struggles financially. Being a two-graduate-degree family means that in addition to current living expenses like food and rent, they pay $1,200 every month toward their student loans, money that otherwise might have gone toward paying down their $20,000 credit card debt—amassed to cover graduate school expenses, wedding expenses, child expenses, and basics like groceries when paychecks didn't quite stretch—saving for an apartment, or contributing to a college fund for their kids.

"That's the bill I resent the most," asserts Charles, who was raised in England and France, both countries where governments heavily subsidize postsecondary schooling. "The student loans are crippling. It seems wrong that we're asked to pay tuitions so out of proportion to what the careers we're pursuing will eventually pay."

Charles's marble-blue eyes, mellow good looks, and trace of a European accent seem well-suited to his first career, in the music industry, but when he was laid off from that job in his midtwenties he decided to pursue a more socially significant profession that would combine his interests in teaching, medicine, and psychotherapy. Though he didn't choose clinical psychology in order to get rich, he says, "Growing up I always believed that if I was well educated and worked hard I would be comfortable. Instead, I'm forty years old and have negative net worth."

Between his medical school research, teaching, and helping with child care, Charles barely has time to sleep and eat, let alone investigate alternative sources of income. He's toying with the idea of looking for a job with a major pharmaceutical company. His research would shift toward developing moneymaking drugs, but brain research is a potentially lucrative arena and he's not convinced that doing good and making money have to be mutually exclusive.

"If someone offered me twice the money to work less than I'm working now, I'd have to take it seriously," he says. But at age forty, he's far less appealing to such companies than he would have been fifteen years ago with smaller salary demands and a whole research future stretching ahead of him.

As for Jessie, even when she does go back to work full-time, she can only expect to make around $45,000 as a licensed clinical social worker, hardly enough to make a dent in their collective education debt.

"It would take a full year's salary just to pay for her degree," Charles points out. "Not counting interest on the loans. "

Charles worries about their financial future, especially funding his own kids' education. Right now, his parents pay for Teresa's part-time preschool, but he and Jessie aren't sure what to do about the underperforming public schools in their area. And they have no idea how they'll afford to send Teresa and Nat to college.

"I like my life," Charles tells me, "but it's hard not to feel bitter. Jessie and I have worked so hard our entire lives and we have nothing to show for it. I have a PhD. I'm a faculty member at a prestigious New York medical school. But it seems impossible that we'll ever get ahead."

Perhaps the most striking characteristic of the educated professional middle class is that we are so shockingly well educated. We hold BAs, master's degrees, and PhDs from Ivy League, sub–Ivy League, and high-end private and public universities. We paid a great deal of money, and took on a great deal of debt, for such educations. In return, those schools, if not society, conveyed a slew of unspoken promises about our financial futures.

But someplace between Western Civ and the rat race, the rules changed. The old standard, "Go to college and you can make something of yourself," no longer applies. College prices are rising, incomes for college-educated workers are falling—dipping over 5 percent between 2001 and 2004—and more and more middle- and upper-middle-class families find themselves swamped in student debt.[1]

It's hard to blame Charles and Jessie for their financial troubles. They worked hard, often holding down several jobs all through college. They both earned multiple degrees from well-respected schools and went on to land enviable jobs. They certainly wouldn't have been better off if they'd skipped college altogether. The wage gap between college- and high-school-educated workers continues to widen, with the college educated earning about 70 percent more than high school graduates.² Nor could they have pursued anything like their chosen careers with only a high school education or vocational training. Most creative, professional, and education-related jobs require at least a four-year degree, and often an advanced degree as well. Life can be tough even with a college education, but it will be far tougher without.

So if Charles and Jessie followed the right rules, what went wrong for them and for so many other members of the educated professional middle class? What does a college education promise these days? How well does it deliver? And at what price?

COLLEGE PROMISES

As a society, we still cling to the vision of college as the great equalizer. Getting an education is supposed to mean that, no matter where we come from or what our chosen career, we can expect to be financially secure. A college education doesn't just bestow knowledge. It bestows status, an instant stamp of class. When the *New York Times* conducted a poll asking people what class they belonged to, not one person with a bachelor's degree or higher described themselves as working class, no matter how little money they made.³

But that promise of financial stability comes with precious few specific details attached. For those who go the MBA or law school route, the assumptions are fairly straightforward. Given this degree, you have the ability to pursue a high-paying corporate or entrepreneurial career if you so choose. But for those with a more liberal or intellectual bent, the road becomes cryptic. There's still the pressure to succeed, but indirectly and somewhat mysteriously. The message is that, given your education, intelligence, and stellar work ethic, you will somehow buck economic trends to achieve financial comfort while never taking your eye off the goal of bettering humanity.

As we ascend the educational ladder, those promises get laid on even thicker. More and more middle-class professions require individuals to have graduate degrees, if not to enter the field then at least to rise up through it. A bachelor's degree has come to be widely regarded in the same way a high school degree was thirty years ago— the baseline for getting a livable job. Today, advanced degrees have become indispensable currency not just for lawyers and doctors, but also for teachers, social workers, museum curators, and librarians. Though wages for those with advanced degrees have stagnated over the past five years, the number of students with graduate degrees is growing over twice as fast as the number with bachelor's degrees.[4] And with the investment of more time and money come still higher expectations. How could six or eight or twelve years hitting the books not land us in some version of financial clover? Perhaps we feel entitled simply by virtue of making it that far.

That expectations bar can rise yet another notch for those who attend the most elite colleges and universities, those that have sustained their reputations as bastions of privilege while holding on to their predominantly upper-income student bodies.[5]

"There was this constant message that I was part of an elite circle, and that I'd stay there once I graduated," explains Melody, an African American studies professor who did her graduate work in the Ivy League. "It sounds stupid, but I bought into the whole idea that an Ivy League education would automatically take me somewhere. No one ever mentioned that an intellectual life could mean struggling to raise my kids on $65,000 a year."

For those emerging from this academic environment, drunk on potential, a crucial message is getting lost. As an investment in our futures, an expensive education is becoming riskier from a financial perspective, necessary as it continues to be. While the price of college and the number of educated job seekers have both shot up since the mid-'70s, middle-class incomes have not. That means more degrees, and more members of the educated elite with school debt, but not more money to pay for it all.[6]

Especially for those who pursue the so-called "softer" liberal arts disciplines like the humanities, social sciences, education, and the arts, college is no longer an investment that guarantees you a middle-class foothold. It's bad enough that an undergraduate degree—and the graduate degree all but required in many professions—can't guarantee us a job, let alone financial security. But, as Charles and Jessie discovered, the debt we acquire in pursuing such degrees means we're actually paying a penalty for having chosen to learn.

AT WHAT COST?

Peter is slim, fair, and tightly wound, a midwestern boy still finding his feet after six months in Manhattan, with round glasses, curly red hair, and a keen sense of right and wrong.

Five years ago, while contemplating his college choices, he knew that his parents couldn't provide much in the way of help. His mother had taken out loans to finish her own bachelor's degree just two years earlier, and Peter's two younger sisters still lived at home. Though his father's job as a construction manager and his mother's as a continuing education teacher earned them enough to disqualify Peter from most need-based grants, their other financial responsibilities limited the amount of money they could actually contribute to his college fees.

Peter had thrived in the more intimate environment of his small public high school in Ohio, and feared getting lost at a largely commuter state university.

"Since I knew I'd be taking out loans either way," he explains, "I chose to go to a smaller, more expensive private college. Tuition, room and board cost $24,000 a year. At eighteen, I didn't understand the financial arrangement at all. I just took what they gave me. I didn't think about what was going to happen when I had to pay it back."

Sallie Mae—the government's primary lender, generating $16 billion a year in government-guaranteed loans and $7.4 billion in private student loans—offered Peter a federal aid package combining subsidized (interest starts accruing after graduation) and unsubsidized (interest starts accruing immediately) Stafford loans. His parents also took out an additional $10,000 in federal loans to help him out.[7]

The federal loans, combined with the money Peter made working at Wal-Mart and as a bank teller, allowed him to eke through his first two years.[8] His junior year he saved money by moving off campus, but it wasn't enough to offset a tuition hike. Peter reached the $23,000-per-student annual cap on federal loans, so he had to take out a high-interest private loan to bridge the gap. Sallie Mae hooked him up with a commercial bank that lent him additional money at prime plus 2.75 percent, though until he began paying it back Peter was under the impression that his private loans—like his federal loans—were at a fixed lifetime rate.

Peter majored in art and communications, "not economics," he asserts pointedly, with the hope of eventually doing graphic design for travel and lifestyle magazines. After graduation, he was eager to escape the Midwest, with its conservative art scene and small gay community. He began searching for a job in the mecca of art and alternative lifestyles, New York City.

Through an online job bank he landed a $35,000-a-year position as a graphic designer for a community-based nonprofit. He found a small apartment with two roommates in an ungentrified section of Brooklyn.

Peter's student-loan payments kicked in six months after graduation. He consolidated his federal loans, or at least he thinks he did, though he's a little confused about why the loan company keeps sending him letters offering to help him consolidate. That means he has two payments a month—$175 for the Stafford loans and $400 for the private. The various payment options offered were difficult to decipher, especially since he couldn't be sure what his income would be for the next ten months, let alone ten years. For simplicity's sake, he chose to pay the same set amount every month for the next twenty-five years. If he continues at this rate, he'll finish paying for his undergraduate degree when he's forty-seven years old.

Peter's sketchy about the exact terms of his various loans, how much he took out—"I think it was $60,000 or $70,000 total"—and the rules of repayment. When he tried to make an early payment, Sallie Mae promptly advanced his regular due date two weeks and raised the amount of the monthly payment by $65. He had to send a written letter to the lender to reestablish his original schedule.

Though he's angry about the cost, Peter doesn't regret pursuing a career he feels passionate about. "I thought about studying something more practical than art and design but the thought of a lifetime at a job I hated was too depressing," he tells me. "My father started out wanting to be a racecar engineer but he got sidetracked and wound up in construction. I saw how unhappy he was the whole time I was growing up. I would pay any price not to be like that."

The combination of high loan payments and small salary make it impossible for Peter to set aside any savings. In an optimistic moment, he opened an apartment account, hoping that in ten years he might save enough for a down payment. It currently holds about $500 and he's already raiding that to make it through to the end of each month. He lives as frugally as he can—we meet for a $6.50 lunch special in New York's Chinatown—but he didn't come to New York to hole up in his apartment.

"I spent all of college eating ramen, watching DVDs and working at Wal-Mart," Peter tells me. "Now I have a job and a degree. I want something a little bit better. "

"I'm about as all-American as you can get," he continues, his voice brimming with stress and frustration. "Two parents, three kids, a dog, a cat, a house, two cars. Something isn't working here. If it's this hard for me to get an education I can't imagine what it must be like for everyone else."

Though Peter seems too young to be negotiating such all-consuming financial stress, he is among the three-quarters of full-time college students who rely on financial aid to fund their education.[9] Gone are the days of dirt-cheap state universities—in the late 1940s my father paid the full tuition of $42 a quarter to attend the University of Washington, an expense he could easily cover with his weekend job parking cars at the racetrack. Gone are the days when subsidizing college education was seen as a way for the government to invest in a richer collective future for the country.

Now college, like washing machines or flat-screen TVs, is something you're expected to purchase out of your own pocket. If you need help in financing this purchase (most people do) and you're looking to get federal aid (most people are) chances are that help will come via the nearly $57 billion offered in government loans. With college costs rising—tuitions have gone up 35 percent in the past five years[10]—and incomes sinking for everyone but the superrich, the average undergraduate today carries close to $20,000 in student debt. If you go on to graduate school, you can expect that amount to more than double to $46,000.[11]

Students coming from low-income families may be eligible for government grants, the largest of which is the Pell Grant program, yet such grants have failed to keep pace with the price of education. In 1986, the maximum Pell Grant covered 51 percent of college fees for a student attending a public university. By 2006, it covered just 35 percent—with the average grant covering just a quarter of costs—requiring more students to take out loans to cover remaining costs.[12]

For middle-class students who come from middle-class families that make too much to qualify for direct aid but too little to pay the full cost, help also comes with a high price. Government-insured Stafford loans provide a risk-free safety net for the commercial banks and private lenders who administer them, but for students they can quickly turn into a hornet's nest of compound interest rates, payment regulations, and unexplained penalties and fees. Peter isn't alone in not understanding what he's paying and to whom. The packages are so complicated—so many different kinds of loans cobbled together, some subsidized, some not, some private, some federal—that many people I spoke to had no idea how much money they'd taken out even as they signed a monthly check to pay it back. And if they didn't know how much money they'd borrowed in the first place, they certainly weren't clear about which of the repayment plans offered by their various lenders made the most financial sense.

When that $23,000 annual cap on federal loans runs out, as it did for Peter, students have little choice but to either drop out of school or turn to private loans from commercial lenders. Private loans are the fastest-growing sector of the student-loan industry, more than tripling over the past five years to reach $17.3 billion in the 2005–2006 school year. Ten years ago private loans made up 6 percent of all money loaned to students, now they clock in at 20 percent. A quick Google search of the term "student loans" turned up private lenders offering me up to $120,000 student debt relief, available in just five days. These private loans come with variable interest rates—meaning that if rates shoot up, so do your payments—and they lack the interest caps offered by federal loans.[13]

Students are expected to begin paying off their loans six months after graduation. For every payment you miss, you amass additional penalties. Loans can be deferred for up to three years due to economic hardship—though unsubsidized loans will continue to accrue interest over that time—but never banished, not even if you declare bankruptcy. Your wages can be garnished, your federal tax refunds or Social Security payments withheld, and your credit score ruined. The only way to get out from under a student loan is to pay it off, become permanently disabled (presuming your condition didn't exist before you applied for the loan), or die. For many students, calls from collections agencies become a regular and perpetually shaming blot on that rosy postcollege future.[14]

"We do walk the line when it comes to legal harassment," says Wes, forty-two, a "recovery specialist" for a debt collection agency in the Northeast owned by Sallie Mae, who—before the laws changed in 2006—abolished his own student-loan debt by declaring bankruptcy. "We call your neighbors, your relatives, your relatives' relatives. We call back every hour if no one picks up the phone. We check your house registration and your credit record. We basically do anything we can to humiliate you and hunt you down. Most people I contact aren't deadbeats. They're working people who just don't make enough money to pay off a five- or six-figure debt."

The high cost of college stays with individuals, and society as a whole, far past graduation day. Student debt can affect career choices, steering graduates away from lower-paying jobs with high social value, like teaching and social work. They cause people to delay marriage and parenthood, forgo buying homes and cars, alter the framework of their young—and consequently older—lives because they feel so financially trapped. Escalating college costs and a lack of affordable aid have also contributed to a widening enrollment gap between white and minority students. That gap, which narrowed to 5 percent in the early '70s, has now jumped to 11 percent between white and black students and 13 percent between white and Hispanic. It's estimated that as many as 4 million low- and middle-income students could opt out of a four-year college education in the coming decade because they simply can't afford to go.[15]

For the large number of not quite so young people who put off college to earn some money first, or who return for graduate degrees once they've spent a few years in the real world, educational debts can stretch well into their forties and fifties, directly clashing with the expense of raising families and the need to put money away for retirement and their own children's education. We can see the beginnings of a spiral, an educational vortex that's sucking down not just the current generation but generations to come. What happens to an educated professional middle class so loaded down with their own student debt that they can't help their children? As Charles put it, pinpointing the anxiety of many: "Ultimately, we're going to be forced to sacrifice our children's education because we chose to get educations of our own."

EDUCATION FRUSTRATION

Jayne never expected money to be an issue, not given her master's degree in chemistry from one of the top math and sciences universities in the country. Fresh out of graduate school, she accepted a seemingly secure corporate job working in the lab at a pharmaceutical company. She got laid off after only a year. When she couldn't find another pharmaceutical position, she wound up moving back in with her parents and getting a job at Pottery Barn for $7 an hour, joining a wave of graduates whose diplomas hadn't opened the door to much of anything. In 2004 there were more unemployed college graduates than high school dropouts.[16]

In search of an alternate career, Jayne eventually started substitute teaching in the local school district for $60 a day. She found she loved the interactive dynamics of the classroom far more than the isolated monotony of corporate lab work. Despite her master's degree, it took her two years to find a full-time teaching job in the New Hampshire public school system. Today, at thirty-two, she earns $37,000 year as a high school science teacher, an amount she supplements by teaching organic chemistry one night a week at the local college and working in her father's office during the summers.

"This is my overeducated life," she explains over a patchy cell phone connection while driving from school to school one Thursday evening. "I always have at least two jobs and I still live paycheck to paycheck."

Such lean living made it impossible to pay off the $30,000 in student loan and credit card debt she had accumulated during graduate school. Even her father, a financial planner, couldn't come up with a budget that allowed her meager paychecks to stretch that far. So, while in the process of launching her teaching career, Jayne turned to a debt-consolidation agency for help. Today, she's managed to pay back nearly half the money she owes. She's also going to school part-time to earn her third degree, a master's in education, so she can make a few extra thousand dollars a year as a teacher.

"Even if I eventually get my PhD, the salary cap for high school teachers is around $70,000," she explains. "And that would be many years, and a lot more debt, down the road. Sometimes it's hard to stay motivated when you're earning so little money. And very easy to just burn out."

Jayne's grateful her job feels secure, in that there will always be a need for high school science teachers. But in her current school system the teachers have been working without a contract for the past year, a fact that makes her nervous enough that she's considering moving to another—hopefully higher-paying—district in another state.

"Worrying about money keeps me up at night," she admits. "This was not how I envisioned my future. I was raised to expect that a job and an education would lead to a certain quality of life. That definitely isn't happening here."

Simple mathematics assures us that Jayne's experience is far from unique. There isn't a skilled job for every skilled college graduate, and the economy can't be expected to shift to make room for more degree-holders just because they exist. A rise in college-educated workers doesn't ensure more widespread financial security. Instead, it means many wind up in jobs that are below their qualifications, and earn corresponding salaries. Today 37 percent of flight attendants, 21 percent of embalmers, and 13 percent of security guards and casino dealers have college diplomas.[17]

The oversupply of qualified applicants means employers have little incentive to make those jobs that do require college degrees pay off. Sure, a few budding bankers and corporate lawyers will take a flying leap into six-figure starting salaries, but the average income for a new college graduate is a far more humbling $36,000. Long-term unemployment is also rising for college graduates, increasing nearly three percentage points from 2000 to 2005.[18]

Sabina, a thirty-year-old teacher who grew so fed up with the U.S.

academic system that she took her master's in education overseas to work in Vietnam, describes the moment she truly began to appreciate the limits to the amount of security her stellar education could actually provide.

"One afternoon, five of us were sitting in our living room in Baltimore. We were all in our late twenties and early thirties. We had eleven degrees between us. And our total income was less than $100,000. That just made me sick."

Among the people I interviewed, those freshest out of school seemed the most optimistic about the future, even saddled with debt and low-paying careers. They, most strongly, believed that financial tangles would somehow work themselves out. But over time, those college-instilled expectations created far more conflicted feelings. I found many people in their thirties and older questioning the value of a college education. People who told me that, given the high cost and uncertain payoff, they regretted getting graduate or even undergraduate degrees. Many had stories of friends and family members who'd skipped college—and the accompanying debt—and were making higher salaries as machinists, welders, court reporters, and even baking bagels. They mentioned encouraging their own children to get a profession or a trade, that college wouldn't be a necessity for them.

"Sadly, I would love to get back to counseling," said Caitlin, thirty-two, who works as a product manager for an aviation company to pay off the $60,000 in government and private loans she took out to finance her master's in social work. "But I could never make enough money to pay off my loans or save up for a house. When I started school, I didn't get the ramifications of having so much debt because I'd never had any before. I certainly didn't understand how much money I'd have to make to pay it off."

At one time, taking financial risks was considered part of the middle-class coming-of-age process. These days, those in their twenties who decide to take a year off to write a novel, to accumulate several thousand dollars in debt backpacking through West Africa, to spend six months in cooking school, or even to waste money they don't have buying vintage comic books or CDs or maxing out their Victoria's Secret credit card can pay a tremendous price. I spoke to people who did all these things and, instead of chalking them up to experience, they're working two or three jobs, agonizing over whether they can afford a house or children, and dodging calls from collections agencies, all in an effort to make up for what they lost.

"I want to go back to school in the worst way," said Amelia, thirty, who left college two semesters short of a biology degree to try to make it as a dancer in New York. Nine years and two ankle surgeries later, she feels closed out of future possibilities. "I want to be a doctor. I applied and was accepted to go back and finish my undergraduate degree, but there's no way I can afford it. I'm still trying to pay off loans from the first time around. Some days I feel optimistic and I think maybe next year. Other days I think I've screwed it up for life."

The postcollege years used to be a time when people had the freedom to test careers, travel the world, screw up a few times before finding their niche. Now, far too often, they exit the ivy-covered walls and make a beeline for the corporate ladder already saddled with enough debt to sink anyone without the luck of, or foggiest interest in, landing a job on Wall Street. Today's graduates never get to know the meaning of the words "fancy free." Instead they're launched into an economic system, a political system, and a value system that teaches its most promising members that the only definition of success is a high-earning job, and that loads them up with enough debt that many young people truly wonder whether there's any other wise choice than the corporate one.

THE STATE OF HIGHER EDUCATION

Though today's education frustration can be largely blamed on broader economic trends, colleges and universities have also done their part to reshape the educational landscape. Schools, competing to win students, spend money on research labs, sports teams, superstar professors, and endowed business schools. With cutbacks in state and federal aid, somebody has to pay for such flashy new additions, and odds are higher than ever that the students themselves will end up taking the hit.

This marriage of education and commerce has far reaching social and ideological ramifications. College education, like many social services, is transitioning into a consumer service, a buy-as-you-go, pay-as-you-play situation. Some colleges have actually raised their tuitions in an effort to boost enrollment, figuring that consumers equate cost with quality.[19] Student debt has become such a competitive and lucrative industry that loan companies are offering school officials "added incentives"—bonuses like Caribbean vacations, iPods, and cash rewards—for sending more students in their direction. Officials at top-tier universities have been caught holding shares in those same student-loan companies they recommend to their students, or accepting gifts ranging from cases of tequila to assistance with graduate school tuition. Such ethically ambiguous ground smacks far more of big business than of the hallowed ivory tower.[20]

I spoke to a number of college educators, every last one of whom went into the field to pursue a love of ideas and the life of the mind, who were having serious troubles making ends meet. With schools requiring more and more money from students—teaching at the college level requires at least a master's degree and frequently a PhD— and having less and less to spend on its faculty, save the occasional celebrity professor, college professors seem to epitomize those caught in the educated professional middle-class quicksand.

"It's a constant struggle, one I see going on for everyone I work with," says Natalie, a recently tenured art and design professor at a major midwestern university who makes $39,000 a year. "I feel like there's been this insidious shift in the whole academic system. Making money is starting to matter more than higher learning. Salaries for professors in the business school are much higher than for those teaching art or English or history."

Natalie's observations are borne out by the statistics. The average engineering professor makes $78,900, and the average business professor $66,760, considerably more than professors of English at $53,090 and the arts at $53,360. Job security for all professors has plummeted, with tenured and tenure-track positions making up just 37 percent of faculty, a drop from 57 percent in the 1970s.[21]

Adjunct professors, paid on a per-class basis, related making $18,000 and $20,000 a year—an amount one history professor broke down to $3 an hour—salaries so slim that they worked a second full-time job, defaulted on student loan and credit card debt, and put their kids on Medicaid just to squeak by. Others admitted aban-

doning their teaching careers early on not because they were disillusioned by the politics or the workload of academia but because they
feared they simply couldn't make a living.

"I'm insanely overeducated for what I'm doing now," admits
Courtenay, thirty-five, describing her decision to forgo dreams of becoming an English professor in favor of a career as a gymnastics
coach. "It's not exactly an intellectually stimulating career, but I
needed to support myself. Sadly, I make twice as much money coach-
ing ten-year-olds than I did teaching college."

Many interviewees feared that universities are losing touch with
their role as centers of thriving creative and intellectual communities,
making it doubly difficult for professors to justify the financial sacrifices they've made for their careers.

"The hardships are even harder," explains Melody, the African
American studies professor, "but the creative center that's supposed
to feed and inspire you has disappeared. I feel like no one at these
schools cares about learning anymore."

There's a problem with an education system that won't even pay
those who form its core support structures—the professors, deans,
administrators—enough to support themselves. And there's a troubling hypocrisy unfolding within schools that don't teach their students about financial literacy, then push tuitions so high that such
economic naïveté becomes a danger to their futures.

I'm not one who advocates turning four-year colleges into vocational centers that spit out students with "practical degrees." I don't
think college should be viewed as job training. It should serve the
same purpose it has for centuries, as a hub of intellectual pursuit.
That hub should be available to anyone who wants to take advantage of it. Instead—between the limited funds available through Pell
and other government grants and the escalating burden of taking on
both government and private loans—it's becoming increasingly out
of reach for a huge segment of the low- and middle-income population. While a good computer skills degree can make you a good systems engineer, I suspect a strong broad-based liberal arts education
enables you to think more deeply, solve problems more effectively,
and hopefully engender more empathy toward human kind, all essential skills no matter what your chosen vocation. Our current edu-

cational system is too bottom-line corporate as it is. The last thing we need to do is make it more so.

But if college, and in many cases graduate degrees, are going to be necessary, they need to be affordable to more than a sliver of the population. Today two out of three students take out education loans, and that doesn't even count those who don't bother applying because they know they can't afford to pay. Instead of trying to curb the high prices set on academic credentials, in July 2006 the government actually made interest rates on Stafford loans 2 percent higher, adding $2,000 to the average borrower's debt.[22]

We've become so accustomed to student debt that we don't question the need to borrow money to get an education. Student loans are the social norm. The alternative—not going to college at all—is infinitely worse. But why should these be the only options? Widespread student debt is a relatively new phenomenon in this country. In 1977 college students borrowed about $6 billion. By 2005 they were borrowing over $85 billion, over fourteen times as much.[23]

In the short run, we need to address the fact that college graduates are drowning in student debt. Too many of them simply don't make enough money to cover current living expenses and pay back their loans. It takes longer than six months, sometimes longer than six years, to find your feet in the working world, particularly if you don't enter a traditionally lucrative profession. A simple first step could entail better adjusting payment plans to take into account things like a graduate's current income, their career trajectory, and whether they have dependents, then giving them more options with respect to repayment.

The loan industry has become bloated with unnecessary costs, which are passed on to borrowers. Why does the government need to offer education loans through private lenders who take their own cut of each transaction? Loans provided directly through the government, or through colleges themselves, could cut costs, lower current interest rates, and ensure such rates remained fixed for the life of the loan. In fact, the government already has such a program in place. The William D. Ford Federal Direct Loan Program, instituted in 1994, provides the same federal loans most students acquire through private lenders like Sallie Mae with identical interest rates and similar repayment options, but no private lenders are involved. Instead, universities originate the loans themselves, with the federal government supplying capital and servicing the loans. The Direct Loan program not only benefits students, it costs the government less as well. For every $100 lent by private lenders, the government pays $13.81 in subsidies, defaults, and other items, but the same amount lent through the Direct Loan program costs them just $3.85. Making all student loans direct loans would save the treasury, and thus taxpayers, up to $4.5 billion. Expanding such a program would seem to better serve everyone involved, except the commercial banks and private lenders, who essentially bribe schools—offering them millions of dollars of subsidized loans for student who wouldn't otherwise qualify—not to participate in the Direct Loan program.[24]

We might also consider a system of full or partial debt forgiveness for college graduates who go into public service. We need to acknowledge that those who embark on education and social services careers serve an essential societal role for which they'll receive relatively little financial reward. Given the debt they're paying to society, maybe they shouldn't have to pay such a heavy debt to Sallie Mae. For example, the Teaching Fellows program, started in New York in 2000, offers adults interested in a career shift into teaching a master's degree, fully subsidized, in exchange for spending two years teaching in high-need city schools. Students could also be given the opportunity to do service work in organizations like the Red Cross or the Peace Corps in exchange for tuition reimbursement, similar to how things work in the military. A loose template for such a program already exists in Americorps. Congress took a laudable step in this direction in September 2007 when it passed a bill overhauling student aid programs, including forgiving loans to graduates who've worked ten or more years in public service professions and limiting monthly payments on federally backed loans to 15 percent of the borrower's discretionary income. The bill was subsequently signed into law by the president.[25]

On a larger scale, we can begin examining alternative models in other countries—Australia, Canada, France, Germany, Holland, Italy, Sweden—all of which manage to supply partially or fully subsidized college educations to their citizens without giving way to economic collapse. In an evaluation of global higher education standards comparing sixteen industrialized countries, the U.S.—though a respectable fourth in terms of accessibility—ranked thirteenth when it came to affordability, coming in ahead of only the United Kingdom, New Zealand, and Japan.[26]

Scandinavian countries in particular have been successful in creating higher education systems that are both affordable and accessible, with Finland often cited as having the best system in the world. Sixty-five percent of Finnish students go on to universities or polytechnics—schools that prepare students for careers in business and the applied sciences—essentially free of charge. The government picks up the entire tuition cost and also provides generous student grants and housing subsidies, spending 7 percent of its GDP on education as opposed to the 2.9 percent spent in the United States. The average student pays slightly over 200 Euros ($270) in education costs, while the average American student pays more than 9,600 Euros ($13,000), almost five times as much. As a result, unlike in the U.S., nearly every Finnish student truly does have the freedom to attend university if they so choose.[27]

Until our current U.S. financial circumstances change, and perhaps even then, colleges and graduate programs also have a responsibility to address the financial realities most students will face when they leave.

"Not once in grad school did someone discuss how to plan financially or live on the salaries most of us would be making," Caitlin tells me about her graduate program in social work at an elite southern university. "The only time anyone mentioned money was when I took a class in human sexuality and the professor told us we could make $100,000 a year as a sex therapist."

"I wish I'd gotten some trace of a financial education," echoes Isabella, a professor with an MFA in film studies, and a single mother trying to raise two children on $50,000 a year. "When money is this tight every wrong choice has enormous ramifications. Right now I feel like I'm just paddling around without a clue."

Part of comprehensive college education should include realistic discussion about income, debt, and the financial choices students may confront. Though college needn't mirror the real world, it should prepare us for what's out there. Given how crucial financial management has become, it is imperative that a required financial literacy class be included as part of every undergraduate and graduate—and even high school—education. It's time to start being honest, with students and with ourselves, about the potential costs of navigating our increasingly polarized economic world.

4

CAREER AND CONTRIBUTION

Society or the 401(k)?

Henry, fifty, is a Presbyterian minister serving as the pastor for a small parish, with about seventy members, just outside Boise, Idaho. His job entails being a ministerial jack-of-all-trades, conducting services, writing the church bulletin, leading adult education classes, all for a base salary of $29,800 a year. His wife, a former public school teacher, now does periodic substitute teaching and homeschools the two youngest of their four children—ages eighteen, fourteen, twelve, and ten. The family essentially lives on Henry's salary.

"Making ends meet is a constant battle," Henry admits. "We have to get creative wherever possible."

"Getting creative" has included paying $40 a year to belong to a Community Food Resource Center, which picks up old bread, produce, and dairy products that grocery stores have pulled from their shelves and redistributes the food to group members. The church provides a house and a $4,300 housing allowance to defray utility costs, a boon in the present but a mixed blessing for the future.

"Not owning a house means no chance to build up any equity," Henry explains. "The church does have a denomination-wide pension fund but it's not enough to support us indefinitely. I worry a lot about where we'll live and what we'll live on once I retire."

Though the church provides health insurance, the cost of additional medical expenses, including co-pays on doctor's visits and the prescription drugs Henry and his wife take for heart problems and high blood pressure, have proved a major financial drain. In addition, as the kids get older, child-related expenses keep increasing, everything from clothes to school supplies to fees for extracurricular activities like Scouts and sports teams. None of these in and of themselves will break the family, but all together it adds up to severe financial strain.

Before moving to Idaho four years ago, Henry was the pastor for a small-town congregation in Nebraska, a parish he loved but had to abandon because it couldn't afford his $25,000 salary. While in Nebraska, Henry and his wife found their credit card and student loan debts getting so out of control that they turned to a debt-consolidation company. In five years, they've managed to wipe out most of what they owed and are currently carrying only about $200 on an emergency credit card.

"We've had some very bleak passages," he acknowledges. "Sometimes we've had to deal with collection agencies, but we've never defaulted on anything. Some way or another we always make it work."

Henry's decision to become a minister was fueled by something he considers far deeper and more significant than monetary concerns. After getting his bachelor's degree, he spent ten years working as an accountant, a job that earned him a fair living but left him increasingly deflated and unfulfilled. Everything he loved, everything that fed his soul, revolved around his volunteer work with the church. So in the late 1980s he and his wife decided upon a career and life change that began with Henry spending three years pursuing his master's degree at the Louisville Presbyterian Theological Seminary in Kentucky. His wife cashed out her retirement plan, they sold their house and paid off all their debts in order to start their new life financially free. With the help of various scholarships, Henry was able to keep his student loans down to $10,000. But even that was a heavy load to carry into a career with an average salary of just $41,210.

Making ends meet has become increasingly difficult for members of the clergy. Among Presbyterian churches, trends indicate smaller congregations getting smaller while the large get larger, drawing parishioners through better-funded education and outreach programs. Increasingly, these small parishes are also having to "get creative" in order to pay a minister. They've developed strategies like yoking churches—two churches sharing a single pastor—and looking for ministerial candidates with second jobs or economically secure spouses, who aren't dependent on their parish incomes as a sole means of support.

Unlike the shrinking congregations, new pastors are graduating from seminary with increasing amounts of student debt—an average of $25,018.[1] With so many churches finding it difficult to pay base salaries, even those who secure a full-time position have little prospect for financial growth. Rather than having to ride out a particularly lean period at the start of their careers, they face economic hardship for the rest of their lives.

"We're living the reverse of the American dream," Henry says, describing his career trajectory. "When my wife and I first got married we were a dual-income family. Once we had kids we became one income, then after I went to seminary we became one lower income. I guess that's the price you pay for doing the work you love."

Despite the financial stresses, there's no question in Henry's mind that he would encourage his children to follow their passions—"the gifts that God gave them"—rather than focus on finding a financially stable career. But it does weigh on him that he hasn't been able to provide for his family in the way he had hoped.

"We don't want to buy a boat or a second car," he tells me. "But a little more money would relieve a lot of anxiety. I would like to take my family on vacation, just once, so we could spend time together someplace fun. I would like my kids to see the ocean. I would like to help them pay for college. That doesn't seem like so much to ask."

Like Henry, most members of the educated professional middle class I spoke to didn't want more money so they could acquire more material possessions. Not a single person complained about not being able to afford a Mercedes or a second home. No one chooses to be a priest or a social worker or a book editor with that goal in mind. They voiced a different definition of success, one in which they could escape the crippling financial pressure under which one unforeseen life blow—a medical crisis, a dip in the housing market, an unplanned pregnancy—could permanently wipe them out.

The idea that the rich are getting richer while everyone slides backward is not just a liberal bromide. It's remapping our entire culture. This middle-class squeeze means that a whole group of society's valuable contributors—those who chose careers based on rewards like autonomy, creativity, and service rather than fat paychecks—risk becoming too busy struggling to keep their heads above water to actually contribute. The potential loss is enormous.

DOING GOOD VERSUS DOING WELL

One benefit of membership in the educated middle class is the freedom to work for rewards beyond just a paycheck. Education opens up a world of jobs that stimulate the mind and perhaps even better society. But today, as personal wealth and ambition trump values like service and generosity, opting to be more socially than financially conscious can require serious sacrifices. There's a noticeable salary gap between careers in which one does good and those in which one does well. The average child and family social worker makes $38,000 and the average high school teacher $54,000—less than she'd make as an elevator repairman. Compare that to a typical sales manager making $99,000 or a corporate lawyer making $110,000.[2] Those who do enter lower-paying, socially significant professions often feel stranded as our country steadily diminishes investments in education, research, arts, and culture. Cuts in social programs affect not only the beneficiaries of such programs but all those working for nonprofit and social service agencies, leading to fewer jobs, lower salaries, and reduced health-care and retirement benefits.

"I have a passion for this work," says Meghan, thirty-one, who makes $42,000 a year as a substance-abuse counselor in San Francisco with no prospects for raise or promotion. "But financially I don't know how long I can continue. If I ever want a house, a family, anything beyond a month-to-month lifestyle, forget it. If you're going to enter social work, the only way to make it is to marry rich or go into private practice."

As finances get tighter and our lives grow more precarious, we can find ourselves wrapped in a heavy, even crippling cloud of shame. Not shame over the work we do. Most people I spoke to loved their jobs and, aside from the financial aspects, were committed to and proud of their careers. Social workers, therapists, journalists, book editors, those populating a wide range of arts organizations, community groups, and nonprofits, all voiced a real sense of nonmaterial reward from their professions. Again and again I heard some version of the assertion that "if I thought I could make a living at it, I would be happy doing this for the rest of my life."

Instead, the shame we feel is a direct reflection of our inability to make ends meet. It stems from our insecurity over whether we can afford to keep these jobs and still support ourselves and raise our families. To complicate things even further, those of us who've embarked upon creative, intellectual, or service-oriented pursuits often feel like we're not supposed to care about money. We're dedicated to loftier ideals—peer respect, a deeper understanding of an issue, informing or aiding the public—and should feel lucky to have the jobs we have at all. And we often do feel these things. But this anxiety over whether it's okay to also want tangible rewards like financial stability and security, decent pay, and benefits, creates added emotional pressure. That shame over not having enough becomes laced with guilt for wanting more.

"I'm always aware of the tension between my desire to have a comfortable lifestyle and my social justice values," say Rafael, thirty-five, a case manager for a foster care agency. "Part of me believes that it's right, even noble, for me to suffer and scrape by for the rest of my life. But part of me resents that I have to live like this when I know I have the brains and skill to acquire wealth. I'm not sure how to resolve that question of wanting money but not wanting money to be the ultimate goal."

Like Rafael, many members of the educated professional middle class view maintaining both a comfortable lifestyle and social justice values as mutually exclusive. In a sort of cultural brainwash, we accept prolonged financial struggle as a nonnegotiable part of the contribution package, rather than envisioning a society that more equitably rewards those who tend to its intellectual, social, and creative well-being. The future of such careers may lie in the balance. Today's college graduates are shying away from public service careers because they rightly assume they won't make enough money to support themselves in the short or long term. Twenty-three percent of public-college graduates and 38 percent of private-college graduates would have an unmanageable level of debt if they attempted to live on the average starting teacher's salary of $31,704. For starting social workers making an average of $27,163, such debt would be unmanageable for 37 percent of public-college and 55 percent of private-college grads.[3]

For Henry, becoming a minister has meant a lifetime shaped by financial compromise. Though he's matter-of-fact about his circumstances, one can't imagine it's easy to be a college-educated professional with a full-time job and still be dogged by collection agencies and have to feed your children out of a food bank. It's not a trade-off many people are willing to make.

For every Henry who has no doubts about staying the course, there are scores of other ministers and substance-abuse counselors, museum curators and foundation officers who find themselves, in their late thirties, facing a stack of bills, a family to support, and nothing to call their own, and wondering if it's too late to change their minds and take up accounting. But even for those who decide that "selling out" is the best way to go, it's often too late. There are precious few jobs out there you can sell out for, especially if you didn't hop on the fast track the second you left school. In today's economy, the fastest-growing occupations don't belong to lawyers or investment bankers, they belong to home health aides, medical and physician's assistants, and computer systems analysts.[4] Members of today's educated professional middle class are finding that there's no laid-out route that ensures stability anymore. Job and financial security remain elusive regardless of how hard you work and how much you're willing to sacrifice.

FREEDOM IN THE AGE OF PERMANENT INSTABILITY

On the surface, Helen and Arthur seem to be a rare success story. Helen, who has two master's degrees and a PhD in education, is a college administrator at a small private school in Minneapolis. Arthur has parlayed his three degrees—a BA in physics and two master's in business and management—into a product-management job for a large Internet provider. They live modestly, following a weekly budget, and can afford to own two cars and pay $750 a month in day care for their two-year-old daughter. Their current combined income is $180,000, placing them comfortably above any definition of a middle-class household. On the surface, they appear to be two of the lucky few to have escaped the insecurity and instability that haunts so many of today's educated professionals.

But a closer look reveals some cracks in their cozy tale. Though they're both in their late thirties, the couple has only $1,200 in savings and $10,000 invested in various retirement accounts. They don't own their own home but instead rent a two-bedroom house in a Minneapolis suburb for $2,200 a month. Most surprising of all, they're carrying over $50,000 in credit card debt. Though the mind may jump to designer clothing binges, lavish cruises to the Bahamas, or wild and wayward college days, Helen and Arthur's negative net worth has a far more prosaic source.

"When Arthur finished business school in 2000, he got a consulting job right away," Helen explains. "Then just over a year later they shut down the unit and he was laid off. That was four days before 9/11. He was out of work for the next four years."

Helen, who was working as an administrator at a community college in Chicago at the time, became the family's sole provider. Their household income fell from $150,000 to $50,000, dropping to one-third its previous level and making them very much a struggling middle-class family.

"We'd just bought our first house," Helen recalls. "I was panicked about whether we could keep it. My mother wound up giving us a tax-free loan so we could pay the mortgage. It was humiliating. We still haven't been able to pay her back."

Though Arthur took various temporary consulting jobs while he searched for something more permanent, for the next four years he brought in less than $30,000 a year. The couple struggled to make payments on everything from mortgage to credit cards to Arthur's remaining student loans. They quickly tapped out their savings and Helen launched a full-scale search for a better-paying position.

"It was stressful for both of us," she recalls. "Arthur got very depressed. After months and months of looking, it's difficult not to take things personally. There was a lot of pressure from my family that he wasn't trying hard enough, and I didn't always know how to be supportive. It's hard to be the spouse of an unemployed person. How do you explain the fact that when I looked for another job, I found something right away?"

When Helen was offered her current position in Minneapolis, with a $20,000 pay increase, the couple figured they had very little to lose. Not only would they be closer to Helen's family but they hoped the fresh job market would also give Arthur a much needed psychological boost. Arthur was still freelance consulting when Helen got pregnant with their daughter the following year, and since she was already in her mid-thirties and had feared she might have trouble getting pregnant, they decided not to wait to have a child.

"Financially, we were more stable than we'd been in the past two years," Helen says. "It was nerve-racking, but who knew if there'd ever be a time when we felt totally financially ready. We would just figure out a way."

Though the couple has finally landed on firm financial footing, the specter of those four lean years remains. They figure it will be five to ten years before they climb out from under their current debt, and the prospect of accumulating enough savings to buy another house seems far, far down the road. Helen doubts whether she'll ever again have a sense of true financial security.

"I worry all the time that Arthur might get laid off," she admits. "The Internet industry isn't exactly stable, and his company profits didn't meet expectations for the past few quarters. Both of us are very mindful of keeping our ears to the ground about shifts in the job market. We never want to get caught again without a plan B."

Stories like Helen and Arthur's abound as the volatility of American incomes continues to grow both more pronounced and more common, outpacing even the rising inequality between the rich and the rest of us. At its 1990s peak, income instability was nearly two and a half times as high as it was in the 1970s, and this instability has risen across the board, striking college-educated workers just as aggressively as the working class. Even if our salaries do eventually rebound, it can take years to recover from both the financial debt and the psychological blows.[5]

Our current economy has been painted as one in which educated working professionals become gloriously free agents, able to move from job to job and custom-design careers confined only by the limits of their imaginations. There may be less support and loyalty from employers, but the payoff comes in terms of more individual freedom. This much praised sense of freedom planted the seed that if you're not making money, you simply need to work harder, faster, and longer in order to do so. The opportunities are out there, around the clock, just waiting for you to take hold. Of course, in order to take advantage of such freedom, workers require the financial grounding to quit their jobs, go back to school to enhance skills and training, or start their own businesses. When they're dependent on every paycheck to make it through the end of the month, and with the possibilities of layoffs and salary freezes perpetually hovering, most people become less inclined to take career risks, not more. The ramifications of loss are too devastating.

Individuals who entered the labor market in the '80s and '90s are 43 percent more likely to change jobs than those who entered it in the '60s and '70s.[6] Though jumping from job to job early in one's career can be beneficial, adding to the depth of skill and experience, workers eventually reach a point where remaining at a job for a longer period of time becomes the more advantageous choice. Staying with a single employer enables you to develop more intricate job skills, and forge relationships with colleagues, clients, and superiors. It puts you on track to accrue raises, benefits, and promotions, not to mention less quantitative gains like establishing long-term loyalty and trust. Though some movement is healthy, studies have shown that workers who change jobs early and often get caught in a permanent job-shift cycle; the more jobs you've had in the past, the more likely you are to change employers yet again in the future. Such chronic instability ultimately prevents workers from moving upward in their careers.[7]

Most people I interviewed who'd made voluntary job transitions weren't attempting to scale the ladder to immense wealth. They either simply couldn't live on what they made, saw no room for raises or promotions—so that moving was less a question of greed than need—or felt desperately unhappy in their current position. Though they didn't want a return to the 1950s model of one job, one company for a lifetime, many were actually seeking what they've been told they're so lucky to no longer have—some sort of job security in this age of rampant downsizing and outsourcing. They wanted to feel that someone owed them something for the time and energy they poured into their careers. No one I spoke to reported feeling confident that they could always find a better-paying position. Instead, they tended to comfort themselves with the idea that they could live closer and closer to the bone if the need arose. They could take in roommates, move in with their parents, get a restaurant job, or fall back on their credit cards, steps that bespoke far less freedom than financial desperation.

As with Helen and Arthur, the prospect of layoffs and job loss haunts the educated professional middle class, becoming a far more powerful motivator than a potential job or salary uptick. I spoke to people who'd been laid off not just once but two, three, four, six times. So often they'd purposely lost count. Many had been young victims of the wave of dot-com layoffs in the '90s, in on the ground floor of startups that folded seemingly overnight. They'd worked for major companies that consolidated operations, shut down units, or outsourced entire departments. Despite reassurances that the economy is booming, to them the job market felt precarious. And despite reassurances, the job market is.

The unemployment rate may not be rising, but the chance of losing your job is indeed going up. Job-loss rates are as high now as they were during the recession of the 1980s, the most severe economic downturn this country has seen since the Great Depression. Spells of unemployment also tend to last longer. In the 1960s the average time spent out of work was twelve weeks; today it's climbed to sixteen. And among those who do find new jobs, half come back at lower salaries and a third experience an income drop of 20 percent or more.[8] Nor is unemployment solely a problem for the young or for those lacking in job skills and education. In the mid-1990s, college-educated workers who were laid off experienced just a 5 percent income drop when they found a new job. But today, educated professionals across the age spectrum are actually the least likely to find new jobs at equivalent salaries and benefits, They experience income losses averaging 20 percent, nearly twice as severe as those who didn't even graduate high school. In addition, more and more white-collar workers are experiencing long-term unemployment. Beginning the day you step off campus and lasting well into the typical retirement years, a college degree no longer buys you anything close to job security.[9]

Even for those who haven't been laid off, the fear of losing one's job hovers. It's happened to too many friends and colleagues for most of us to feel immune. Few educated professional middle-class families have the recommended three-month, or even three-week, cushion to fall back on. Homes, child care, healthy credit, and financial solvency all lie in the balance. As one TV producer I spoke to put it, "We'd be screwed."

This escalating economic instability means financial insecurity shadows even those who currently make enough to live comfortably. In a life characterized by regular income swings, long-term investments seem too risky. How can you feel confident that you'll be able to pay monthly mortgage and child-care bills, that you'll continue to have money for taxes and school tuitions, if your earnings are so reliably inconsistent from year to year?

"I've never earned this much in my life," says Kayla, an alternative health practitioner. Together she and her husband, a research scientist, made over $100,000 last year. "But we're still living in a rented apartment because we're too afraid to buy a house. We're still choosing between getting dental work done and paying down our student debt. My work depends on a healthy economy. When times get tough, alternative medicine is one of the first luxuries to go. My husband's position relies on him getting new grants every year. What if we commit to a thirty-year mortgage and the next year our income is cut in half?"

A number of people I spoke to took the edge off this perpetual insecurity by working multiple jobs, a survival strategy they share with many members of the working class. In addition to full-time white-collar professions, they moonlighted teaching, writing articles, babysitting, doing construction work, or waiting tables. Again and again I heard the phrase, "I work constantly but still can't see to make enough money."

Others found a perverse sort of security in one of the most traditionally insecure job sectors, freelance and contract work. The popularity of temporary work (essentially any job in which there's no implicit or explicit contract for long-term employment) has shot up since the '90s—when the phenomenon was so rare the Bureau of Labor Statistics didn't even bother tracking the numbers—as businesses shift their emphasis from stability to flexibility. Full- and part-time contingent workers now comprise 33 percent of the workforce.[10] Today's population of freelancers combines those who offer a specific skill to an array of clients—journalists, graphic designers, computer programmers—and those who work for a single company that wants to maintain regular employees without providing typical employee benefits like health care, retirement, or paid sick and vacation days. In 2000, one-fifth of Microsoft's workforce was made up of contingent workers, even as the company succumbed to a lawsuit filed by temporary workers demanding benefits available to permanent staff.[11]

Allegra, thirty-four, has an MFA in creative writing from one of the top liberal arts colleges in the Northeast, and earns her living as a freelance copy editor and proofreader, working seven days a week when the work is available. Her yearly take-home pay is about $30,000 before taxes. She charges clients—a mix of publishing houses and marketing firms—$30 to $35 an hour, five times the state minimum wage. Nevertheless, her meager paychecks have led to severe financial floundering.

When she got pregnant with her son a year and a half ago, finances were so tight she had to apply for state welfare programs, WIC and Medicaid, to afford food and medical care. Because her freelance income varies so widely month to month, she had no problem qualifying. But even with WIC paying for food, formula, and her son's medical expenses, things are tough. Her child's father does construction and electrical work but Allegra's freelance income is responsible for covering the bulk of the family's expenses.

For Allegra, holding down multiple white-collar jobs, with the ever-present option of taking on yet more work, feels like the best possible option for making ends meet. Though she doesn't make much, it's still more than she earned in her previous job as a field coordinator for a nonprofit women's organization.

"I feel more in control," she explains of her current situation. "At least if I lose one client, I still have other paying work to fall back on."

Allegra also prefers freelance work because it gives her more flexibility to arrange child care. And there's always the possibility of making more money, given the proper amount of hustle, luck, and lack of sleep, which you can't do if you're locked into a salaried position. She's constantly looking for more work—full-time, part-time, freelance, whatever is on offer—to add to her current responsibilities and maybe somehow scrape by. But she doesn't know what she's going to do when her deferred student loans reappear a year from now or she has to begin making car payments on the Nissan Sentra she bought this past summer to replace her ten-year-old Honda.

Allegra admits that freelance work is the definition of economically volatile. You can wait months for checks. There's no such thing as benefits or paid leave of any sort—she started back to work when her son was only two days old. It's nearly impossible to come up with a short- or long-term budget, since you only have the loosest idea what you'll be making in the coming year or years. Getting a decent rate on anything from a mortgage to a car loan becomes that much trickier if you don't have what's considered a legitimate job with the pay stubs to prove it. Everything in this country, from Social Security to health care to the tax system, caters to those who have a traditional job with a traditional employer-employee setup. For the increasing number of people who operate outside that box, the liberating lack of dependence on a single employer comes with an equally powerful sense of being financially trapped. When I spoke to Allegra during the period around Christmas and New Year's, when work slows and expenses rise, such income volatility had come close to breaking her.

"This month I just couldn't deal so I didn't pay the bills," she said, ticking them off on her fingers. "Con Ed, gas, phone, cell phone, Internet, credit cards. I didn't even open them. What are they going to do? Come and shoot me? I paid the rent so we won't be out on the street. And that's about all I can handle right now."

Having lived through the economic booms and busts of the '80s and '90s, members of today's educated professional middle class are having trouble buying into the fact that we are more individually empowered. Wearing jeans to work and not having to set the alarm clock hasn't been enough to offset the fact that we also have to pay for our own health care and could spend two years without a job. These days, we may be encouraged to pursue the work we love, but that pursuit often comes at the steep price of our short- and long-term financial security. Which provokes the question, Are we really any freer after all?

THE TRUE CREATIVE CLASS

There's one subset of the educated professional middle class that has always lived near the edge. Creative people aren't supposed to care about money, at least not quite as much as the rest of us. They are the freest of free agents, with a natural affinity for operating outside conventional societal boundaries. Since the dot-com boom of the 1990s, the business world has been abuzz with reports of a new and flourishing creative class. Unlike in the 1950s, when conformity and routine comprised core educated professional middle-class values, in the New Economy you earn points by being innovative and original. Think Bill Gates. Think Google. If anyone should thrive in this age of individual accomplishment, surely it's those most willing to take the creative path.

In truth, there's a new creative class in the same way that there's a new career freedom. Artists haven't suddenly come into their financial own, we've just opened up the term "creative" to include a slew of new members. The notion of a New Economy–fueled creative groundswell was popularized by urban studies theorist Richard Florida and his 2002 book, *The Rise of the Creative Class*. For Florida, the term "creative" encompasses scientists, engineers, computer programmers, advertising executives, mathematicians, basically anyone who works in a field capable of innovation. He even goes so far as to include health-care professionals, sales people, lawyers, and financial operators.[12]

As this new corporate creativity has gained prominence, a career based on old-style individual creativity—the kind exercised by writers, painters, dancers, actors, musicians, filmmakers, and all those who support them—has grown even tougher. Financial security has never been part of the creative package, but today a polarization is occurring among artists that echoes the polarization within the rest of the educated professional class. While a precious few people acquire extreme wealth, even moderately successful artists face a life of economic insecurity and instability, a life that is becoming increasingly difficult to sustain.

Alice is a hip and wiry forty-four, with short spiky brown hair, tight jeans, and a languorous energy that echoes her Chattanooga, Tennessee, roots. She's a painter and a screenwriter who's made her living as an artist for the past fifteen years.

"Back in the early '90s my then husband was working for an investment bank and he got a big bonus," she recalls. "We decided to take the next year and live on that money while we both pursued our dreams. I got a show right away and sold every painting. I quit my day job and hoped I'd never look back."

When Alice and her husband divorced four years later, she moved from their three-bedroom house to a small apartment in an industrial section of Los Angeles where she still lives today. Her work—which at that point consisted of large, brightly colored abstract paintings— adjusted accordingly and she began producing smaller, more condensed pieces she could do on her kitchen table. Meanwhile, Alice's second career dream of becoming a film director led to periodic jobs writing and rewriting screenplays, for which she earned anywhere from $2,000 to $10,000 for a couple months' work.

Though Alice is far from a household name, from a critical and creative standpoint her career has flourished. She's sold out solo shows at galleries in Los Angeles, New York, and Chicago, and her work has received strong reviews in prestigious art journals and papers like the *LA Weekly* and the *New York Times*. Several of her screenplays have been optioned by small production companies, and her paintings are included in a number of prominent embassy and corporate collections, collections that she hopes might someday wind up in museums.

"People have this stereotype of the flaky artist who falls apart when it comes to managing the business end of her career," she says. "But that's not me. I've taken care building and protecting my reputation. I always delivered exactly what I promised exactly when I promised it. I paid attention to which galleries represented my work and which collectors bought it. I've always thought in terms of not just this one sale, but building a career."

Despite her success, Alice has always struggled financially. Her critical coups have provided no economic security, "nothing, zero, none, none, none." Her annual income, which ranges from $25,000 to $50,000, can easily drop by half from one year to the next, and she never knows when that will happen until it does. Even when her biggest New York show sold out—"That was the year I felt I'd truly made it as an artist"—once she'd covered her expenses and given the dealer his 50 percent cut, Alice wound up making only $30,000.

She lives month to month, with never more than a couple thousand dollars in savings and not a cent stowed away for retirement. Her fixed expenses include $1,500 rent for a small one-bedroom apartment "with mice" and $225 a month for health insurance through a writer's union. She's sold everything of value, right down to her engagement ring, and her working-class family neither understands nor is in a position to help support her creative career. Over the years, particularly those lean early years, she's bridged the financial gaps by turning to her credit cards. She now owes over $30,000.

"All I'm ever doing is buying myself more time," she says. "I'm forty-four years old and I have no assets, no investments, nothing. There are plenty of days when I panic that I could wind up on the street. Financial security? What's that? It's all just one big maybe."

Because she needs to sell each painting as soon as she finishes it, Alice hasn't been able to build up enough work for another show in recent years. Though she likes being in Los Angeles, in close proximity to the galleries and dealers with whom she trades, she's considering moving to a smaller town where the cost of living might not be quite so prohibitive—though at this point even the cost of the move itself seems out of reach. She's even ready to look for her first regular job in fifteen years, ideally part-time so she can continue to paint and write, but she has few practical job skills to fall back on.

"I've run my own business for over a decade, but in today's marketplace I'm pretty much useless. I doubt I'm even qualified to answer the phone at a gallery for $10 an hour."

Alice sees her own financial struggles, and those of nearly every creative person she knows, as reflecting major changes in the art world in the past few years, changes she sees echoed in other creative fields as well.

"Problem number one," she explains. "All the grant programs have dried up, so everyone is dependent on their income to survive. That means we all become a lot less creative and a lot less generous.

"Problem number two: the art world keeps getting more and more market driven. It's become all about the collectors and very little about the work. These Wall Street types pay ridiculous amounts for an artist someone else tells them is hot. They're looking for an investment, not a piece of art. There's only room for the supertrendy and the superestablished. All of us in the middle, even if we're selling work, are left struggling to put bananas on our oatmeal."

Alice, who has no children and has been single since her divorce eight years ago, is beginning to seriously question her choice to put art front and center in her life. The sacrifices seem so far out of balance with the rewards.

"I work all the time, six and seven days a week. I work so hard I haven't had time for a life, which is something I really regret. Yes, I love being an artist. But at the same time, every morning I wake up and ask myself: I'm smart, I'm talented, I'm as committed as they come. So how did I end up here?"

The financial crunch leveling artists like Alice stems from the same one-two combination hitting the rest of the educated professional middle class. They are making less at the same time they're expected to pay for more. In addition to the stagnant earnings and increasing fixed expenses they share with all college-educated professionals, those who enter creative professions face a massive reduction in government and private subsidies of the arts. At the same time, it's become harder to live that low-overhead alternative lifestyle—even if you're willing to sacrifice middle-class comforts like vacations and large homes—that used to be the signature of the artist's existence.

For the most part, artists never had access to those luxuries, like expensive cars and private school educations, that were the reward of becoming a doctor or a lawyer. But as the counterculture of the '60s and '70s has given way to an era characterized by rising economic inequality and the dominance of the free market, artists have lost the one luxury they could count on, the luxury to live and work cheaply. Bohemian existence—from Paris in the early 1800s to America in the 1960s—embraced a free-spirited ethic, an emphasis of pleasure over production and a disinclination to follow traditional societal rules. But it also embraced a lifestyle. Because money was not a priority, people didn't tend to have much of it. So bohemians figured out ways to live cheap and on the fly. In its extreme, such alternative living landed people in communes. But it also encompassed families and friends sharing cheap apartments, often in ethnically and culturally diverse neighborhoods, and spending less so they could create more. Though essential for the cultural health of a society, these creative types contributed relatively little to the consumer-driven market economy.

Not only were such bohemian enclaves hubs of affordable living, they were also key centers of creativity. Artists in particular tend to depend on a communal life that runs counter to the emphasis on individual ambition and personal responsibility so in vogue today. In creative fields, "research and development" entails testing material with other artists, getting feedback, continually honing and refining your way toward a finished product. Creativity tends to flourish through interplay of ideas and inspiration, the sort of cross-pollination that gives birth to a generational style or a new school of art. Hence the periods of concentrated creative flowering throughout history—from Florence in the Renaissance to Paris in the mid-1800s, Elizabethan England to early-twentieth-century Greenwich Village—eras that don't necessarily line up with periods of great market wealth and prosperity.

Though the U.S. has a relatively weak history of supporting the arts, FDR's New Deal of the 1930s provides a telling national example of how artists can respond to communal and societal support. As part of its commitment to subsidizing employment and public works, the Roosevelt administration provided financial and organizational opportunities to a range of artists through the Federal Theatre Project, the Federal Art Project, and the Federal Writers Project. By providing a steady income and subsidizing creative works, this period in American history engendered the careers of John Steinbeck, Richard

Wright, Arthur Miller, Dorothea Lange, Walter Evans, Jackson Pollock, and many others. The country itself experienced a surge in cultural prosperity despite, and perhaps even because of, the accompanying economic hardship.

Today, artists face just the opposite situation, with major cutbacks in arts-related funding by state and federal governments, corporate backers, and private foundations. Most other Western countries—including Canada, France, Germany, and the U.K.—subsidize the arts far more generously than the U.S, designating large chunks of national and local government funding to support filmmakers, painters, museums, theaters, and symphonies. The German government, in the city of Munich alone—population 1.2 million—supports seven full-time professional orchestras, two opera houses, a ballet troupe, and two full-time theaters.[13]

America's pale facsimile of such subsidized arts programs, the National Endowment for the Arts, is still reeling from the 40 percent budget cuts it suffered in the '90s, and political controversies surrounding the kind of art it chose to fund. In 2005, the total amount of NEA available programs funds was just over $100 million, a meager, almost nonexistent drop in the bucket when compared to the $401.5 billion base budget for the Defense Department, or the $554 billion in military expenditures that year. In the past, private foundations and corporate backers picked up some of this government slack, but these too have cut their funding in recent years, in particular since 9/11. In 1994, 9.5 percent of corporate philanthropy was directed toward supporting the arts. By 2004, that number had dipped to just 4 percent.[14]

This lack of external support combined with the escalating cost of living makes it nearly impossible for creative types to forge a bohemian life in cities like New York, Los Angeles, and San Francisco that have long nursed diverse creative communities. In the past, clusters of artists were always the first to pioneer underdeveloped urban neighborhoods like SoHo and Chelsea in New York and San Francisco's Mission District, where they could find cheap space to set up studios and apartments. When their more moneyed counterparts followed them in, jacking up prices, they simply moved on. But today, as real estate prices rise and those low-rent neighborhoods disappear entirely, artists find themselves being pushed out of these major creative hubs altogether. A single adult living in Manhattan in 2004 required $40,000 just to meet bare-bones needs. In neighboring Queens and Brooklyn—areas to which many artists once fled when priced out of the city—it took $22,000 and nearly $25,000 respectively.[15]

"I moved to New York because both my producer and my record label are here," says Kelsey, a singer-songwriter with five albums and a handful of international tours under her belt, who still works as an office temp between gigs and gets her health insurance through Medicaid. "I feel like it's essential for my music career that I be here, but in every other way it's a constant struggle. I don't look too far ahead anymore because it's too depressing. Eventually the cost of living in New York will break me. I guess I'll just stay as long as I can stay."

Though these cities can still support their major cultural venues, those operating on the fringe—from artists like Alice and Kelsey to small theater companies and music and dance venues—simply can't sustain themselves. New York has already begun to see this cultural slippage with the shuttering of institutions like downtown rock club CBGBs and the Upper East Side's Beekman movie theater, both victims to rising rents and redevelopment. Less visible, but potentially even more damaging, are the streams of individual artists leaving town in search of a more economically feasible environment. If only the thin top lid of financially successful artists can afford to stay, these cities risk losing their future creative capital. They will become vendors rather than incubators of art and creativity.

Even in less expensive cities, the rising cost of living can prohibit pursuit of a full- or even part-time artistic career. Like Alice, most artists work for themselves—nearly 70 percent of authors and over 50 percent of both artists and photographers are self-employed,[16] and as such they're responsible for covering their own health care and retirement. In addition, they're hit with heavy self-employment taxes. Many other creative types work for small nonprofit companies —theaters, galleries, design firms—that can offer only low salaries and no benefits. In addition, it's become so difficult to make ends meet in the typical fallback careers like teaching, journalism, or working in an arts-based nonprofit that often these incomes require supplementing of their own, which leaves precious little time for the artwork that's supposed to be supplemented.

As the business of art is consolidated into a handful of major corporations—Time Warner, Bertelsmann, Sony—there's an increasing emphasis on money, marketing, and commercial success. The artists who traffic in riskier material, who aren't making blockbuster films or writing Top 40 hits, are falling into a widening creative limbo. They find there's simply no time to work full-time and then some, plus raise a family, plus pursue an avocation that produces little or no financial reward. Creative fields are no longer seen as a realistic career choice for members of the educated professional middle class.

"As creative fields get more money focused, the work produced gets more bland," says Alice. "I hear and see this across the board— from artists, from writers, from musicians. You rarely see anything rebellious or original. By necessity, everything is about 'how much can I sell this for?'"

To measure art only in terms of its financial impact is to make a strong statement about our current cultural values, or lack thereof. Art serves as an essential form of communication in a civilized society. It provides a forum through which we can challenge conventional wisdom, expand our perception of self and others, and acquire a more complex understanding of how the world works. The most successful art is not always the art that earns a great deal of money, which is why it's crucial that artists have resources outside the free market in the form of government and private subsidies. If generated purely for financial gain, art grows stagnant. Even worse, it ceases to provide a venue for controversy or social critique. Artists must be risk takers. But as things stand now, with individual financial choices more and more limited, those in creative fields are joining the rest of the educated professional middle class in growing increasingly risk-averse.

5

TO HAVE OR TO HOLD

Money, Marriage, and Children

Like many educated professional middle-class couples, Tessa and Richard decided to wait until their careers and finances had stabilized before having children. They met in graduate school, still harboring dreams of becoming a professor and a poet, and lived together five years before getting married. Tessa got her master's degree in history, then tested jobs in the nonprofit and legal fields before choosing, just over a year ago, to become a high school history teacher. Richard transitioned from the art world to Web design and now works as a Web manager for a nonprofit. They were married four years, both in their mid-thirties, when Tessa got pregnant. When she and I spoke on the phone one mid-July morning, their daughter's birth was just two months away.

"I always wanted to have kids," Tessa tells me. "And we thought a lot about when would be the right time. Eventually we realized things would never feel right. There's never going to be enough money saved up or a good time to take a career break. You just have to jump in and hope you can figure out a way."

Integrating career, family, and finances proved tricky from the start. While pregnant, Tessa took part in a rigorous yearlong training program designed for adults interested in making a career switch to teaching. She spent her days working in a public school an hour's commute from their house in South Boston and her evenings in class at a local college. A $500-a-month stipend replaced the $40,000 she'd been making working for a women's nonprofit organization; the couple essentially lived off Richard's $70,000 salary.

"Financially, it was a scary time to be cutting back," Tessa admits, "but I knew that if I was going to be in a position to launch my teaching career, I had to do it before the baby came.

"It was a really rough year," she adds after a moment. "It definitely took a toll on our marriage."

In an ideal world, Tessa would like to give birth this fall, take the next year off, then look for part-time teaching work when their daughter is twelve months old. But spending two years as a single-income family is simply not a financial option.

"Our savings are almost gone as it is," she explains. "I'll start looking for something part-time in December, once the baby is three months old. At this point, I'm just hoping we can swing it so I won't have to go back to work full-time until she's in preschool."

To save money, Tessa and Richard are trying to figure out a way to sidestep child-care costs, a major financial drain for most educated professional middle-class families. On average, child care in the U.S. eats up over 10 percent of the family income. In Boston, full-time accredited day-care centers can run close to $2,000 a month.[1] Since Richard works at home, they plan to split the child care between them, with Tessa finding a part-time morning job then taking the baby in the afternoon, and hopefully hiring a sitter willing to watch their daughter for an hour or two in the middle of the day when their schedules overlap.

As new parents, they're eager to cut every corner possible, since they have precious little room for financial maneuvering. The couple's main asset is their two-bedroom house in South Boston, which they bought three years ago and fixed up themselves—"It was a wreck," Tessa emphasizes, "we went five months with no bathroom"—and which has since doubled in value. When they do sell it, probably in two or three years, they plan to move to a smaller and hopefully more affordable city. Though they like Boston, their current neighborhood has underperforming public schools and housing prices are out of reach in all the more affluent suburbs. The rest of their sparse savings consist of a $10,000 second mortgage, and $11,000 in Richard's 401(k). They're also carrying $7,000 in credit card debt, most of which accrued in the last year while Tessa was in school, and paying off $600 a month in student loans for both Tessa and Richard's undergraduate and graduate degrees.

Tessa tells me she's terrified that parenthood will mean sinking deep into debt, that the decisions to go back to school and spend the next few years working part-time are foolish and irresponsible.

"I can't see how we can possibly save anything. We're living right down to the bone as it is and we're still swimming in bills." Bills including student loans, mortgage, gas and heating, house repairs, car insurance, health insurance, and the list goes on. "I just don't look too far ahead, because it's too easy to panic."

"It's overwhelming," Tessa confesses, "I used to think differently, but now I'm sure I only want one child. I don't think we could afford—financially or emotionally—to do this all over again."

In recent years, it's become harder to navigate the financial intricacies of being a dual-career educated middle-class couple. The prospect of then introducing children into such an equation stirs a snake pit of worries and fears. This intersection of economic and cultural institutions has left many of us grappling with the decision of when —or whether—to have families and panicking over how to pay for them. We're looking differently at who we marry, if we marry, and how to merge and preserve our financial futures. We're having fewer children later in life and in the case of 20 percent of American women—the highest rate since the Depression—we're not becoming parents at all.[2]

The pressure to pick a financially viable career in order to support a family is nothing new, but that range of viable careers is narrowing. Today, some members of the educated professional middle class have serious doubts about whether it's possible to raise kids, or even share a comfortable life with a spouse or partner, while pursuing many of those careers that combine personal fulfillment with a service to society—careers in education, nonprofit work, journalism, or the arts. For couples and families today, the economic cushion that used to be furnished by a dual-income household has proved elusive, and having two parents at work has added to the child-rearing package, upping our need for assistance with child care and other domestic duties.

For those like Richard and Tessa, who are already struggling to maintain their financial stability, taking on the expenses of parenthood on top of paying off mortgages, school, and credit card debts and trying to save for retirement can seem an insurmountable burden. Often, young professionals now confront a choice that nothing in their comfortable backgrounds and college degrees prepared them to have to make, between having children and having a house, a rewarding career, a secure financial future, and other facets of the educated professional American dream. The contradictions between our cultural freedoms and our financial limitations—so many choices, none of them as viable as they once were—leaves many of us feeling paralyzed.

"Thank god for the biological clock," said one forty-year-old mother of a two-year-old son. "Because if it were left to logical decision-making, no one in their right mind would take on the financial risk of having a kid today."

THE CHANGING FACE OF PARTNERSHIP AND MARRIAGE

Once upon a time a typical middle-class couple met young, married young, and pooled their finances straightaway. Even if they started out as dual income, the husband usually earned more and the unspoken plan was for the wife to quit work as soon as the children inevitably arrived. The going models were *Leave It to Beaver* if you lived in the suburbs and *I Love Lucy* if you hailed from the big city.

But since the combined sexual and feminist revolutions of the 1970s, the shape of the American family has undergone cataclysmic change. For the first time, married people are in the minority—49.7 percent of households consisted of married couples in 2006[3]—as individuals delay or forgo marriage and instead coalesce in all variety of alternative families and living situations. The number of cohabitating couples rose 72 percent between 1990 and 2000, and these days 41 percent of nonmarital households include children.[4] Given the increasing legal and social acceptance of marriage alternatives, individuals face a slew of options. They may marry soon after falling in love, wait until they're ready to have children, divorce several times, or never marry at all. Today, most educated professional middle-class couples are not only dual income but also dual career. The recent media attention surrounding the issue of same-sex marriage has led many to question the meaning and even the necessity of such an institution in today's world. In the modern era, one's personal life seems dictated by a single word: choice.

But beneath this new array of options, many of today's educated professionals are finding that financial constraints have a way of putting a crimp in social freedoms. For those struggling to live on single salaries, the freedom not to marry is often counteracted by a financial pressure to partner up. Buying a house, paying down debt, or saving for a viable retirement can seem like insurmountable obstacles for one person alone. The single life is no longer necessarily the embodiment of freedom. Instead, for many, it's marriage that comes to be viewed as the great liberator.

Tameka is thirty-seven, never married, with a BA from a respected liberal arts college and eight years of charitable-fundraising experience. She currently makes $40,000 a year raising money for an arts organization in Los Angeles. Her salary covers her basic expenses but—between rent for her one-bedroom apartment in the San Fernando Valley ($800), gas ($80–$100), car payments ($250), and insurance ($140) on her Toyota Corolla, plus food and utilities—there's little left over at the end of the month to invest in her future.

Though she has a 401(k) through work, into which she feeds about $100 a month, Tameka has only $1,000 in accessible savings. It's enough to cover a minor bump, like getting her car towed, but leaves her economically vulnerable to any larger blow like job loss or medical problems. She likes her job, but the nonprofit she works for runs at a deficit, so she doesn't envision making more money anytime soon.

"I'm extremely concerned with being able to take care of myself in the future," she admits. "I always imagined I'd feel more secure than I do now, even if I wasn't married. I thought I'd earn more money and that money would take me further. I had worries about being alone, but they weren't money worries. The two—being single and being financially secure—didn't seem like a contradiction in terms."

Instead of reveling in her freedom or taking pride in her financial independence, Tameka worries about the future. She fears that she'll never be able to afford a house or condo or manage to put away enough to take care of herself in retirement. Her parents have both passed away and there's no family money to call upon, especially since her older brother and sister both have families of their own to support. She has little faith that either the government or her employer will step in to help. Some days, the sense of financial isolation seems relentless.

"My emotional security hinges on my financial security and right now there's not much of that," Tameka explains. "As a single woman in her late thirties, I have to accept the fact that I may be taking care of myself for the rest of my life. Short of marrying for money, I can't imagine how I'm going to do that."

As public resources for everything from health insurance to student loans grow slimmer, our private relationships are seen as absorbing—or not—the added monetary stress. Today, domestic arrangements can make or break your financial future. New questions enter the equation. How do our economic needs shape what we seek in a mate? How do we navigate partnerships composed of careers with equal prestige but unequal salaries? Who's marrying, or deciding not to marry, for money these days?

"I'm getting so I only date someone who makes more money than I do," admits Courtenay, thirty-five, whose relationship history has included a string of talented but struggling artistic types and whose $50,000-a-year income has left no room for long-term savings. "I have real ideological issues with thinking that way. I feel like I've stepped back into the '50s. I consider myself a strong, successful woman, but I also know that long-term financial independence is a pipe dream. If I'm ever going to own a house or be able to afford children, marrying a provider seems like the only way to go."

I heard from a number of single people like Courtenay and Tameka, men and women who saw partnering up as the only possible path toward economic relief. But this fantasy of financial salvation is, in many cases, exactly that. Fantasy. Marriage is not a guaranteed protection from economic hardship. In fact, when adjusted for added expenses, the average couple's income actually falls when they begin living together, as they face higher taxes and fewer public benefits and are more inclined to take on added financial burdens like home ownership or having children. With both partners pursuing full-time careers, dual-income families do earn more today than families did thirty years ago. But given the rise in fixed expenses like education, mortgage, child care, health insurance, car payments, and taxes, they actually have less discretionary income than single-income families did in the '70s.[5]

Though many of the single people I interviewed fantasized about finding a partner to absorb their financial burden, among those who lived with a significant other just the opposite phenomenon seemed to take place. Most cohabitating couples (and some married couples), even those joined at the hip in every other way, expressed a real reluctance to combine their finances. They shunned joint bank accounts and tended to split living expenses down the middle—with each partner writing a check for half the rent, the electric bill, the food shopping—or to prorate living costs according to who made more money. Often they had little grasp of their partner's economic situation, leaving it to each individual to control spending, pay off student loans, and navigate credit card debt. In their minds, sharing finances seemed to signify something more permanent and potentially explosive than any other sort of union.

"The way we think about money is not the same," says Rafael, a social worker, about his boyfriend, a photographer in the process of getting his MFA. Though the two share a house, a personal life, and presumably a future, they make a point of discussing money as little as possible because of the tension it sparks in the relationship. "We have different backgrounds. He spends, I save. His parents can help him out and mine can't. I make more money than he does. It just seemed simplest, for the health of the relationship, to keep our financial issues to ourselves. I don't want money to dictate anything about who we are together."

For today's educated professional middle class, it can seem shallow and gauche to let financial concerns shape a relationship, especially for those of us who early on shed the idea of entering big business to pursue what we'd hoped would be intellectually or spiritually fulfilling careers. We are not "money people," and we like to think our relationships are deep, rich, and healthy enough to transcend such tawdry details. But when money gets tighter, it matters more, and financial compatibility begins to weigh heavily against more modern concerns like life goals, value systems, and how two people mesh on an emotional and intellectual level. Perhaps unmarried couples are reluctant to commingle their finances because they know how easily money can shift from an issue to "the issue." Many married couples I spoke to said that money was the thing discussed, worried about, and fought over the most. And if coming together can be a financial choice, staying together can be one too.

"Not an option," says Ruth, thirty-eight, a freelance grant writer who works for several nonprofit organizations, when I asked her if she ever worried about how she would support herself and her daughter if anything happened with her husband. "We've had our difficulties, but we just find a way to work through them. There's no way I could keep our house as a single parent. When it comes down to it, we simply can't afford to divorce."

It's hard not to project where these trends might lead us, if money keeps pinching and the possibilities of pursuing a meaningful career and supporting a family continue on their divergent paths. Among those I spoke to, both single and with partners, the practical benefits of getting and staying together seem to be gaining ground on romance. It's not too hard to envision a future where the marriage of financial compatibility starts to edge out the marriage of intellectual or emotional compatibility, where members of the educated professional middle class begin to search out mates according to earning power because the alternative feels too daunting. I like to think that financial security will never truly trump falling in love, but it also seems naive to insist that our partnerships will suffer no consequences whatsoever when the scarcest and most desirable quantity, the brass ring of the relationship ride, isn't social but financial freedom.

Even those educated middle-class couples who do manage to achieve some sort of financial balance can find the stress manifesting in other aspects of the marriage. One of the few financially viable models I encountered was one of economic polarization within the marriage itself. In a twist on the '50s concept of the single breadwinner, today I found a flowering of power-imbalanced couples where one person earned enough money to float the other while he or she pursued a creative, intellectual, or "meaningful" career. It's no longer just that you need to marry a provider in order to stay home with kids, but that you need to marry one in order to have a creative or service-oriented job.

Unlike the 1950s model, this economic imbalance is fashioned under the guise of a "marriage of equals," no matter who earns more money. Families have lost the cushion provided by the knowledge that mom can go out and get a job if money gets too tight. In fact, today a woman might easily find herself already playing the provider role. These modern twists mean that, though couples with one solid breadwinner may be more financially secure, that security comes at a price. Tensions can emerge when both partners have careers that require equal investment of time and energy but one makes significantly more money.

"I hate, hate, hate that, even if I'm working, I can barely contribute," says Vickie, an adjunct college professor and freelance writer who makes $20,000 a year and whose husband supports them both on his $90,000 salary as a software engineer. "He could get by if I wasn't there, but I'm entirely dependent on him. Even though I've worked just as hard to build a career. It's very difficult to accept that I can't get by without him. It's not how I was raised or, I like to think, who I am."

Unlike their predecessors of the '50s, '60s, and even '70s, most educated professional middle-class partnerships today are rooted in the premise of equality. The divisional split—men bring home the bacon, women fry it up and then do the dishes—has all but disappeared. But given today's financial stresses, the definition of equality gets trickier and trickier to pin down. Do we mean equal income? Equal responsibility? Equal respect? Equal commitment to home or to career? How equal is the marriage if one half is financially independent and the other is not? Who is more likely to be called upon to take off work to care for children or an ailing in-law? Who has more power to make decisions about where you live and what you spend? If push comes to shove, which career and financial future will be seen to matter more?

"I have tremendous guilt about not contributing more financially to the marriage," Vickie admits. "My husband gave up his dream career to do something where he makes a decent living. I'm lucky that he's so generous. But clearly, it's not fair that I haven't had to do the same."

This idea of what's fair resonated among most of the polarized couples I spoke to, the question of how to restore that sense of fairness to your marriage of equals that now so clearly isn't. We all live in a culture where money symbolizes power and status. For men at the low-earning end of a power couple, the blow to the ego that comes from a smaller paycheck can be particularly harsh. For generations, Americans held a cultural belief system that positioned real men as providers; the roots of this system are too deep to be dug up in the few decades in which we've sown equality.

This equality question also taps into deeper concerns about how to navigate economic need in a marriage supposedly based on higher values like love, compatibility, and trust. From early on, members of the educated professional middle class—men and women—have learned to embrace financial independence. Such independence lends us the ability to marry late, have children late, leave a bad relationship, or form an alternative family, the sorts of personal choices that shape our current lives. We may marry for a thousand other reasons—love, companionship, a warm body in the bed—but being financially dependent on another person, to any degree, undercuts our sense of individual success, perhaps the core educated professional middle-class value. In today's culture, the one thing more shameful than thinking "I don't know if we can make it together," is thinking, "I don't know if I can make it on my own."

With our financial position in marriage feeling so precarious, just the idea of transitioning from a couple to a family can generate a flood of financial anxiety. Middle-class couples who are otherwise highly qualified to be parents—educated, employed, responsible—have serious questions about whether they can adequately provide for their children. By the time they reach their mid- and late thirties, with financial circumstances still tenuous, some couples are no longer just considering pushing back having kids but wondering whether it's the right thing to have them at all. Their vision of good parenting entails creating a secure environment for their children both emotionally and financially, a set of expectations that often clashes with economic reality.

"I don't anticipate having children," says Luis, forty-one, a northern California acupuncturist who makes between $45,000 and $50,000 a year. "It's not that I don't want them, but unless I met someone who made a great deal of money, I'd have to work all the time just to pay the expenses. I'd have no relationship with my children at all, and in my mind that's no way to create a healthy family."

Some individuals and couples I spoke to struggled with what they considered a highly sensible degree of financial responsibility. If it's wrong to have kids when we can't afford them and if we are still in a shaky financial state, the logical conclusion is that maybe it's best not to become parents at all. How, when we can barely swing rent or mortgage, when our 401(k) is still in the four figures, when we haven't even finished paying off our student loans, can we possibly contemplate parenthood at thirty, thirty-five, even forty?

These are honest and troubling concerns. Raising a child to age eighteen costs a middle-class family $237,000, an enormous hit for a couple already struggling to preserve their middle-class status. Ninety percent of those who file for bankruptcy qualify as middle class, and those in the worst financial trouble—across the board—are families with children. They are more likely to be late on credit card payments, have their cars repossessed, and their homes foreclosed upon. Married couples with children have more than three times the debt level as those without, and nine times the debt level of all childless adults.[6]

"We think about money all the time," Tessa tells me just before hanging up the phone. "Every month we ask ourselves, how can we possibly do this? And we haven't even bought a single diaper yet. The emotional pressure is tremendous. It's the worst possible feeling, worrying you won't be able to take care of your children. It's entirely different from not being able to take care of yourself."

THE HIGH PRICE OF FAMILY VALUES
When Gretchen and her husband, Linc, both in their midthirties, found out they were pregnant with their daughter, finances weren't the first thing to jump to mind.

"We'd been trying for eighteen months," Gretchen explains in a throaty voice with a Deep South twang. It's five o'clock on a mid-winter Friday evening, the only day she could arrange to have her husband pick up their now two-year-old daughter at day care so we'd have time to talk. "And let me just tell you we were nothing but thrilled."

Gretchen graduated with a BA in communications from the University of Arkansas hoping someday to write for film or television, and spent her early professional years doing communications work for various nonprofits and accounting firms in Little Rock. She comes from a working-class family—her mother was a secretary and her father ran a pest-control business out of their garage—and she paid her own way through college, shouldering over $30,000 in student loans and taking breaks along the way to earn money selling clothes at Ann Taylor and waiting tables at T.G.I. Friday's.

"When I graduated from college I was sure that degree meant I could support myself with no problem for the rest of my life," she says with a laugh. "Boy was I wrong. Right out of school, I had to move in with my mother because I couldn't get a job. I distinctly remember picking up my shoe and throwing it at the diploma hanging on the wall. I told my mother, 'that thing isn't worth the paper it's written on.'"

Before she got pregnant, Gretchen was working in a tedious and stressful job for a small accounting firm, where she spent her days negotiating plenty of office politics and no room for raise or promotion.

"My boss and I mutually parted ways when I was seven months pregnant, which probably wasn't the smartest move but I was getting too big and too tired to be that unhappy."

Though she would've loved to take a break until after her daughter's birth, Gretchen knew there was no chance the family could survive even for a few months on the $24,000 Linc made at the time, managing a record store. From the outset, there'd been no question that they would always be a dual-income, two-full-time-job family.

"Linc doesn't have a college degree, so I knew I'd probably make more money than he did," Gretchen explains. "Combining work with motherhood was never not an option."

Skeptical that anyone would hire "a big, lumbering, waddling, about-to-give-birth pregnant woman," Gretchen did freelance contract work from home for the last two months of her pregnancy. She only brought in a fraction of the money she'd earned before and those few months proved a major financial strain.

The biggest hit came via the benefits Gretchen lost when she quit her job and shifted to a COBRA plan, which required her to pay $800 a month out of pocket for the same benefits she had received through the company health insurance plan. She and Linc couldn't afford the coverage, nor could Gretchen afford not to be covered with the impending birth and all its associated bills. Desperate, they finally turned to their parents for help covering the monthly payments.

"When our daughter was born we couldn't afford to add her to my insurance, so I got a major medical plan for her and one of those dollar-a-month life plans," Gretchen says. "Basically we paid all her medical bills—checkups, immunizations—out of pocket for nearly two years. At one point her pediatrician's office told us we couldn't bring her back until we paid up, and we owed them over $400. It was heart-wrenching to bring home $56,000 combined but not be able to get insurance for our child."

A few weeks after their daughter was born, Gretchen was already out searching for a full-time job. She found a position with another accounting firm, not her ideal environment but steady enough to pay the bills. A year and a half later, Linc shifted careers, taking a job as a salesperson for an accounting-software company where he makes $30,000 a year plus full benefits that cover both him and their daughter.

"When I heard that," Gretchen tells me. "I almost cried. He was upset that he had to pay $190 a month out of pocket and I said, 'Mister, that is the supersweetest deal ever. You will never, ever leave this company. They will have to drag your dead body out of your cube.'"

Since then, Gretchen has moved to a position as the communications and PR director for the local branch of the Boys & Girls Club. She typically works fifty- to sixty-hour weeks, often firing up her home computer for a few hours after her daughter has gone to sleep.

She loves the job and hopes there might be room to move up in the organization, but her $44,000-a-year salary, though the most she's ever earned, still makes it tough to make ends meet.

Initially, Gretchen placed her daughter in a nearby church-run child-care center. When it inexplicably shut down six months ago—leaving Gretchen thirty days to find a new caregiver while working full-time—she switched to a home-based day care on the outskirts of Little Rock, about twenty minutes from their house, for $460 a month. The monthly payment is tough, but Gretchen acknowledges that it could be a lot worse.

"I think God saw to it that we found this place, because I don't know how we could have afforded anything more."

Good day care was important because both Gretchen and Linc put in long office days, usually working from 8:30 to 5:00 or 6:00. They have fine-tuned their schedules to minimize their daughter's hours away from them. Gretchen drops her off every morning on her way to work, then, depending on who can leave the office earliest, they split the pickup, doing their best to always get there before six. When things get especially busy, Gretchen picks up her daughter and brings her back to the office for an hour or two before heading home.

Home is a two-bedroom, one-bath house in a historic district of Little Rock, purchased just a few months before Gretchen learned she was pregnant. To meet the $109,000 asking price, they took out a thirty-year fixed-rate mortgage with payments set at $1,200 a month. They're also paying down over $30,000 in credit card debt spread across ten cards, some of it left over from Gretchen's college days, the rest accrued paying for their daughter's birth and fixing up their home.

"We bought a crib, furniture for the house like a bed and a couch; basically anything extra went on a card," she explains. "Most of them are maxed out, which is good because it means we can't work up any more debt. But I live in fear of some major expense. Our heater has been leaking and we're scared to death to call the repairman. If it needs to be replaced, I have no idea what we would do."

Though they do have a savings account, it empties as soon as it fills. And Gretchen has stopped even thinking about the $28,000 in student loan money she still owes. "There's no money to pay them so what's the good of worrying?"

She feels fortunate to have a beautiful healthy daughter, a husband she loves—"the only thing we ever fight about is money"—and a fulfilling career. But she hates that the future, be it tomorrow or ten years from tomorrow, is one giant and terrifying question mark.

"Things were tight before. But since my daughter was born, much as I love her, it's been close to impossible," Gretchen says, her voice growing quiet. "I feel like we're hemorrhaging money and I have no idea how to stop the leak."

For couples already teetering on the edge of the middle class, having a child is a serious financial blow right up there with losing a job or the death of a spouse. It costs roughly $10,000 a year to support a child under five, close to double that for two children. Previous generations may rightly point out that it's always been tough, but statistics show that the cost of raising kids has increased 15 percent since the 1960s. And despite the shop-happy stereotypes of modern parents, this rise isn't fueled by couples snapping their infants into hand-knit Parisian baby wear. Today's parents actually spend less on toys and clothes, and more on fixed expenses like health care, housing, and—most of all—child care.[7]

The increased cost of raising children means an increased need for both parents to work in order to pay for it all. Today only 30 percent of families with children under eighteen meet the traditional model of male as sole breadwinner. But despite our cultural rhetoric about family values, the modern workplace doesn't tend to facilitate family-friendly lives. Career-track jobs demand more and more working hours, particularly for middle-income families. Hours worked by prime-aged couples with children has risen 30 percent since 1975, making Americans' average workweek longer than any other industrial country, including Japan.[8]

Because we are having children later, often for financial reasons—American women over thirty are having babies at the highest rate since the 1960s[9]—early parenthood frequently clashes with key career years when earnings are climbing, critical promotional decisions are made, or, for those in professions that require extensive training or schooling, a professional identity is just forming. For either parent, cutting hours or taking a year off at such a pivotal moment can risk permanently derailing your professional future.

Just taking a standard twelve-week maternity leave often means a cut in family income and, over time, can lead to job loss or demotion. Female executives who take as little as 8.8 months in combined maternity leaves—for three children that is less than the twelve weeks per child designated in the federal Family and Medical Leave Act— have been shown to suffer permanent setbacks in career advancement and earning potential.[10] Like Gretchen, many women also risk losing their health benefits if they change jobs or take a longer leave than mandated. Such financial blows can be devastating when coupled with the added costs of a new baby, not to mention juggling a mortgage, student loans, car payments, and school or child care for other children.

Even getting pregnant has become costlier. Women who wait until their late thirties and early forties to have kids face an increased chance of needing fertility treatments, the most expensive of which often aren't covered by insurance. One round of in vitro fertilization (IVF) runs between $10,00 and $12,000, and with success rates hovering around 30 percent, many couples are in for repeat cycles. For couples eager to start a family and fighting a ticking biological clock, this option can seem far more necessity than luxury.[11]

"We took out a home equity loan to pay for IVF," says a thirty-four-year-old television producer, "and now in three months we'll have a daughter. It may put us in debt for the rest of our lives, but how can anyone tell me that was the wrong financial choice?"

It's no wonder that many new parents feel a panicky pull to get back on the job. But though going back to work as soon as possible can seem the most sensible decision under the circumstances—and 70 percent of women today do return to work within six months after giving birth to their first child—it hardly guarantees a return to financial solvency. Returning to the office means hiring someone else to watch the baby, slicing a considerable wedge out of that second income. Today child care costs between $4,000 and $14,000 a year.[12]

Since child care is not an item that any responsible parent wants to consider scrimping on, families often wind up paying far more than they can afford if they're lucky enough to find a situation that meets their needs. Others find themselves continually scrambling, arranging and rearranging their schedules, compromising work, compromising family, just to try to make all the pieces fit. Locating affordable day care can be especially challenging for parents who do freelance work or have otherwise irregular schedules. Many childcare centers require a commitment of a certain number of days per week or hours per day, and they charge by the minute for parents who pick up their children late or drop them off early.

"It's been a nightmare," says Allegra, a freelance copy editor earning $30,000 a year, about finding decent, affordable care for her two children, both of whom have been in day care since they were a few months old.

In under two years she's entrusted her children's care to a distant relative of her boyfriend's, who left after a family falling-out; an in-home Christian day care that turned out her kids after three months when they discovered Allegra and her boyfriend weren't married; a caregiver who stole her children's clothes, extra diapers, and bottles; and another who took her children on a visit to see friends in another state and didn't return them home until one in the morning. The stress and panic of finding safe and affordable care—added to the stress and panic Allegra and her partner, as new parents, were already facing on all other financial fronts—has been tremendous.

Allegra laughs. "It sounds crazy, but it was almost a relief when my boyfriend lost his job and wound up staying home with the kids."

Though they've certainly created this middle-class time and money crunch, neither the government nor private employers have stepped in to help relieve it. For the most part, today's families still have the same social support and protection designed for single-income, dual-parent households of the '50s, programs that assume one parent is at home to tend to illnesses or other emergency situations or to jump into the workplace in a pinch. The sole major legislative change, the 1993 Family and Medical Leave Act, requires that companies with fifty or more employees provide twelve weeks of unpaid leave to those who have worked there for at least a year. If there are pregnancy complications, if there are health complications with mother or child after the birth, if you can't find good child care right away or if that child care falls through, you risk losing your job—and job benefits—with no recourse. If you work for a small company, you are entirely at the mercy of your employer. And, big company or small, only one in eight workers are offered employer-subsidized child care.[13]

Such "you're on your own" child and family policies are unheard of in other industrialized countries. We're not just talking about blond, well-scrubbed socialist utopias like Sweden. The United States is one of only two industrialized countries in the world that doesn't offer paid maternity leave to its citizens. The other, Australia, gives women a full year guaranteed unpaid leave instead. In an international work and family survey compiled by the Project on Global Working Families, out of over 168 countries studied, 96 guarantee paid annual leave, 45 also guarantee some form of paid paternal leave for fathers, and 37 mandate paid leave specifically designated for caring for sick children. The U.S. is not among them.[14]

Our government should be deeply concerned about falling so far behind the curve, but it's not. Instead, decisions about providing child care and family leave have been passed on to individual employers, as if caring for and raising a country's children were a bottom-line decision. When our anemic Family and Medical Leave Act was passed in 1993, surviving ten years of debate and two presidential vetoes, corporations still bitterly fought what they saw as a gross infringement on the free market. Unfortunately, this surviving attitude has meant that the bottom is exactly where child and family leave policies usually wind up.

By the time kids reach school age, it's easy to find yourself in a serious hole. But the escalating costs don't stop there. In the 1940s, when my mother walked home from her first day of kindergarten and told my grandmother she didn't want to go back, my grandmother said okay, and kept her home until she was ready for the first grade. Today, unless you plan to quit your job to homeschool your children, forgoing preschooling isn't an option. Early childhood education is no longer just a homespun convenience or an opportunity for small children to socialize. It's become a necessary step in preparing middle-class children for regular school. Parents, in particular parents in large cities with competitive school systems, feel the pressure to have their children in the right school by age two or risk falling out of the loop. Such preschools can easily cost more than tuition at the state university.[15]

"You can't compromise on preschool," says Stella, a graphic designer living in Brooklyn, who tells me she and her lawyer husband carried debt on their two children's preschool for years. "Preschool preps them for kindergarten and that sets them up for the rest of their educational lives. It sounds ridiculous, but if they fall behind when they're three you really do worry they'll never have the chance to catch up."

When it comes to early schooling pressures, it's difficult to separate the parental hysteria from legitimate worry about the future of a child's education. Surely many children do quite well in life even without the benefits of an expensive preschool under their belts. Nevertheless, since middle-class children don't qualify for federal programs like Head Start, their parents do need to negotiate some sort of early education for them, and that education often comes at a heavy price.

Once through the maze of preschooling, many professional middle-class parents must then grapple with the reality that they can't afford to educate their children the way they were educated. Their incomes simply don't have room for private schools, or even a more expensive house in a more expensive neighborhood with high-quality public schools. To ensure their children's futures aren't compromised, families are twisting themselves into financial knots they may never manage to untangle.

"My son got a scholarship, so I only had to pay $2,000 a year for this incredible education. How could you pass that up?" says Isabella, thirty-nine, a single mother with a twelve-year-old son and seven-year-old daughter. She works two jobs—teaching and designing education curriculums—and squeezes her family into a single-bedroom apartment on the northern tip of Manhattan to make her $50,000-a-year salary stretch far enough to send both children to private schools. "I couldn't put my son in private school and tell my daughter 'tough luck, we can't afford it.' So I pay $12,000 a year for her to be in one, too. Once they're there and they're happy, you do everything humanly possible to make sure you don't have to take them out again."

Isabella's parents came to New York from the Dominican Republic—she's the first in her family to graduate from college—and she admits to a constant sense of shame that she's not more successful. Her parents, seeing that she makes what they consider "good money," can't understand why she struggles so hard to raise her kids. She carries no health insurance and the children are covered by New York State's Child Health Plus, a program they qualify for only because Isabella applied during the summer, when her teacher's income was at its lowest. Her credit is shot, though she's slowly working her way through the thousands of dollars in debt she and her ex-husband accrued during their tumultuous marriage. And she has no idea how she'll pay off the remaining $30,000 in loans she took out to fund her own graduate degree, let alone considering any sort of college fund for her kids.

"I'm bitter," she admits. "When I finished grad school and started creating a family, I had no idea that I would be so poor for so long."

Though she's invested as heavily as she possibly can in her children's education, Isabella feels torn about just how much security that schooling will provide. Is she doing right by her kids in continuing to value education above all else? Or is she setting them up for the same sort of financial disillusionment she's experiencing herself?

"I know I won't be in a position to help them out once they reach college," she says. "But I'm not sure what to tell them about how to handle the future. I no longer believe that if you study hard and do well in school it guarantees things will turn out okay. These days there are no guarantees."

Few parents I spoke to had much money stored away for college and, like Isabella, many couldn't conceive of starting a college fund until they'd finished paying off their own student loans. They worried about the ramifications of passing down a legacy of financial hardship and possibly saddling their children with their own insurmountable debt.

They also worried about what they would teach their kids about the value of money, about need versus want, and about how to measure success. Children today grow up with higher consumer expectations than those raised in the '60s and '70s. The economic polarization among educated professionals is reflected in our children too, and our educated middle-class kids often interact with peers sporting iPods, handheld video game systems, cell phones, designer clothes, and digital cameras before they hit the double digits. Given their proximity to such luxuries, how far will our children's sense of entitlement outstretch our own? Will they have less money and a greater hunger for things?

"I've talked to them about immediate gratification, and about not buying so much," says Stella, the Brooklyn graphic designer, about raising her two daughters ages six and eight. "I want them to understand that life is not about stuff. I have less than my parents had, and I can foresee them having less then we do now. I worry about how to prepare them for that, given the world we live in."

If we feel torn between money and values, imagine the pressures our financial anxieties will place on our kids now and in the future. How do we reconcile our children's tentative and fragile personal development with the sense that kids today need to be smarter and more competitive than everyone else if they're going to succeed? How fully do we propagate those ideals that left so many of us disenchanted: the sense of entitlement, the idea that hard work and fair play will automatically get you somewhere, the virtues of meaningful work, generosity of spirit, and a life of the mind? Much as we might relish having grown up in an era where possibility was the watchword, can we say we're responsible parents if we encourage our children to do as we did, bypass financial security and focus on following their dreams?

THE GENDER CARD

Though the arrival of children can reshape the finances and values of an entire family, parenthood is not a gender-neutral question. Women are still far more likely than men to be single parents, to choose lower-paying career paths that make it harder to support children, to devote more hours to domestic responsibilities, and to require parental and family leave to care for children or elderly parents. Though women without children now make 90 cents to every male dollar, women with children still make only 73 cents and single mothers make just 56 to 66 cents. Mothers are 35 percent more likely than childless home owners to lose their homes, and three times more likely than childless men to go bankrupt. If educated professional middle-class families are being pushed over a financial cliff, then mothers are being catapulted.[16]

Professional women today experience an unprecedented tug-of-war between work and family. The rise in family incomes since the 1970s has been largely due to women's entry into the workforce, and women in middle-income families have seen a more dramatic rise in their working hours than any other sector of the population. It's a sign of progress but also added stress. While women have stepped out into the workforce en masse, the household duties that used to fall under their responsibility have not simply disappeared. Though home and child care are split more evenly between couples than they used to be, women still take on the bulk of the domestic responsibilities, picking up roughly two-thirds of all at-home duties. A 2005 time-use survey conducted by the U.S Department of Labor showed the average working woman spends an hour more per day than the average working man on household activities like cleaning and cooking, and over twice as much time caring for children.[17]

Even as women feel pressured to commit endless time and energy to career preservation, they're running up against a modern-day "cult of motherhood" that insists good parenting entails hands-on attention and lots of it. Women I spoke to felt overwhelmed by the new definition of a good mother, encompassing everything from pureeing organic baby food, to supplementing their children's education with at-home activities, to making sure their kids join sports teams and learn a second language—the list proves endless. The definition of good parenting has changed since our parents' generation and that change has not only emotional and psychological but also financial ramifications.

What other options are there? For one hot second in the 1980s, popular attention focused on the idea of sequencing, advising women to take time out midcareer to have kids then rejoin the workforce once their children were in school. But that path left many women earning far less than before they'd had children, struggling to get back onto career ladders that wouldn't accommodate a gap of several years. Many couples like Gretchen and Linc are already stretched too thin to cut their income in half even for a few months, nor can they afford to lose job benefits, particularly with a new infant. But even for those women who can swing things on the financial front for a year or two, there's no guarantee that career will still be waiting when a mother is ready to return. Unlike in many other industrialized countries, employers in the U.S. are under no obligation to hold a spot for a woman who wants to take more than the legally mandated twelve weeks leave. Smaller employers are under no obligation to hold their position for them at all. Among mothers hoping to return to work, national surveys have shown that only 40 percent were able to find full-time, mainstream jobs. Those who'd been out of the workforce for at least three years typically suffered a salary drop of 37 percent.[18]

"Ideally, I'd love to take a year off," say Chloe, thirty-five, a San Diego art teacher who's eight months pregnant with her first child and plans to return to work when he's four months old. "Financially we might be able to manage. But there's no way the school is going to hold my position. Jobs like mine get snapped up the second they're available. If I quit, I don't know if I could ever find a situation like this again."

The advent of "flexible scheduling" has been trumpeted as another savior of the working mother, but as of 2004 only 27.5 percent of total workers—male and female—reported such schedules, a drop of more than a percentage point since 2001.[19] Even if mothers work for companies where job-sharing or part-time work is an option, accepting such positions, even temporarily, can often spell professional suicide. Clients forget, responsibilities are reassigned, benefits are sliced, and you're surreptitiously derailed from the promotional track.

Given this dearth of choices, working mothers go in on weekends, work nights after their children have gone to bed, and take six weeks or even six days maternity leave, not because they prefer work to parenting but because the alternative can mean compromising their entire professional and financial future. Anyway they turn, today's educated professional middle-class women face a maternal catch-22 we were supposed to have hurdled decades ago.

"I'm in a constant state of shock trying to both work and have kids," says Celeste, thirty-five, who balances a full-time job in the health-care industry with raising her four-year-old son and five-month-old daughter. She and her husband are still struggling to pay off the $35,000 in credit card debt they amassed trying to make ends meet during Celeste's two unpaid maternity leaves—five months for their daughter and three for their son. "The career world just hasn't caught up to women who need to do both. To be successful you have to be 110 percent dedicated to your job, and you can't do that and take care of children. But you also can't afford to not work at all."

The pressures are immense, and for most educated professional women I spoke to, shouldering them was not a matter of choice. Despite a recent surge of attention in the popular media, not a single interviewee had "opted out" of the workforce, electing to stay home and raise her children. Women in most cases wanted and in every case needed to work either full- or part-time in order to support their families. Even for those who did express the desire to stay home, if only for a few years, financial realities dictated otherwise. Opting out was never an option for the working poor and is increasingly not viable for the educated professional middle class either.

But the prohibitive cost of child care and our country's lack of community, employer, or federal support does lend this opt-out question an added wrinkle. It's created a sector of professional women with small children who stop working for a very different reason. Because they can't afford to stay on the job. The money they would earn going back part-time or picking up a low-salaried career can't cover the costs of child care. Rather than opting out, new mothers —and occasionally fathers—are being pushed out by a system that hasn't adjusted to a world in which dual-income families have, by necessity, become the norm.

When Britta, thirty-seven, returned to work after the birth of her second child, the private high school where she taught was willing to arrange a quarter-time schedule the first year, offering her a single class that met three times a week, plus management of the school's newspaper. But the $9,000 salary for nine months work didn't come close to covering the $1,400 a week she paid to have an infant in day care. The following year Britta expanded her hours to teach an additional class and her salary rose accordingly. But the $23,000 she now made still only just covered child-care costs. Her son had some health problems, and every day she missed—though she found her own substitute teacher—the school docked her pay. Eventually, unable to continue working at a financial loss, she quit to pursue freelance journalism she could do from home.

"The administrators who had children, particularly the one working part-time, understood, but they didn't have the power to do anything about it," Britta recalls. "One man told me his wife wasn't working because they just couldn't afford to do that. Can you imagine looking at a job as something you can 'afford'" to do? But the reality is, for very many careers, the cost of quality child care really means you work for free. Ours is probably also the first generation of people who can't count on support in the form of child care from grandparents either, because many of our mothers work, or are taking care of their elderly parents. It's really quite a difficult problem. I don't know what the answer is."

For professional middle-class mothers, returning to work full-time also means returning to financial independence. In the longer term, this might be one of the smartest choices they can make. One of the key freedoms gleaned by women's march to work in the '70s was that wives and mothers no longer had to remain dependent on their spouses, nor wind up broke and helpless should something befall the marriage. Though no one wants to factor this one into their personal future, today's high divorce rates—43 percent of first marriages end in divorce[20]—mean there's a high probability that married couples who have every intention of forming a traditional two-parent family will instead face the financial and psychological cost of breaking up.

Divorce is not just an emotional assault, it comes at an enormous financial cost. Immediate expenses can include lawyers' fees, court costs, buying and furnishing a new home, and expanded child-care arrangements. Given the trauma of the divorce itself, parents are often exceedingly reluctant to shake up their children's lives with further cost-cutting changes—like moving to a smaller home in a less expensive neighborhood, switching schools, or cutting out extra-curricular activities. And though both members of a couple suffer, women with children overwhelmingly bear the financial brunt.

Even today, with the majority of wives and mothers already in the workforce, divorced women are more likely to earn less money than their ex-husbands, meaning that they suffer greater loss of income when they split, typically between 35 and 50 percent. They're also more likely to assume a larger portion of the postdivorce child care, mortgages, tuitions, insurance, and taxes. If they don't have a lucra-tive full-time career to support them, the ramifications for both parent and child run deep.[21]

Katia, thirty-nine, earned her BA in sociology with a minor in so-cial work. She and her husband, Kyle, married shortly after she grad-uated from college in her midtwenties, and for the next two years she supported them both while he finished flight school. Kyle signed on to become an Air Force pilot, a job requiring them to move some-place new every two years—New Mexico, South Dakota, Louisiana —making it difficult for Katia to develop a career of her own. She continued to work, finding counseling or child-care positions in the local public schools, and also took primary responsibility for raising their son. When her husband was sent to Iraq in 2003, Katia cut back her hours so she could spend more time at home with her then nine-year-old boy.

A year ago, Katia and Kyle divorced after twelve years of mar-riage. The emotional turmoil has been difficult. But it's the financial hit that proved most devastating.

"I don't have a master's degree, and though I worked nine of the twelve years we were married, I was never in the direct social work field," explains Katia. "When I went out to find a full-time job to support my son and myself, I found out that it's almost impossible to get back into the workplace once you've been gone."

Katia moved back to Albuquerque, where she grew up, and even-tually found a job working thirty hours a week as a social worker for a nonprofit organization that helps the disabled. The position pays $20,000 a year. Even with the $700 a month her husband pays in child support, it's nowhere near enough for her and her son to get by.

In the past year, Katia's gone through every last cent of her savings and she owes $8,000 on her credit cards. She officially defaulted on her student loans, and the government has started taking money out of her tax returns.

"I feel like such a loser," she tells me over the phone one Sunday afternoon while her son is off visiting his father. "My credit is shot. I have collection agencies calling like crazy. I just ignore them. I don't know what else to do."

She loves everything about her job but the paycheck and hopes there might be some room for a small raise in the next year. But given that salaries are reliant on grant money, she's not holding her breath. She's also considered getting a roommate to share the two-bedroom house she rents for $1,000 a month, but fears that might be too disruptive for her twelve-year-old son. For now, her main focus is making their life together seem as stable and secure as she possibly can.

"I try to hide from my son how tight things really are," she confesses. "I don't want him to be ashamed or embarrassed. I feel like we live in a culture where having financial troubles equals failure, and he's been through so much already. It would break my heart for him to feel that way about our family."

ALTERNATIVE FAMILIES IN A REACTIONARY AGE

Of course, raising children as a dual-income married couple is far from the only choice out there. Today, married couples with kids occupy fewer than one in four households, half the number they occupied in 1960 and the lowest level ever recorded by the census.[22] Experts predict that 50 percent of children in the United States will spend part of their lives in a household that doesn't include both biological parents.[23] The "married with children" model may still occupy a key position in our image of the American dream, but gone are the days when it's a reliable gauge of the real world. The loosening of social strictures about family—which began in the 1970s as both divorce and cohabitation rates began to rise—has unveiled a long hidden truth. The conventional nuclear family often doesn't meet our intimacy and partnership needs and desires, nor does it necessarily adhere to the realities of contemporary life.

These freer social rules have had a particularly profound effect on the possibilities available to educated professionals who find themselves partnerless but still eager to have children. Individuals—primarily women—who reach their mid- to late thirties or early forties without having met the love of their life no longer have to resign themselves to a childless existence, should they desire children. They can mix up the traditional order of things, kids first, relationship, possibly, later. Literature from organizations like Single Mothers by Choice reveals that having a child on one's own is rarely the ideal or even preferred choice, but for many women it seems the best choice under the circumstances. For educated professional women born and raised in the socially progressive '60s and '70s, it's a natural leap to feel that we are entitled in this department too, entitled to motherhood and the right to shape our own families without the rules and expectations of others interceding.

But though social strictures may be dissolving, the financial constraints faced by single mothers can be severe. The widening acceptance of single motherhood as a life choice has been accompanied by narrowing financial options, leaving many single women feeling as trapped as they did generations ago. Social dependence on a partner may have faded but economic dependence still runs strong—the gains won by women in the workplace seldom equate to incomes that stretch far enough to pay for two. It can be impossible to fathom even coming up with the money for a sperm donor, IVF, or adoption, let alone taking on the long term-financial commitment of raising a child. The fear many interviewees expressed that it's irresponsible to plan a child when you're nowhere near financially stable applies doubly, triply, when you're on your own. Given our liberated social times, surprisingly few women I talked to were willing to even consider raising a child on their own, purely for financial reasons.

They are right to be concerned. Today's single parents are in the job market, the housing market, the child-care market, the college-tuition market, the food and gas and insurance market, competing against dual-income families who themselves can barely afford a middle-class lifestyle. And though the gaps in social acceptance of alternative family structures have certainly narrowed, the earnings gap between single mothers and married parents is greater than it was in the '70s, with single mothers typically earning $41,000 less than married couples with children.[24]

With no second earner to catch them should they slip, single mothers are also far more prone to financial distress and even bankruptcy. Having a child is the single best predictor that a woman will go bankrupt. Over two hundred thousand single mothers file for bankruptcy every year and they are primarily middle-class women over thirty with educations, established jobs and careers, even their own homes. A single mother who's been to college is 60 percent more likely to go bankrupt than one with a high school education.[25] When questioning where to turn for help, single parents in the U.S. have few options. Beyond the twelve weeks mandated unpaid maternity leave you might receive if your employer falls under the Family and Medical Leave Act, American families receive no federally mandated help at all. If you're lucky your employer might be willing to help you structure a more flexible work schedule or a longer maternity leave, giving you a fraction more time to bond with your child and arrange for satisfactory child-care arrangements. If you're extremely lucky there could be child-care subsidies or even on-site day care available through work.

None of the single parents I spoke to were extremely lucky.

"My parents have helped me out a lot," says Savannah, forty-one, an Ivy League–educated book editor and single mother of a two-year-old son. "But they're getting old. Eventually the story is going to flip and they're going to need me to take care of them. I don't know what we'll do then. I've gone from feeling completely blessed to feeling completely exposed. That's not what I expected motherhood to do for me."

If they're to reach any sort of financial security, today's families need help. They need paid maternity leave and affordable and trustworthy child care. They also need paid family leave to tend to elderly or ill family members, because our current care crisis extends up the age spectrum as well as down. As our parents age, facing loss of income and steeper medical costs, membership in what's been called "the sandwich generation" is growing—40 percent of those taking care of elderly parents are parents themselves.[26] That same twelve weeks allotted by the Family and Medical Leave Act is still our only recourse if we require time off to care for a sick or aging relative.

Not only do we need more generous government and company policies, but we also need corporate culture to come to a more universal acceptance of those policies. It's not enough just to offer perks like flexible scheduling and paternity leave. If six months maternity leave means you miss out on years' worth of raises, bonuses, and promotions, families will wind up paying a severe economic price for taking advantage of this so-called benefit.

Though the fact that the United States falls behind nearly every other industrialized country when it comes to providing family leave benefits to its citizens is certainly alarming, it can also provide considerable grounds for hope. It means that we're surrounded by multiple models for child care and family leave programs that are proven successful. For example, in Spain, France, and the Netherlands, mothers receive sixteen weeks fully paid maternity leave. In Panama, Senegal, and Cameroon it's fourteen weeks. Sweden, often held up as the penultimate in family-friendly societies, provides 480 days in combined parental leave, 390 days at 80 percent pay rate and the final 90 days at a government mandated flat rate, essentially freeing parents to stay home with their children for the first sixteen months of their lives. Not only does this provide new families with much needed time together, it also significantly diminishes the need for early child care, state sponsored or otherwise.[27]

In all of these countries, the costs of paid parental leave are covered by the government in the form of tax-funded social security programs. Other nations, including Germany, Korea, India, and the U.K., combine government and employer contributions to cover similar leave programs. As our own government moves forward in determining what we as a nation value and choose to spend our money on—be it war, defense, or an increase in domestic social programs—we can do well to look to some of these other nations and the family-oriented value systems they have chosen to put in place.

6

WHAT WERE THE BENEFITS?

Health Care, Retirement, and Everything Else
the Government Was Supposed to Help Provide

Over the fifteen years I've spent in the workforce, I've been personally responsible for covering most of my own health care and all my retirement savings. In my twenties I either went without health insurance or carried a high-deductible major medical policy, what my father called "hit by a bus" insurance, which (fortunately) never kicked in. For a brief time I was eligible for insurance through a professional union, an early brush with the HMO system that I found so confusing I mostly just didn't use it. In my thirties, feeling less cavalier about my good health, I paid thousands of dollars for a COBRA plan off an old job until I became eligible for a group benefit package through another professional organization. From there I began a long cycle of hopping between the various plans it offered, always trying to find something cheaper that still gave me decent coverage. I kept two sets of doctors and swapped between them depending on which insurance carrier I was with at the time.

Today, I pay over $500 a month for a group plan with a major New York area provider. There was a less expensive choice—one with no prescription-drug coverage and no out-of-network options, one that gave me a considerably diminished list of doctors to choose from—but sitting in my Manhattan apartment with the various options, printed on candy-colored paper, strewn across my bed, trying to speculate about my medical future, I decided that there was a good chance prescriptions could factor in. Visions of the $1,000-a-month chemotherapy drugs my mother had taken several years earlier loomed large. So did the idea that if, God forbid, I got sick or hurt—really sick or hurt—I wanted to go to the doctor I wanted to go to, not someone chosen and defined by my "plan."

So I shelled out. And I still do. I pay more for health insurance than I do for anything but rent. And if you pool what I also pay for what's not covered, from visiting an out-of-network therapist to acupuncture treatments that are considered an alternative luxury, my health costs often outscale rent. Paying for decent health insurance and decent health care means I don't spend on other things. I don't go on vacation, to concerts or movies, or out to eat. I don't buy clothes unless something falls apart. I reliably rack up credit card debt around the months that the insurance payment is due. I am, overall, a healthy person. I eat well and practice yoga and stay pretty clear of alcohol or drugs. Nevertheless, the cost of potentially losing that health has come to dominate my economic life. Even more frightening, despite having insurance, I have no doubt that a genuine health crisis would shatter whatever tenuous financial balance I've somehow managed to attain.

As for retirement, my story reflects the situation of many freelance workers. I don't have any savings. Because most of my jobs have been on a freelance basis, no employer has ever offered me a 401(k), let alone a pension, and I've never had enough extra money to set up an IRA for myself. For a long time my plan was one of committed passivity—hoping that something might change between now and my seventies. In recent years, as I near my forties, I've felt the urge to take a more proactive stance. In part, I was driven to write this book by a real desire to understand what we as a society must do so that circumstances for those in situations similar to my own might change.

My tangled financial relationship with health and longevity is hardly uncommon. Perhaps nowhere has the idea of personal responsibility reared its head so prominently and done so much damage as in the arena of social benefits. These days many high-opportunity, high-potential members of the educated professional middle class, those with solid careers and multiple degrees, feel that their health insurance and retirement plans—if they're lucky enough to have them—are woefully inadequate. And as we enter our thirties and forties and we have not just ourselves but also our families to consider,

going without insurance seems foolish in the extreme. If we're looking for what's changed in the past two decades, making a secure
middle-class lifestyle more difficult to sustain, we need look no further than the high cost and limited payout of social benefits like
health insurance. Today the responsibility and cost of social services
has largely shifted from the government and employers to individual
workers.

Despite all the individualistic rhetoric tossed in our direction these
days, personal responsibility has not always been the American way.
We have a long history of social responsibility. Over the course of
the twentieth century, as we morphed into a more complex industrialized and democratic society, we came to realize the need for a
government that cares for its individual members. The tradition of
government-backed social insurance was to a large degree spawned
by the dramatic financial inequalities of the 1920s and the subsequent suffering of the Depression. In the face of such glaring need,
FDR's New Deal created government-subsidized insurance policies ranging from Social Security and unemployment insurance to
minimum-wage and child labor laws, all of which gave workers the
sense of something far more powerful than themselves watching their
backs. At the same time, physicians and hospitals began setting up
private group insurance plans to make their services more affordable,
one of the earliest and most successful of which would become Blue
Cross.[1]

On a broader plane, the onset of social insurance set us on a path
toward becoming a society that functioned best—both economically
and morally—by pooling the shared risks of its individual members.
The idea was that the healthy supported the sick, the wealthy supported the poor, and the active workforce supported the young and
the elderly. This concept of social instead of personal responsibility
continued to evolve in the coming decades. In 1965, Medicare and
Medicaid joined the social insurance roster, supplying government-
backed health insurance to the elderly and to low-income families
and rounding out the idea of a government responsible for helping
those least able to help themselves.

In the early twentieth century, an evolving sense of corporate responsibility also helped create a safety net for workers, regardless of

their means or background. Our parents and grandparents came of age in an era when employee loyalty, consistency, and long-term service were valued and rewarded. An employer felt it was good for business to keep a worker healthy and happy. Low turnover meant more skilled labor and less time spent training new employees. Benefits like pensions and health insurance—regulated by the government and subsidized by tax breaks—were created to keep workers loyal to companies over the long run. By the 1950s, the Eastman Kodak Company in Rochester, New York, was providing benefits including company housing, in-house health programs, employee profit sharing, and production planning to minimize layoffs.[2]

Even in the late '70s and early '80s, though the middle and working classes experienced a drop in salaries, employers worked to preserve increasingly costly employee benefits. But by the end of the '80s, as the price of benefits continued to grow and the value placed on employee loyalty and longevity sank, employers began opting to cut benefits rather than absorb the rising costs.[3] In the past two decades, the government- and employer-provided shields that once helped protect us from financial harm have succumbed to deregulation and a freewheeling market economy. Job security, health insurance, and retirement funding are now viewed as too costly to be taken on by government or employers. The provision of such benefits has fallen into the hands of for-profit entities—from banks to insurance providers—who concern themselves with high profits, not communal well-being.

By default, in a "free society," we're increasingly expected to see to such insurance on our own. Pension plans have been replaced by IRAs and 401(k)s that rely on worker contributions. Employer-provided health care now involves co-pays, deductibles, and employee contributions, meaning a smaller and smaller portion is actually provided by the employers themselves. Many of today's benefits, including 401(k)s and health savings accounts, require that individuals put their own money into tax-protected accounts, so that they only really benefit those who have money to spare. Such a perva-sive shift toward individualism is not an automatic offshoot of a free market economy. We had a free market economy when we enacted child labor laws, eight-hour workdays, Medicare, and Social

Security. What's been lost is the vision of a society that cares for its own, a baseline of collective responsibility.

Perhaps most troubling is the fact that our society has begun backpedaling from its moral and ethical code under the auspices of providing its members with increased personal liberty. Freedom is the new buzzword, but its meaning has been twisted almost beyond recognition. The intangible perks of being a free agent, able to move from job to job and design our own careers, have replaced tangible benefits like health care, retirement, and generous paychecks. The awkward truth is that there's very little personal freedom involved when subsidies and tax breaks go to corporations while the individuals receive increasingly little. If corporations, with their increased profits, are having trouble paying for benefits, where do we get the idea that individuals staggering under stagnant wages and a rising cost of living will be able to absorb this additional expense?

In reality, far from making us more liberated, our current lack of social supports is gutting everyone from the educated professional middle class on down. In addition to the two biggies—health care and retirement—the government has cut investment in the sort of community services that benefit all of us, from public schools, parks, hospitals, and libraries to roads and transportation, all those public spaces that are not part of the marketplace but instead contribute to quality of life.

These days, in privatizing and individualizing social services, we've turned them into market-ready consumer products that work like any other consumer product from doughnuts to blue jeans. The private sector is defined by competition. It flourishes because it doesn't strive toward equality, because the market angle always obscures the human angle. Somewhere along the way, we've lost sight of the fact that health care and retirement should not involve any sort of cost-cutting, profit-chasing race to the top. Life and longevity are not expendable commodities.

HEALTH CARE: THE COSTS

Two years ago, at age twenty-nine, Bethany was well placed on the path toward pursuing her educated professional middle-class dreams. Her high school and college years had been tough—she lost her mother when she was sixteen and her father three years later—but now she finally felt like her life was on track again. After several trying years working in customer service for Internet companies, dodging layoffs right and left, she'd returned to graduate school to study her true love, art history, with the hope of eventually pursuing a career as a museum curator. She'd moved to the Northeast from her native Michigan and was supporting herself through school with a full-time job working in a cultural embassy near her New England university. Sure, there were financial pressures, like the $80,000 in student loans she'd taken out to finance her undergraduate and graduate degrees, never mind food, rent, and other living expenses. But she thought that buckling down for the next few years seemed the only means to the proper end.

One thing did nag at Bethany's sense of responsibility. She had tried getting health insurance first through school and then through her job, but as a part-time student and new hire, she wasn't eligible in either place. And she earned too much money to qualify for any state programs.

"I was gravely concerned about getting health insurance," she explains. "I went to the school and tried to pay for it out of pocket, but they said no, that I had to be a full-time student to get insurance. I killed myself trying to find some plan I was eligible for. But there was just nothing out there."

Though she knew going without wasn't the most prudent option, she didn't know where else to turn. For the next three months, until she qualified for her employer-provided package, she'd just have to be sure to take her vitamins and look both ways before crossing the street.

Then one late night that November, about a month before her insurance would've kicked in, Bethany, a friend from graduate school, and the friend's mother were driving along a well-traveled strip of highway near the friend's hometown in New Jersey. The exact details of what happened are still hazy, but Bethany remembers her friend's mother grabbing at the wheel and her friend calling out "Mom!" The next thing she knew, the car had spun out of control, flipped over, and slid on its roof across seventy feet of highway. Once the car stopped moving, Bethany managed to crawl free through the blown-out back windows, cutting her hands on the shattered glass. For a long moment, she just stared into the blurry darkness, unsure what to do.

"Luckily, there were a lot of other people on the road that night, and tons of people stopped to help," she recalls. "My left arm was broken in three places and my right shoulder was broken as well. Once I'd crawled out of the car and the pain hadn't hit yet, I was sitting on the ground and I realized I didn't have any health insurance, and I started to cry. Someone who'd stopped to help asked if I was in pain and I wailed, 'I don't have health insurance!' I just sobbed. A cop walked past and heard me and said, 'Don't worry, the driver's insurance will cover you. This wasn't your fault.'"

It turned out the cop was wrong. The driver's insurance covered only $2,500 of Bethany's $55,000 in medical bills. She was responsible for paying for most of the surgery, the six-day hospital stay, the titanium rod and two screws put into her left arm, the titanium plate and seven screws in her right shoulder, and the painful months of physical therapy. On top of such staggering medical bills, Bethany missed nearly two months of school. She was fired from her job and wasn't physically able to take on something new for another six months, during which time her debts—medical and otherwise—spiraled.

As soon as she learned that the driver's insurance wouldn't cover her, Bethany used the little money she had left to hire a lawyer, a family friend willing to cut his fees, to sue the driver's insurance company for one-third of the medical costs. The lawsuit took a year and a half to come to court and required getting thirteen different medical billers—among them EMS, the hospital, the surgeon, orthopedist, radiologist, anesthesiologist, and physical therapist—to agree to reduce their costs. In the meantime, despite a letter from her lawyer asking them to hold off until the suit was settled, five of those billers referred Bethany's case to collections agencies. Her credit was ruined, and the annual percentage rate (APR) on her Visa card leapt from 9.99 to 32.9 percent.

"Up until then I was superresponsible financially," Bethany tells me. "I paid at least the minimum on my credit card every month. I didn't have any outstanding debt. I was a very good financial risk.

Suddenly my credit rating was severely compromised due to all those delinquent accounts. I wrote letters to the creditors, and my reports all say 'paid' on these accounts, but two years later my rating is still only fair and I'm rejected whenever I apply for a new credit card."

Today Bethany is thin and pale, though she's regained nearly full usage of her shoulder and arm. I have no trouble believing her when she tells me she's living on ramen and peanut butter and jelly, still struggling to get out from under the debt, medical and otherwise, that mushroomed from her accident and the six months she spent out of work. She has a job she loves as an assistant curator for a small museum specializing in the decorative arts. But she earns just $36,000 a year, hardly enough to live on let alone cut into her debt load. Two years later, her credit report still carries the black mark of unpaid medical bills. She's still carrying $9,000 in credit card debt but after hours spent with the credit card company on the phone—"I literally asked them 'how do you sleep at night?'"—she got her APR reduced to its original 9.99 percent. She's now paying $383 a month for a COBRA plan on the insurance she got as a full-time student in her final year of grad school, and in three months the policy for her new job will kick in. She's not sure what she'll do when her deferred student loan payments pick up later in the year but even that seems small fare when compared to what she's been through.

"The whole thing has really given me serious doubts about the health-insurance system we have in this country," Bethany says. "How can we be this great nation when this kind of stuff happens? I mean, I did everything I was supposed to do according to the rules: I went to college, I got a master's, I got a good job, I was never late on any of my bills. I even had it a little rougher than most because I lost both my parents when I was a teenager and had to really struggle for everything early on. But I was successful. So it really kills me that through all my struggles financially, I was always able to maintain good credit, and now it's shot. After this accident happened, which was out of my control and not my fault, somehow I'm the one who gets punished. It makes no sense to me."

Today, finding and affording health care has evolved into a nightmare for all but the wealthiest Americans. Just consider the statistics:

46.6 million Americans lack health insurance, nearly twice as many as in 1980. There's a clear correlation between this rise and the climbing costs and reduced availability of employer-provided coverage. In 1980, the majority of medium to large employers paid 100 percent of the premiums for health coverage. Today, fewer than a quarter pay full coverage for individuals, and only 9 percent of firms assume full family coverage for their employees. The 2005 Census showed more disturbing trends: an increase in the number of children without insurance, a decrease in those covered by employer-based insurance, and a decrease in the overall percentage of people with health insurance.[4]

The souring state of health care has always been an issue for immigrants and the working poor, but increasingly it's becoming a middle-class issue too. More than a third of those uninsured have household incomes over $40,000. Thirty-five percent of households with incomes between $50,000 and $75,000 report having trouble paying medical bills and health insurance. And more than a third of those who carry both insurance and medical debt have either college or graduate degrees.[5]

It's not hard to figure out why health care has become such a precious commodity. The costs of both insurance and medical care are skyrocketing. Family premiums have increased 87 percent since 2000, compared to an 18 percent rise in inflation and a 20 percent rise in wages. As of 2006, only 61 percent of the population had employer-provided insurance, down from 69 percent in 2000, meaning that more and more people are expected to figure out how to cover these rising costs on their own.[6]

And things only seem to be getting worse. Even the largest companies with the healthiest profits are expecting workers to assume more coverage costs. They're increasingly opting for plans with high deductibles, reduced services, and no prescription-drug coverage, requesting that employees pay up to a third of the costs themselves, and refusing to subsidize premiums for spouses and children. Though relatively few companies are going so far as to cease coverage altogether, what they offer is becoming harder for their employees to afford.[7] Meanwhile, fewer small businesses are willing or able to provide health benefits at all, with just 60 percent of companies employing fewer than one hundred people offering any sort of insurance plan.[8] Increasingly, those working for nonprofits or small companies are expected to cover much or all of the health-plan costs on their own, whether or not they can afford it given the salaries they're paid.

Even if you are fortunate enough to receive health benefits from your employer, extra expenses—co-pays, deductibles, employee-paid premiums, out-of-network providers, and services not covered such as mental health, dental, and alternative care—can easily run more than the cost of the plan itself. Seventy percent of those with medical debt actually had insurance when they accrued it, and 51 percent of insured Americans still spend more than 10 percent of their income on medical care.[9] These costs can be especially pervasive for those with chronic conditions that affect their ability to work. But if you get sick enough that you have to quit your job, there goes your insurance.

If you're not covered by an employer, the costs of coverage becomes astronomical and the policies at times difficult to secure at any price. Over the past three years, 89 percent of adults who sought health coverage on their own were either rejected for health reasons or couldn't afford what was on offer. For those who do sign up for plans, over half pay more than $3,000 a year on premiums and about a third pay upward of $6,000. If you happen to have a preexisting condition—those who need health insurance the most—premiums can run to thousands of dollars a month, if you can find anyone to insure you at all.[10]

Our current system of employer-based benefits ignores the health needs of those who are between jobs or unable to work, as well as the rising number of freelance, temporary, and contingent workers, who comprise 33 percent of the workforce. Such "nonstandard" workers are far less likely to receive health benefits from their employers, and far less likely to be able to afford such benefits even if they are offered.[11]

"I make $18,000 to $20,000, for what's basically a full-time job" says Leslie, twenty-eight, an adjunct English professor at a midwestern university. "Yes there's a benefit package included with my job but it's basically worthless. Maybe the school feels better being able to offer me something, but I can barely afford food and rent, let alone paying for health insurance out of my own pocket. I haven't been able to afford it since I was a student, and at this rate it's going to be a very long time before I ever will."

A few budding professional organizations like the New York–based Freelancers Union provide benefits for contingent workers, but they only offer plans in a limited number of states at a cost that's still difficult for many to meet. The cheapest standard plan the Freelancer's Union provided in spring of 2007—one that included no mental-health coverage, a $50 co-pay for office visits, a $100 deductible on prescription-drug coverage (generic brands only) and a $3,000 deductible for in-patient care—still cost individuals a hefty $205.69 a month and for families ran a full $608.95.

As Bethany experienced, assuming these rampant health care costs on our own can decimate our financial lives. The under- and uninsured often have little choice but to turn to credit cards to absorb the additional financial burden, sinking them further and further into personal debt. Twenty-nine percent of low- and middle-income families who carry credit card debt report using those cards to pay for illnesses or other necessary medical expenses. In the past twenty years, the number of families declaring bankruptcy in the wake of a serious illness or other medical crisis has risen an almost inconceivable 2,000 percent.[12]

The whole health-care fiasco has left even the educated and employed with a mounting sense of helplessness and very little in the way of alternative plans. A forty-two-year-old acupuncturist I interviewed summed it up after explaining that as a self-employed practitioner making $48,000 a year, he simply can't afford to carry health insurance.

"It's certainly not ideal," he told me, "But I don't see any other choice. There is simply no care option out there for someone like me. I figure that at least I'm one of the lucky ones. I know a lot of people who I can consult to keep me well."

THE DISAPPEARANCE OF VALUE AND VALUES

Under our current model, health care has undergone a full-scale transformation from obligatory (public) social service to lucrative (private) bottom-line industry. Insurance has been consolidated under a handful of providers each enrolling millions of members and raking in billions of dollars. While millions of Americans are unable to afford coverage at all and many more—from the poor to the squarely middle class—struggle to find proper care, drug companies, hospitals, and insurance providers, from Pfizer to WellPoint, Johnson & Johnson to UnitedHealth, continue to report record profits.[13]

Rather than improving patient care, the majority of these profits are channeled toward lobbying, political contributions, prescription-drug advertising, and administrative costs. In the past fifteen years, health-care companies—including insurance providers, hospitals, and pharmaceutical companies—have contributed millions of dollars to political campaigns, donating more than the energy industry, commercial banks, or big tobacco. They've consolidated to form a powerful medical lobby on Capitol Hill, pouring more money into courting politicians than any industry but the combined finance, insurance, and real estate lobby. They've also established a major presence on Madison Avenue. Between 1994 and 2004, spending on consumer drug advertisements leapt from $266 million to $2.5 billion.[14]

Is private insurance at least better and more efficient than government-sponsored health care might be? Not likely. When compared to seventeen other industrialized nations with similar economic conditions, all of which provide significantly greater public health care to their citizens, the U.S. comes up decidedly short. Though we have the highest per capita spending on health care—15 percent of our GDP—we have one of the lowest life expectancy rates and the highest infant mortality rates, measurements commonly used to assess the health status of a country.[15]

For example, in Canada health care is provided to every citizen, regardless of medical history, age, income, or employment status, through a group of socialized health-insurance plans that are publicly funded—through personal and corporate income taxes—and administered by individual provinces and territories according to federal guidelines. Individuals receive free preventative and primary care as well as access to hospitals, dental surgery, and prescription drugs. The main principles of the Canada Health Act are universality (all citizens are eligible for care), comprehensiveness (all necessary services are covered), and accessibility (all citizens can get access to such care). These are all areas in which insurance in the U.S. consistently falls short. In addition, Canada spends just 9 percent of its GDP on health care, as compared to 15 percent in the U.S, yet Canadians have a life expectancy of 80 years, 2.8 years higher than ours, and an infant mortality rate of 5.4 deaths per year compared to our 7.[16]

When you break it down, our largely private, for-profit care system is at best wasteful and at worst dangerous to its patients. It's laced with unnecessary middlemen—since 1970 the number of doctors in the U.S. has increased 40 percent while the number of medical administrators has gone up 3,000 percent—all of whom must receive a cut in order for us to purchase care. Today, nearly one in three dollars spent on health care goes toward administration costs. It's been estimated that if we switched to a single-payer system we'd save $161 billion on paperwork alone.[17]

The increasing number of private hospitals are run on a business model, where patients have become "customers." Their cost-control measures include cutting back on employees, from critical-care nurses to the janitors who clean the operating rooms, under-ordering supplies, limiting hospital stays to a night or two even for such serious conditions as stroke or congestive heart failure, having low-paid call-center operators with no medical training determine whether a patient should see a doctor, and relying on insurance-company employees to determine the length of a patient's hospital stay. Death rates in private hospitals are significantly higher than in their non-profit counterparts, and both environments are becoming increasingly dangerous. Today, in hospitals both public and private, six times as many patients die from medical mistakes as from HIV/AIDS.[18]

In such a mind-set, health care is not viewed as an entitlement provided in equal measure to all members of a civilized society but as a personal responsibility individuals can and should take care of on their own. Insurance is no longer about collective risk-sharing—everyone putting money in the common pool but only those who fall seriously ill having to withdraw it—but corporate risk avoidance. Instead of making efforts to help those who are underinsured or uninsured, the health-care industry takes advantage of them whenever and however they can. The less insurance patients carry, the more they're charged for medical services. Because they aren't eligible for the volume discounts negotiated by the insurance companies, uninsured patients can wind up paying two, three, five, even ten times as much as insured patients for the same care and services.[19]

Like student loans, mortgages, and credit cards, a good chunk of the health-care system's power lies in its being incomprehensible or, at the very least, difficult to understand. Confusion abounds regarding what we're supposed to pay on a given claim, which services are covered, which doctors we can visit, and what recourse we have if we can't pay. There's often no clear sense of what sort of care we're entitled to, and rather than do battle with a string of customer service representatives, we typically simply pay whatever bill happens to arrive. Insurance companies add to the confusion by delaying, reducing, and denying claims or sending their patients bills for services already covered.[20]

Not surprisingly, when it comes to health care the government has passed the buck. As of 2003, according to the Economic Policy Institute, only 25.3 percent of the American population was covered by government health care, compared to 100 percent in countries like Switzerland, Canada, Australia, Italy, Japan, and the United Kingdom. The U.S. government is focused on reducing cost rather than improving access to quality care. In a 2007 radio address, President Bush, after acknowledging that the rising cost of health care was indeed a problem, suggested that we "treat health insurance more like home ownership" by providing tax incentives for individuals who purchase insurance out of their own pockets rather than relying on government or even employers for help. Not that what we have today could be considered a free market health system. The health-care industry receives generous tax subsidies; in essence the government pays companies to make it look like free market medicine works more efficiently than it does. This is particularly frightening given how inefficiently it works even then.[21]

The situation has grown so dire that individual states are stepping up and attempting to partially or entirely fill the chasms, among them Massachusetts, and to a lesser degree California and New York. Such local action is a positive and proactive step, while also signaling that both politicians and individual citizens feel our health-care system has truly reached a crisis point. However, this move toward state-provided care should not negate the federal government's responsibility and role in providing universal insurance to all its citizens. Successful models in other nations, such as Canada, rely on some degree of federal funding and regulation to assure consistency and quality of care. Though Massachusetts and the other states moving to follow in its footsteps should be lauded, the federal government should not be allowed to leave the financial and administrative burden of health care solely to individual states.[22]

Even corporate America seems to be reaching a breaking point, as companies struggle to keep apace with international competitors based in countries whose governments subsidize health-care costs. A few large companies are taking steps to ameliorate the problem on their own, opening private on-site health clinics to tend to their employees' basic health concerns without needing to turn to—or pay for—outside care. But this is a patchwork remedy, not a feasible long-term solution for most companies, nor does it address the needs of small-businesses or freelance workers.[23]

In addressing the health-care crisis, the federal government has seized upon the economic theory of "moral hazard," which dictates that if consumers don't have to pay for something themselves—i.e., if insurance pays their medical costs for them—they are far more likely to spend recklessly and overconsume on items that aren't needed. It has created a false portrait of a medically bloated American population running around ordering up tests and checking into hospitals willy-nilly, and uses this image to support the claim that government-sponsored universal health care would be impossible to finance.[24]

One of the government's favorite cost-cutting instruments has become the health savings account (HSA), a program in which individuals put money in a tax-free savings account and then withdraw it over the course of the year to pay for their medical expenses. The idea is that if you're paying for health expenses out of your own pocket, you'll think twice about spending on frivolous visits to your doctor. Of course, there's already a serious flaw in the premise that we can distinguish a frivolous visit from necessary preventative care. Is a mammogram really necessary? Having someone check that pain in our lower back or those persistent grinding headaches? How much prenatal care does a pregnant woman really need?

An added kicker to the health savings account setup is that you must already have health insurance—high-deductible, bare-bones, "catastrophic" insurance—to open up an account in the first place. Which makes over 46 million Americans already ineligible. Yes, the money you place in that health savings account is tax deductible, but along the spectrum of health-insurance benefits, that one seems pretty minimal. The plan seems a hard sell under any tagline: "Put aside money you don't have to pay for medical services you can't afford"; "We'll give you a few tax breaks if you'll pay all your medical expenses on your own."

Not surprisingly, research shows that people with HSAs wind up spending more out of pocket and feeling less satisfied than those carrying more traditional plans. Also not surprisingly, HSAs have been slow to catch on among both employers and employees. Though they've been widely available since the mid-'90s, today only 6 percent of employers offer HSAs, though that number is growing as traditional plans grow more and more expensive.[25]

Health savings accounts are good for the banks that administer them—in fact, the American Bankers Association is a major lobbying force in favor of the plans. They're adequate for the healthy—those fortunate enough to need only the most routine care—and the wealthy—those who have the easiest time contributing to an account and run the least chance of having to actually tap it. But the added personal risk makes little sense for anyone else. Unfortunately, HSAs seem perfectly representative of the direction in which our health-care system is traveling. In today's fragmented care climate, the value placed on actual health is dropping all the time.

FINDING A REAL HEALTH-CARE SOLUTION

The current tangle that is the health-care system can leave individuals feeling like helpless victims of a gross injustice. But though it's easy

to understand why we feel as if we're drowning, there are a few rescue boats on the horizon. More than anything I've discussed so far,
health care is a policy problem with existing policy solutions. There
are other alternatives. Progressive economists, social scientists, community groups, and presidential candidates have come up with an array of viable proposals, ranging from broad suggestions to highly
detailed plans.[26]

Americans know what we want—affordability, control, choice—
and we know what we think is fair—a system in which every citizen
is covered. We don't want more scaffolding to buttress up an aged
and buckling system, we want core-level fundamental change. Despite all the administration rhetoric against "socialized medicine," in
numerous polls Americans have approved the idea of a national
health-care system providing universal coverage, even if it means
raising their taxes to pay for it.[27]

In part, health-care costs have risen in recent years because medicine is more expensive now than it was fifty years ago. Innovative
surgical techniques and courses of treatment save lives, but they also
tend to cost more money. In addition, the money spent by pharmaceutical companies on lobbying and advertising, plus rising malpractice insurance for doctors, is passed down to consumers. With people
living longer, chances are that they'll have to pay for more health care
than in any time in our history. It's more essential than ever that we
formulate some sort of social insurance to help manage these costs.
We have to demand a shift from thinking of health care as a consumer item to thinking of it as a social service available to all citizens
regardless of their economic status.

One obvious point, given the fact that so many employees are ineligible or can't afford it, is that the model of private, employer-based
benefits doesn't make sense anymore. Private insurance certainly isn't
more economically feasible. We spend more on health care than any
other industrialized nation, $2 trillion in 2005, yet we also have the
highest percentage of population that goes without health care due to
the phenomenal individual cost.[28] Nor is private insurance more
straightforward. In fact, our current system proves less transpar-
ent than any sort of single-payer or government-based system because money is routed through private insurance companies, tracked

only as tax breaks or deductions from take-home pay rather than through highly visible financial pipelines like the federal tax system. We stick with private insurance because it's more lucrative for the medical lobby and because politicians and even individuals seem overwhelmed by the enormous task of instituting any nationwide change.

But change need not be such a massive or frightening prospect. Among the many proposals out there, the simplest and most sensible I came across was Yale political scientist Jacob Hacker's "Health Care for America" plan, which posits extending a Medicare-like program to cover the entire population for a lifetime. Not separate programs for the poor, for children, for the elderly. One population, one system.

The first and most obvious reason to extend Medicare is that it works. Americans with Medicare consistently report being happier with nearly every aspect of their insurance than those who rely on private insurers. Medicare boasts lower administrative costs than any private plan on the market. And the Center for Medicaid and Medicare Services is already the single largest insurance provider in the country. What it dictates shapes hospital and insurance policies. With an even larger pool of insurees, the government could negotiate lower rates on drugs and services. It could spread the risk most evenly because everyone will be required to take part.[29]

Centralized health care will help corporate America, too, removing at least part of the health-care burden on both small businesses that can't afford to provide benefits and larger ones that are being drained by today's employer-based coverage options. Even if companies are taxed to help pay for a national system, it will still cost them less than providing private benefits on their own.

Of course, any transition to a new health-care system will have its rough spots. However, instead of an unrealistic jump to socialized medicine, Hacker proposes a much more feasible gradual revamping of an existing program to take into account those whose needs aren't being met. Delivery of care would still be the same. We'd go to the same doctors and hospitals. There would even still be an option of private coverage for those who want to pay for it. And it would be relatively easy to implement because the whole structure is already in place. Most doctors already take patients on Medicare. Everyone would pay in through either general taxes or payroll taxes, but coverage would not be reliant on continued employment. Health-care for America would ensure coverage even if you lost or changed your job.[30]

The stakes have grown too high for us to risk letting health-care reform sink into yet another morass of bureaucratic and political bickering. A growing percentage of the population—more than half of adults earning up to $75,000 a year—worry that they cannot afford a serious illness or secure quality medical care if and when the need arises.[31] Among those I interviewed, health care figured as an ominous and persistent threat. A medical emergency lay within the terrifying arena of things that could tip you over the edge into financial ruin. The slim sense of security provided by health benefits of any sort had people holding on to jobs where there was little prospect of raises and promotions, and stretching and knotting themselves to somehow pay out of pocket for what those plans couldn't cover.

Health-care reform is indeed an issue rife with moral hazards. Providing medical insurance to all citizens regardless of their health or economic status, pooling, spreading, and sharing the risk, is quite simply the only morally sound thing to do. To place those risks back on individual backs is costly on all levels, from the economic burdens of a society saddled with higher bankruptcy and personal debt to the psychological suffering weathered by those who can't manage such spiraling economic risks on their own.

THE UN-RETIREMENT GENERATION

At fifty-four, Lewis is the epitome of the old-style, hardworking educated middle-class American. He was born and raised in St. Louis, married his high school sweetheart, and the two of them have raised three children together. Lewis studied psychology in college but, when a number of his friends who'd gone into the field reported being disenchanted, he switched over to business, which seemed a respectable pursuit with which to support his growing family.

Lewis landed a good job out of college and for the next twenty years worked in sales for a major manufacturing corporation. He climbed the company ladder by doing whatever they asked of him, moving his family thirteen times and traveling up to 90 percent of the year to cover sales territories stretching across the Midwest and the South. He did well financially, working his way up to a six-figure salary, and his family never wanted for anything. All three children went to college on scholarships and two went on to earn graduate degrees.

Then, in the mid-'90s, corporate cost-tightening prompted massive layoffs from management on down. The company closed its Midwest regional offices and Lewis lost his job, receiving what was known as "the golden handshake" with a year's severance pay and plenty of time to look for a new position.

"It was unexpected, but I wasn't unduly worried," he recalls. "I figured that with my history and sales contacts I'd be sure to find another job."

But Lewis was reentering the labor market at a time when values like experience and company loyalty were at an all-time low. Corporations were focused on getting lean and mean, hiring inexperienced workers at lower salaries instead of paying what more seasoned workers like Lewis would merit. For Lewis, the ensuing years proved a roller-coaster ride of layoffs and new hires, each job bringing a cut in salary. Lewis and his wife moved to Texas, but when he got laid off from that company in under a year, they decided to return to St. Louis for good.

"I'm sure that did limit my employment opportunities, but my mother was unwell at the time and family seemed more important than a job I might not even get or keep.

"I've had eight jobs in the past six years," he continues, his voice the model of midwestern stoicism. "I've gone from six-figure salaries to earning less than $35,000 a year. I've been laid off seven times. It's depressing and demoralizing, but there's nothing else to do but get back up again."

The small companies Lewis worked for typically gave him no severance at all, while the larger ones offered up to a few months tops. The toughest patch was the full year he spent out of work, during which time he did anything he could find to bring in some cash, from temp work to handyman jobs. He and his wife have had to empty their savings accounts and drain everything they had set aside for retirement. For the first time in their lives they're deep in debt, carrying $20,000 in credit card debt, most of it amassed in that year Lewis spent unemployed.

Over the past decade Lewis has grown thoroughly disillusioned with the corporate world and its capacity to care for its own.

"I feel like most of the companies that hire me now just want to milk me for my contacts and then push me out. They give me huge sales territories and impossible quotas—my last job expected me to make thirty sales calls a week across seven states—but I have no choice but to accept their conditions."

He's currently working in sales for a small company that manufactures factory safety equipment, but the job feels unstable at best. His employers recently restructured the pay scale, setting stringent new quotas for the sales force. If Lewis can't make those unreachable quotas, his $30,000 salary will be cut in half.

"I think they're hoping to either be bought out or to push us out because they can't afford to pay us. I send out résumés every week. I have for the past seven years, just to cover my bases. But by now I have too much experience. My age and knowledge count against me. Human resources people tell me that they would feel obliged to pay me too much and that's why they can't offer me a job. Meanwhile, I have to worry about how to take care of myself and my wife for the rest of our lives."

For the past five years, Lewis's wife has worked for the St. Louis city planning office, a government job that pays $40,000 a year. It provides them with health benefits and will supply a small pension when she retires, though hardly enough for the couple to live on, let alone pay off their debts.

As Lewis nears retirement age, he has no idea what will happen to him and his wife, how they will support themselves. He only half-jokes that he might wind up as a greeter at Wal-Mart. They've already cut back all they can, reducing their spending to bare-bones expenses like the mortgage, food, gas, oil, and heating. If either of them loses another job or can't continue working, there is no cushion whatsoever to fall back on.

"We have no savings. We've come close to losing our house several times. I have no money left in my IRA and just $6,000 in a 401(k). We're down to the bottom of the barrel. If I ever was a proud man, I've lost all that by now."

Lewis hates that he's left himself and his wife in such a perilous position. Even more, he hates that his grown children worry about their parents' financial future even as he worries about theirs.

"My daughter is an English professor and a talented writer who continually struggles financially," he tells me, his voice a mix of admiration and frustration. "She works very hard. It breaks me up to see her struggle so and not be able to do anything to help."

I feel ridiculous asking him about his plan for the future—as if there were any choices left—but I pose the question anyway. He pauses for a long moment and then laughs.

"I don't have any plan. What could it possibly be? I worry daily about how we're going to make it. I figure I'll just work as long as I can. It's tough. Having gone to college and gone to work, having worked this long and this hard at good jobs for respected companies, but to have nothing to show for it. Absolutely nothing at all."

The question of retirement is the educated middle-class skeleton in the closet, still buried deep for many younger members but a potentially enormous problem as more and more of us find ourselves in positions similar to Lewis's, with no savings, no recourse, and little pride left, just hoping we'll remain healthy enough to stay on the job for the rest of our lives. As incomes and savings drop and life expectancy rises, a growing number of American households, 43 percent, risk being unable to sustain their standard of living in their retirement years.[32]

For members of our parents', grandparents', and even great-grandparents' generations, retirement was a much simpler undertaking. Employer-provided pension plans guaranteed fixed monthly payments that took care of professional and unionized workers in their waning years. Company-funded pensions were initially adopted by the railroads in the late nineteenth century as inducements to attract and maintain long-term employees. By 1916, 50 percent of railroad employees were covered by pensions and soon other industries—banks, public utilities, manufacturers, insurance companies, and department stores—followed suit.[33] With the establishment of Social Security in the 1930s the role of such pensions shifted. They became a necessary supplement to the retirement income supplied by the government, ensuring that those who'd worked hard their entire lives were rewarded with comfort and stability until they died.

For the next fifty years, pension plans remained popular among both workers and employers. In 1974, Congress further cemented stability among retirees by passing the Employment Retirement Security Act (ERISA), which provided government insurance to back up corporate pensions. By 1980, more than 80 percent of large and medium-size corporations offered traditional defined-benefit pensions, guaranteeing benefits based on a worker's income and years on the job and ensuring a predetermined monthly payment for the remainder of their lives.[34]

But, as with health care, in the ensuing decades the rising cost of such defined-benefit plans began to seem less and less worthwhile in an increasingly cutthroat business climate. Today, less than a third of companies provide traditional pensions and only 16.2 million workers are eligible, down from 22.2 million in 1988.[35] Instead, companies have shifted toward defined-contribution plans such as 401(k)s or the nonprofit equivalent, the 403(b). Under such plans, workers are responsible for voluntarily contributing a portion of their salaries to tax-free retirement accounts, typically invested in stocks and mutual funds, in which returns are neither predictable nor assured. Once again, personal responsibility has become the buzzword. When it comes to retirement savings, individuals today are expected to assume the risk and responsibility themselves.

At the same time, the government has rolled back its already baseline aid package. Cuts in Social Security in the past two decades, not to mention continual uncertainty about its future health, mean individuals are increasingly pressured to see to financing retirement on their own. If they're to live out their retirement years in anything approaching comfort or security, workers need to depend on something more than what the government now provides.[36]

This shift toward defined-contribution plans has worked out splendidly for employers—it's cheap and easy. Even employers who offer matching contributions to their employees wind up paying far less than they would funding traditional pensions, especially since one-third of workers who are offered 401(k)s never take advantage of them.[37] But though they consider the new setup perfectly adequate for their workers, it's not necessarily the path the head honchos choose for themselves. While everyone from managers on down have been relegated to personal responsibility, big-time CEOs are landing increasingly grand pay packages including huge guaranteed pension and retirement benefits that, rather than requiring the typical years of service, kick in their first minute on the job.[38] Meanwhile, middle-income workers, despite decades in the workforce, are finding it harder and harder to build up the sort of income needed for them to retire in security, if they can retire at all.

Once upon a time, the rule of thumb for adequate retirement savings was that you needed to bring in at least half your working income. Not only do 21 percent of college graduates fail to meet even this criteria, but given the financial straits provided by our current incomes, experts have started to seriously question whether that's enough. How many of us feel that we could live on half of what we make now? In recent years, factoring in longer lives and added costs for health care not covered by Medicare, advisers have upped the amount most people will need to retire comfortably to 85 or even a full 100 percent of their current income.[39]

The amount of money Americans actually have in retirement savings has been hard to pin down, though there seems little question that it's not nearly enough. Yale's Jacob Hacker found that roughly three-quarters of 401(k) holders in 2002 had stashed away significantly less than the widely cited average of $47,000. The median among account-holders—a better measure of what's typical, since it can't be skewed by a wealthy few—was just under $20,000. Among African American families, the rate of retirement savings is even worse, with black account holders typically contributing $254 a month versus $306 for whites.[40] And all these figures only include those who have 401(k)s. Just 53 percent of workers have access to a defined-contribution pension plan, and only 42 percent of those find the extra cash to actually contribute. As with many of the personal-responsibility crusades, the advent of defined-contribution plans has chiefly benefited the wealthiest portion of the population. Today about 70 percent of 401(k) and IRA assets rest in the accounts of the richest one-fifth of Americans.[41]

This lack of retirement savings can strike regardless of age, employer, education, or background. It's not something that's theoretically going to rear its head thirty or forty years down the road when today's young and strapped become tomorrow's senior citizens. It's happening now. Retirement wealth among seniors has dropped for all income levels, except those with over a million dollars in net worth.[42] These retirees face the same financial stresses as the rest of us, bringing in less money while having to navigate increased costs for housing, gas and oil, taxes, and especially health care. It's estimated that if a couple aged sixty-five today attain the average life expectancy of seventy-eight years, they will have to pay $300,000 out of pocket for medical expenses alone. If they're hale and hearty enough to last into their nineties, that figure jumps to $550,000.[43] Most existing retirement accounts for all but the wealthiest slice of the population couldn't even begin to cover such costs.

There's a pervasive notion in recent media that, though retirement security might be a legitimate concern for low-income workers, when it comes to the middle class, lack of savings is a question of more discipline and less procrastination. If only educated professionals could start saving early and sensibly, they'd be fine. But stories like Lewis's reveal the flaws in this sort of logic. The reality is that stagnant salaries and higher health-care, housing, child-care and education costs make it very difficult for even educated middle-class professionals to save anything at all. Because we're pushing so many major financial decisions to later in life—in the hopes that later will be when we can finally afford them—those high-cost expenditures are bumping up against our retirement years. With so many people going back to school later, having children later, and buying homes later, the balance of our financial ecosystem has changed. Retirement can hit at the same time we'll be trying to put our kids through college, and before we've managed to pay off our mortgages. Not only is there less to stow away these days, but there's less time in which to do it.

"I got started late," explains Ernest, forty-eight, a high school

guidance counselor with two sons who earns $51,000 a year. "I fin-
ished graduate school at thirty-six and had kids in my early forties.
That means I'll be in my sixties when my son graduates from college.
There's going to be a major choice there. Do we help him with school
or do we help ourselves in retirement? Because there's no way there
will be enough money for both."

Even for those of us who do manage to build up some retirement
savings, if we encounter one unexpected financial blow, like job loss
or illness, that 401(k) or IRA may be the only source of cash available to keep us solvent in the here and now. In order for a defined-
contribution retirement account to get full and stay full, an educated
professional middle-class family needs to have experienced remarkably smooth financial sailing.

Despite the prevalence of stories like Lewis's, the middle-class
families I spoke to were far more concerned with their immediate financial difficulties than with their retirement funds. Except for those
in their fifties and sixties, looking their golden years square in the
eyeballs, retirement wasn't their primary concern. Plenty of people
confessed that they knew they should think and plan and worry
about it. But given their current financial stresses, retirement just
seemed too far away to merit serious contemplation. Some took
comfort in the fact that a life laced with economic volatility had
taught them to live close to the bone if need be. Many more opted for
the fallback plan of staying on the job as long as they possibly could.

"We can't afford to retire," explained Susannah, thirty-five, a
pharmaceutical marketing executive with two children under five
whose husband works designing maps for the city of Houston.
"We've both decided that we're just going to work until we die."

Things are simply too tight in the present to consider what to do
because we might run into serious health problems in our seventies
or live to be ninety. I think that way myself. It honestly seems the
most sensible choice under the circumstances. Maybe something will
change between now and then—our government, my income level, a
solvent partner. Or maybe I will die and it won't matter. I suspect
that, like me, many middle-class professionals would rather live for
now than later, since they can't figure out any possible way to live
for both.

It's easy to con ourselves into believing that retirement isn't as serious a problem as it is. We look at our middle-class parents and grandparents and they seem to have somehow figured out a way. But the costs and challenges of retirement have changed, sometimes dramatically, and our current system will have to change along with it if we really are to survive. It's not realistic to posit a return to the old pension system, not given the strain such costs put on companies of all sizes and the increasing population of freelance and contingency workers. But we can begin to think in terms of formulating a required rather than voluntary contribution system that will provide workers a retirement income beyond Social Security. A system that won't punish those who move from job to job, rely on freelance and contract work, or suffer gaps in employment. One that guarantees there will be something left over for people like Lewis who've worked hard their entire lives.

Alongside his Healthcare for America plan, Jacob Hacker has ventured an intriguing proposal for a universal 401(k) administered by the government and available to all workers regardless of their income or employer. Government tax breaks could reward employers who offered their workers, particularly low-wage workers, matching contributions, protections would be put in place against excessive investment in company stock, and the default investment would be a low-risk combination of stocks and bonds. This single account would remain intact for an individual's entire working life, regardless of whether they changed jobs or spent time unemployed.[44]

More immediately, we can focus on easing some of the current financial pressure on the working poor, the missing class, and the middle class. Freeing up discretionary income in the present will give us something to save against the future. If education, housing, health care, and child care were less of a collective financial drain, even defined-contribution plans would become a more viable option for some of us. But if we don't get further support in managing our current needs, we will be far more likely to require costlier aid somewhere down the line.

For many members of the educated middle class, like Lewis and Bethany, a decreased availability of health and retirement benefits has begun bumping up against a sometimes alarmingly increased need. We need to worry about the sort of benefits that aren't available to the middle class, pushing us further and further into financial instability. But we also need to look at some of the social benefits that educated professionals are taking advantage of these days. As we have less money and less long-term support, the combination of high costs and high debts makes it increasingly likely that some in the middle class might need the sort of emergency aid supplied by social services designed for the poor and disenfranchised who don't have the educations, the opportunities, or the jobs. It's troubling that a handful of the middle-class professionals I spoke to were already turning to food banks, WIC, Medicaid, and other state-based health-care programs.

Preserving our health and longevity is essential to preserving our economic, psychological, and social stability. Pressuring Congress on social issues such as retirement and health care should be at the top of our political list. We need to encourage lawmakers to pursue the sorts of changes that are important to those who use our social benefits system, not just those who run it. With plans like Healthcare for America and the universal 401(k) fully formulated and on the table, it's clear that we're living in a transitional time, one that can and should give us serious cause for hope. Not only do we understand the kind of change that needs to happen, we have a road map for how to execute it. As individuals, our role now lies in pressuring Congress to act upon what is clearly one of the most pressing social issues of our time.

7

BRIDGING THE GAPS

Saving, Spending, and Debt

Natalie, forty, is an assistant professor of art and design, teaching photography at a major midwestern state university. She holds a bachelor's degree in fine arts and an MFA from the University of Iowa. She currently makes $39,000 a year, up just $3,000 from her starting salary five years ago since, shortly after Natalie's arrival, the school curtailed across-the-board raises due to funding cuts. Her husband, William, who is equally well-educated, with a BS in psychology, a professional teaching certificate, and a soon-to-be-completed master's in gifted education, earns $30,000 as a third-grade teacher in a local public school.

Neither Natalie nor William comes from an affluent background and they made considerable sacrifices to pay for their educations. Natalie chose Iowa in part because it offered her a teaching assistantship, which waived out-of-state tuition and came with a monthly stipend. While she was in school William put his own education on hold and worked full-time as a bike mechanic to pay their living expenses. In addition, Natalie took out nearly $30,000 in student loans.

"You take on this incredible amount of debt for an education that's required in order to enter a field that pretty much guarantees you'll spend the rest of your life underpaid," is how Natalie sums up the situation. "It's not like going to medical school where down the line all that education leads to a big-money career. I don't anticipate our incomes changing dramatically at any point in the future."

After graduation, while Natalie launched her teaching career with part-time positions at several universities, William returned to school for his teaching degree. Given their financial situation, neither of them considered attending an expensive private university. Even so, their higher education costs—Natalie's close to $30,000 in tuition plus $400–$500 a month in art supplies, and William's $10,000 given the discounts he got for attending school where Natalie was on staff—coupled with their low-paying academic careers left behind a pile of debt they're still struggling to get out from under.

Living expenses in their college town are less than they would be in a major metropolis like New York or D.C., but life is far from cheap. Two years ago they bought their house from William's mother for $150,000, figuring that taking on a $1,200-a- month mortgage was preferable to continuing to pay rent. They own two cars, a 1991 Subaru station wagon and a 1997 minivan they bought from Natalie's parents, both of which have over 100,000 miles on them and will need to be replaced soon. Though their ten-year-old daughter attends public school, they pay several hundred dollars a month for her extracurricular activities including violin lessons and membership on a local junior swim team. Though they've worked hard to cut down the debt they accumulated in their student days, they still carry about $5,000 in credit card debt.

Despite expenses, William and Natalie also try to maintain at least a thousand dollars in savings in case of emergencies, much of which winds up going to house repairs like a recently installed new roof. Natalie also has to budget a bare minimum of $4,000 a year for professional expenses, none of them covered by her university, including photography supplies, shipping costs, and entrance fees for art shows around the country. She describes such professional expenses as nonnegotiable, the art department's version of publish or perish.

"In order to hold on to my job, I have to keep producing and showing my work. Regardless of the expense, it's expected that as a professor you will maintain an active research file."

Natalie grew up in a small industrial town south of St. Louis and was the first in her family to get a college education. Both her parents worked in accounting at the local mining company, and her father spent thirty years in the same job, long enough to accrue a healthy pension and benefits. They had a comfortable life—far less financially strapped than Natalie's own—including a house with a yard and a new car every few years. They were even able to save enough to help pay for Natalie and her sister's undergraduate educations, something Natalie is unsure she'll be able to do for her own daughter.

Natalie's family always valued community and social responsibility over financial success, a value system she embraces and hopes to pass down. But, though she chose teaching because of the opportunities it provided to study, explore, and practice her art, Natalie always assumed a graduate-level education would lead to a certain degree of financial security as well.

"I suppose I'm doing better than my parents in some ways," Natalie tells me. "In terms of educations and job fulfillment, I'm better off. But when it comes to money, we definitely struggle more than they did. They never worked longer than a forty-hour week. I work fifty or sixty. But still every extra expense is a huge obstacle. I guess because no one in my family was educated, I really bought into the idea that getting a college degree was the key to a better lifestyle. But times have changed. I didn't expect to be rich, but I also didn't expect us to struggle so hard to get by. I'm forty. William is forty-four. We have good jobs. By this time, weren't we supposed to be enjoying a solid, secure, middle-aged lifestyle?"

Plenty of theories exist about why families like Natalie's—educated, professional, and middle class—are saving less and digging themselves deeper into debt. Most of them tend toward the simplistic, and more than a few verge on the insulting. For example, there's the irresponsible-and-immature theory: If this current generation were more patient and financially responsible, like their hardworking and frugal forebears, they too could save up enough to afford big-ticket items like homes, comfortable retirement, and college for themselves and their children without slipping into five- and six-figure levels of debt. It's all a question of discipline and delayed gratification.

One of the more popular examples used to illustrate this arrested-financial-development theory is the "latte factor." The latte factor posits that if today's financially strapped could just get it together to forgo their daily $3 latte habit and tuck that extra money in a savings account instead, they too could save up enough money to buy something truly meaningful. This may be useful advice to some degree, but it's hard to imagine that saving a few dollars here and there will ever add up to a home of your own. If you saved $3 a day—every single day, with no treating yourself, no vacation, no trips to Starbucks when your coffeemaker broke down or you ran out of beans— by the end of the year you'd still only have pocketed $1,095, not even enough for Natalie and William to pay a single month's mortgage. The only thing this theory seems to accomplish is making us feel guilty for enjoying even small pleasures, when we definitely can't afford the larger ones. Forgoing a fancy cup of coffee can't ameliorate the fact that wages have stagnated and the cost of most major items has risen.

Then there's an equally demeaning sister theory—particularly popular with the media—that we can't save because over the past twenty-five years we've turned into a society of rabid overconsumers, all of whom need three digital cameras, two cell phones, and a flat-screen TV. This one insists that we're in financial trouble because we have no impulse control. The overconsumption theory isn't totally unfounded, but it has some serious holes. The biggest one is that, though we spend our money differently these days, we're actually not spending any more on consumer items than we did in the '70s.[1] We may buy more clothes, but those clothes have gotten cheaper. We may eat out more often, but we compensate by spending less on groceries. Today we don't spend as much on smaller consumer items like furniture and clothing and instead spend more on basics like health care, child care, gas, and housing.[2] This is a critical shift. Frivolous one-offs like three-piece suits and bedroom sets can be given up in the name of tightening the budget. Items like a mortgage, health care, tuition, and child care require a consistent financial commitment that still must be met even if we lose our jobs, get divorced, or have another child.

Most people I spoke to worried constantly about the lack of money they'd set aside. It wasn't that they didn't have the desire to save or didn't think about saving, but that there was just nothing left over. If the choices are live now or live later, there's really no choice at all. You have to live now. Nor were most of them complacent about their debt. To the contrary, many of them fantasized about paying it off, and woke up nights haunted by escalating balances and unpaid bills. They spoke of the shame and sense of failure tied to not being able to pay back what they owed, of hiding financial details from their parents and children. They longed to be as financially scrupulous and conservative as their parents and grandparents had been, to wait and scrimp and save and buy nothing until they could afford it. One woman relayed, with joy in her voice, a story about her grandfather hauling a laundry bag full of dollar bills into the dealership to purchase in full his first car. Today's educated professional middle class is sliding into debt with alarming speed. They're engaged in a constant tug-of-war to wipe out credit card balances, to pay mortgage, credit card, and student loan bills on time, to slip something, anything, into that 401(k). But as quickly as they can pay something off, that debt just seems to accumulate again.

The one thing all these theories have in common is that they position increased debt and decreased savings as optional personal choices. But for the working poor, the missing class, and now most middle-class professionals, the range of choices presents itself in a very different light. Take on debt or forgo a house, a car, an education, child care, even children—all the components of a secure educated professional lifestyle. Too often, if we have any hope of hanging on to our middle-class status, spending beyond our means feels as if it really is the only choice we have left.

OUR CONSUMER SOCIETY

Debt may be an individual choice but in the past few decades it has also become an entrenched cultural paradigm. From a federal government that owes nearly $9 trillion to individuals who owe $9,000, debt today is the American way, a logical, even necessary offshoot of living in our consumer society. Fostering a sense of wanting and needing—and the more those two overlap the better—is integral to sustaining a healthy capitalist economy. In order to keep producing more, we also have to manufacture a never-ending desire for more. Both the public and private sectors will do all they can to ensure we continue to spend, even if that means spending beyond our means, because individual savings is far less profitable than individual debt.[3]

Our free market economy relies on its citizens always feeling as if they never have enough. With the panoply of choices available in everything from digital cameras to peanut butter, college loans to life partners, we've become geared toward wanting to have, do, and experience it all. Freedom is no longer the ability to choose anything, but the right to have everything. With such endless options available, we can live in constant fear that we've settled for too little, missed our golden opportunity. In a country so steeped in consumerism, it's difficult not to fall victim to the belief that the more we have and the more we buy, the happier and more secure we must be.

Has this ever-escalating consumer push made us more materialistic than we used to be? Probably. When questioned about what constitutes "a good life," in 1975, 38 percent of respondents to a Roper poll said "a lot of money," while an equal 38 percent said "a job that contributes to the welfare of society." By 1996, 32 percent answered a job that contributes while those voting for a lot of money rose to 63 percent. More people voted for a vacation home, a second TV, a swimming pool, a second car, a job that pays more than average, and "really nice" clothes, all the trappings of a material life. Meanwhile, fewer people checked items like a happy marriage, children, and an interesting job.[4]

But being more materialistic today doesn't have to mean spending more, not with the influx of cheap consumer goods that line the shelves of big-box stores. For the educated professional middle class, the dangers lie less in harboring a constant hunger for more things than in harboring particular tastes and expectations. We were schooled to anticipate high levels of success as well as specific possessions—a home, one or two cars, yearly vacations, occasional restaurant meals, and private schools for our children, just to mention a few. Many of us made friends in college who came from wealthy families who could provide them with all these trappings and then some. Whether consciously or unconsciously, many of us still look to those affluent lifestyles as an ideal and feel acutely aware of all the ways in which we fall short.

Not only do we as a society have to manufacture these material wants, but we have to finance them too. And we don't do this by giving people more money. We do it by giving them access to debt and then persuading them to acquire it. Our economy depends on pushing back the moment when consumers have to pay off their debts, on supplying yet more credit, refinancing yet another mortgage, so the buyer can continue to buy. The banking and credit card industries go out of their way to encourage all of us to get mired as deeply as possible. Beyond just making debt easy to acquire, they've set up a financial system where it's actually better to have debt than not. When I was twenty-four years old I had to get my father to cosign my apartment lease because at that point I still paid off my credit card every month. The problem wasn't that I hadn't proved myself financially responsible. In fact, just the opposite. With my short and quite responsible financial history, I hadn't acquired enough debt to have a credit score. In my midtwenties, without the help of either my debt or my family, I would've been unable to find a place to live.

This continuous encouragement of consumption and debt has worked its magic brilliantly. Today 76.4 percent of Americans are in some kind of debt. Household debt has risen so high that it's now 30 percent greater than disposable income. And of course more debt means less money to save or invest in the future. The personal savings rate in 2006 was at negative 1 percent, the lowest it's been in seventy-three years. Less than half of American households own any sort of stock market investments, including a mutual fund or a 401(k). In fact, today roughly one in six households has zero or negative net worth.[5]

Almost none of the educated middle-class professionals I spoke to had enough savings to float them beyond a month or two if they lost their jobs. Those who'd already suffered through gaps in employment, even if they'd found a new position in under six months, were usually still struggling to get out from under the debt they acquired at the time. These individuals fit in squarely with the national trend. The number of middle-class households that have at least three months of their income stashed away has slipped dramatically, dropping from 28.8 percent in 2001 to 18.3 percent in 2004.[6]

Today, saving has come to operate more like trading. If you manage to save in one arena, you usually wind up sacrificing in another. Pay off student loans, but don't add to the 401(k). Pay off your credit cards, but have nothing saved for your children's education. Sell the house to pay for your children's education, but then there's nothing to see you into retirement. By middle age, when we've piled the costs of raising a family on top of the costs of buying a home on top of health care on top of our own education loans, we're often at our peak debt level instead of beginning to emerge out from under it the way middle-class middle-age couples were a generation ago. Spending more than you make and turning to others—from banks and credit card companies to family members—to help you fill those financial gaps has become a simple, unavoidable fact of life.

FAMILY MATTERS

Sam is a documentary filmmaker in Chicago who produces history programming for cable television. He's worked for the same media company for seven years and makes $60,000. His wife, Bliss, an associate curator for a small art museum, earns $33,000.

"We chose our careers according to what interested us, not the income potential," Sam says. "And you do wind up paying a price for that."

Between the $450 monthly payments on the student loans they took out to finance their graduate degrees and the credit card debt accrued making Sam's thesis film and setting up house, Sam and Bliss could never manage to set aside any savings. So four years ago, when they began to consider major middle-class decisions like buying a home and starting a family, they knew they were going to need help. The house they found in one of Chicago's fringe neighborhoods was small and needed work. Even so, the asking price of $179,000 was more of a stretch than they could handle. They took out a mortgage (twice refinanced since) and a home equity line of credit (tapped to replace a car that died and to pay for fertility treatments). To close the still-existing gap, they turned to a source that keeps many educated middle-class professionals even partially afloat: they borrowed from their families.

"My parents gave us a $10,000 loan to help cover the 5-percent-down on the house," Sam explains. "They lent it to us at a very low interest rate, and we haven't had to think about paying it off until now." Their current family mortgage payment totals $210 a month, as opposed to the $1,400 check they write to the bank.

Sam's parents weren't affluent but they were soundly middle class.

His father was a tax attorney who did a great deal of pro bono work. His mother worked part-time as a speech therapist. The family always lived in a nice house with two cars and took yearly vacations. Money was tight on occasion, but neither Sam nor his sister ever wanted for anything. Sam had always imagined a similar situation in his own life: a household that valued happiness over money yet still managed to comfortably get by.

"At thirty-four, with a good job, I never envisioned that I'd still be struggling so hard," he says. "I hated having to turn to my parents for help, but given our debts and the kind of money we were making, if we wanted to own a house and eventually start a family there was no other way."

One thing, besides education, that divides much of the educated professional middle class from their working-class counterparts is that many of us have middle-class families who still possess a house, some investments or savings, and are able to help us out in a pinch. We often own homes and cars or have shed our earlier debts only because those middle-class parents could provide in the way of gifts or loans. Today, 34 percent of adults age eighteen to thirty-four receive annual financial support from their families. Parents typically pay over $2,000 a year to help out children in their midtwenties, and $1,500 for those in their midthirties. Once a child has left for college, parents can still expect to pay over $40,000 toward higher-education costs and to support their children into their early- and even middle-adult years.[7]

Among those I spoke to, parents and other family members had frequently provided gifts or loans with little or no interest to buy homes, pay for graduate school, or wipe out high-interest debt. They'd sold their children cars and houses on the cheap, provided them with housing and child care, set up investments in their names, and helped to pay for their grandchildren's education. Most people who turned to their families for help weren't lazy or unaccomplished. Like Sam and Bliss, they had educations and jobs and they worked hard, but when it came to pursuing bigger-ticket items, from first homes to school tuitions, they still came up short. Turning to parents wasn't what they wanted, but what they needed, to do. My own parents can't buy me a house, but they do pitch in when I have trouble paying for my health insurance and to buy me a much-needed new pair of shoes or a load of groceries from time to time. For that, I count myself extremely grateful and lucky. But I also find it disturbing that this thin generational string seems to be all that's holding so many of us up.

Barbara Ehrenreich writes of the middle class being the one social class that members aren't born into.[8] Every successive generation must earn, or purchase, their class status all over again. So what happens when that new generation can't afford the membership dues? Our middle-class families may have the means to prop us up temporarily, but unlike the upper classes they rarely have a bottomless resource pool. Parents in their fifties and sixties may be downsizing their lives—moving to smaller homes, accessing long-term investments, and in the process freeing up some capital. But eventually the financial weight their children are placing on them will prove too heavy. What will we do when our parents have worked through their diminished savings and must confront their declining health, when they need our financial help to support them instead of the other way around?

"It's scary," says Oliver, a Brooklyn-based playwright whose middle-class parents are helping to support both him and his two brothers, all of whom are over thirty-five. "Not only are we not making as much as our parents did, but we're actually reaching back and dragging them down into this financial hole along with us. That can't be a good thing for society in either the short or the long run."

More and more in America, the land of opportunity, your financial status depends on your family history. In order to get rich, it helps to be born rich. Inherited wealth has been on the upswing in the past quarter-century. In the early '70s, 56 percent of total wealth held by those in their late thirties had been passed down to them by their parents. By 1986 that number had shot up to 86 percent. Today, nearly $200 billion is passed down annually in the form of bequests. But, like all other forms of wealth, this too is becoming highly polarized, with just 7 percent of estates accounting for half the money.[9]

For the rest of us, the size of our inheritance stands to be severely limited by the increasing life expectancy and decreasing retirement savings of our parents. For many members of today's professional educated middle class who struggle to get by on just their own incomes, the financial future will hinge on how long their parents live and how much of their wealth, if any, they're able to pass on. If we're tapping that wealth now, it won't be available to us later. In fact we may find ourselves having to provide for our parents' food, housing, and medical care in their old age.

Many of those I interviewed reported that they weren't doing as well financially as their parents had. This conclusion came not just from those like Sam and myself who grew up in comfortable middle-class families, but also from a number of people like Natalie who came from working-class upbringings, whose parents had helped put the first generation of the family through college and were now continuing helping to support their middle-class children as they scrambled to make financial ends meet.

"I grew up in the '50s and '60s," says Keisha, fifty-eight, a marketing executive in the fashion business. "And that sure was a different time. My father raised four children on a grade school education and we never wanted for anything. Back then hard work was enough to get you by. A family like mine could never, never happen these days."

Where does this need for family help leave those who are struggling to maintain their middle-class status and don't have parents, grandparents, and aunts and uncles to fall back on? The financial advantages of those who benefit from the middle-class success stories of previous generations tilt the scale against those like Natalie and Keisha who are the first in their families to reach educated professional status. This can be a particularly powerful blow for black and Hispanic college graduates making their way into the middle class. Though minorities have achieved a solid middle-class presence since the 1960s due to hard work as well as civil rights legislation and affirmative action policies, they still tend to congregate at the lower earning end of that middle-class spectrum, holding more sales and clerical jobs and fewer high-end professional positions like doctors and lawyers. There remains a marked disparity in financial health between white families and families of color. In 2004, 13 percent of white households had zero or negative net worth, compared to 29.4 percent of black households. Black households also possessed just one-tenth of the wealth of white families.[10]

Because members of the white middle class are more likely to come from money, there's a higher chance that there will be someone who can help them with large-scale expenses like paying for school or buying a house. They don't have to take out as many loans or acquire as much debt early on. As the struggle to remain in the middle class increases, black and Hispanic families face the highest risk of dropping out of the bottom end. Even if earlier generations did reach the middle class when opportunities for minorities first flowered in the 1970s, their children and grandchildren will have, and in a number of cases are already having, trouble maintaining the homes and lifestyles their parents worked so hard to achieve.[11]

"I feel like things have been tougher for me in a lot of ways because of where I come from," says Mercedes, thirty-one, the third of four daughters born to Puerto Rican parents who moved to the U.S. when they were teenagers. She grew up in subsidized housing and she and her two sisters are the first generation of her family to graduate from college. She now makes $56,000 a year working for a national civil rights organization. "A lot of the white kids I went to college with had families who could help them pay for tuition so they didn't have to take out loans or lean on their credit cards. None of them had to do what I did, cash out their 401(k) to pay off all that early debt. From the very start, because there was more money in the family, they had an advantage."

When Mercedes and I met at a speaking event in New York, she was immediately curious as to whether I'd be discussing the particular challenges faced by those members of the educated middle class who come from families of color. She asked whether we could talk expressly so that she could explain to me how things had been different for her.

"Even culturally," she explains, "the family pressures and expectations are different. I think for a lot of families of color, you're never on your own. In a good way and a bad way. If some cousin is in trouble and needs money or if we need to send something home to family in Puerto Rico, we all talk on the phone about who's got something to spare and then we send it. There's an expectation that because I have a good job and make decent money, I'll be able to contribute. And I always do. I don't see it as a burden. It's part of my culture and I'm proud of it. But it does need to be factored in to your financial life. These are the kind of pressures most white people I know don't face. It's just a different way of looking at responsibility and family."

It's hard to know how to model ourselves after our parents and extended families, what advice to accept and what to reject as irrelevant in our changing times. There's a definite generation gap between what's possible for individuals and families today, including the compromises required, and the educated professional middle-class experience twenty, thirty, forty years ago. Members of today's struggling middle class are having to map out not just a new series of financial choices but the kind of values we, too, want to embody and pass down.

"My parents don't believe in debt," says Heidi, twenty-eight, who works as a counselor for a nonprofit organization helping underprivileged teens and attends grad school part-time to get her master's degree in education. "They both grew up with Depression-era parents who taught them to work very hard and spend very little. They really took pride in stretching a dollar. They always felt a strong sense of duty and paying dues. And I really feel like that's the right way to go."

Heidi has followed in her parents' footsteps in a number of ways. Her father worked as a school psychologist and her mother as a vocational counselor in the prison system, and Heidi has embodied their dedication to civil rights and social service in her choice of career. But she's found the combination of moral values and debt-free financial philosophy they managed to fashion for themselves thirty years ago impossible to sustain today.

Though Heidi still agrees that, like her parents, she doesn't believe in debt, the fact that she and her husband, who works in retail, together make less than $60,000 a year, has made it almost impossible to practice what she and her family preach. When they found an incredible deal on their first apartment two years ago, the couple had to borrow over $20,000 from Heidi's parents to make the down payment. Upon going back to school, Heidi purposely chose the program that offered her the largest tuition breaks even though it didn't necessarily provide the best education. But though it makes her "very, very uneasy" and she plans to pay it off as soon as possible, she also decided to take a out a student loan so she and her husband could hang on to a small financial cushion, just a few thousand dollars, in case of any emergencies.

"It's hard to imagine any couple just starting out being able to get by these days without help from their families," she admits. "I want to live like my parents did, being financially smart and sensible. But I also want to be like them in dedicating myself to making the world a better place. I'm just not sure if the two can go together anymore like they did once upon a time."

THE LURE OF THE FANTASTIC PLASTIC

For those of us whose families can't provide help, or can't provide enough of it, there's really only one option left. Debt. And, as the credit card generation, we're accruing piles of it. U.S credit card debt has risen 31 percent in the past five years, with Americans now owing nearly $800 billion. Middle- and low-income households owe an average of $8,650, with a full third of them owing over $10,000. In 2000, Americans reached the dubious milestone of possessing 1.5 billion credit cards. That's an average of ten cards per user, signifying that the "more is better" ethic has infiltrated our consumer lives on every possible level.[12]

Not surprisingly, the middle class carries the bulk of today's credit card debt.[13] We make enough money to access high credit limits and multiple cards, but not enough to fully pay off our bills each month. Nearly everyone I interviewed was carrying or had carried credit card debt at some point in their lives. And most of the time that debt wasn't accumulated purchasing frivolous luxury items. In your early twenties, when you're getting used to managing your finances, student-loan payments haven't kicked in yet and expenses are low, credit cards may lead to Barneys and Best Buy splurges or weekends in Cancun. But by the time the educated middle class settle into their thirties, plastic is more often called upon to handle groceries, new refrigerators, health care, and other necessities. In fact, most credit card debt accumulated by middle- and low-income families goes to pay for necessities like medical expenses and car and home repairs.[14] Credit cards have become the default rescue brigade, responsible for everything from financing our major life decisions to bridging the gaps when we can't make it to the end of the month on our paychecks alone.

Mariko, thirty-seven, has accumulated $100,000 worth of credit card debt setting up her own business as a therapist in Denver. Her startup costs covered training and home-office overhead, but the biggest hit she took was in lost income. Before setting out on her own, Mariko had a corporate job in sales management with a high-tech firm. She earned enough to buy a house and put money in a Roth IRA, which she has now drained. But when she was laid off three years ago after the company moved to California, she knew she couldn't take another corporate position.

"The choice was do a job that I hate and could lose at any point in order to make halfway decent money. Or figure out a way to do something that feels like I'm bettering the world."

Mariko's new career has taken off, and in the past three years her practice has doubled annually. But, though the figures are gratifying on a personal level, her current income of between $20,000 and $25,000 provides little comfort in the financial realm.

"If my income kept doubling each year, yes, I would reach a point in a few years where I could pay off that debt," she agrees. "But that's not a practical or likely solution. There are only so many hours in the day and eventually that growth curve has to flatten out. The fact is that I've chosen a career that's personally rewarding but means I will struggle financially for the rest of my life."

Mariko's partner of fifteen years, Colleen, runs her own graphic design firm. Though she has a few regular clients, she, too, has been victim to economic volatility, finding much of the work she used to do now assigned in-house or outsourced overseas. The pair lives month to month with few luxuries—no new clothes, no eating out— and little room to further trim expenses. Most months, it's a struggle to even pay the minimums on Mariko's five credit cards.

"I hate that I'm carrying this sort of debt," she admits. "I alternate between depressed and desperate. I've always been extremely financially responsible. I started saving for college when I was eight, and it's been a longtime dream to run my own business. I do believe I'm providing a much-needed service, but it seems like these days that's not enough to ensure you'll get by."

The psychology of credit card debt is a complicated one. Credit cards can buy us something far more valuable than a new outfit or even a new car. They can buy us status and a lifestyle that stretch beyond the restrictions of our actual financial means. Those little plastic rectangles are the road to all those things our educations and our society told us we could and should achieve. That might mean driving a new Volkswagen, but it can just as easily mean doing the work we're passionate about, sending our children to a reputable preschool, or affording the kind of medical care that will preserve our health and longevity. Credit cards allow us to don the clothing of middle-class respectability and opportunity even as we struggle to stay afloat.

Credit cards also serve as one of the most effective masks of class differences. The teacher and the corporate lawyer can both charge a new refrigerator or a trip to Hawaii with no one but the bank any wiser about how much of that purchase they can actually afford. For the many of us who feel ashamed or inadequate about our financial shortcomings, credit cards allow us to hide our debt from friends and family.

And, perhaps most important of all, credit cards can buy us a degree of freedom we can't afford on our salaries alone. Not just to consume more, but—as with Mariko—to quit miserable jobs, go back to school, move away from our families, marry, or have children. This new kind of ready available debt is supporting not just our financial, but in many cases our personal, intellectual and creative lives.

The ready availability of consumer credit has altered, at a core level, how Americans think about saving, spending, and debt. With the advent of such anonymous, ever-ready purchasing power, the ethos of buy now, pay later has replaced the ethos of saving for the future. As a result, the direct line between working, saving, and spending has been fractured, occluding the trail of financial responsibility and the repercussions of truly not being able to afford what you choose to buy. It's all too easy, whether you whip out your card to finance a new business or a new muffler, to forget that down the line you will actually have to pay cash money for what you're purchasing, not to mention a slew of fees and interest payments. The whole point of credit cards is to get people to spend beyond their means, to flirt with being richer and more successful than they really are.

Among educated professionals, credit card use, and credit card debt, starts early. Ninety-one percent of final-year college students have a credit card, and they're already carrying an average balance of nearly $3,000. Card companies market heavily on college campuses, setting up recruiting tables alongside the swim team and student government and offering kids everything from free pizza to T-shirts to coffee mugs if they sign up. In his exposé of the credit card industry, *Credit Card Nation,* Robert Manning quotes an interviewee explaining how she found a flyer for her first credit card stuffed between the pages of a freshly purchased textbook.[15]

Those early established habits of charging and debt, coupled with the financial strain of setting up a career, household, and family, has sent card debt among those eighteen to thirty-four escalating 55 percent between 1992 and 2001. The average indebted young adult now spends nearly a quarter of his or her income on debt payments.[16] And the accumulation of debt hardly stops there. As the cost of living continues to outpace earnings, these same households find that once they're in debt, it can be next to impossible to get out again. Increasingly, the phenomenon of credit card debt spans age, ethnic, and class lines. Credit card debt as a percentage of income runs particularly high among black and Hispanic households, where wealth and earnings levels still lag behind their white counterparts. And overall debt among seniors over sixty-five more than doubled between 1992 and 2004, with increased credit card debt one of the top factors in the rise in seniors filing for bankruptcy. In the face of declining retirement wealth and rising health-care expenses, one in three seniors possessing credit cards do not pay off their bills each month.[17]

Credit cards may be more anonymous than what came before—a loan from the local bank or credit extended from the store down the street—but they're also less forgiving. Job loss, illness, a new baby, none of it matters when payment to the Chase or Citigroup piper inevitably comes due. Credit cards have played a major role in the recent rise in middle-class bankruptcies. One-third of those filing for bankruptcy, nearly 90 percent of whom are middle class, have credit card debt equal to or above an entire year's salary.[18]

Though many of us may be unclear about how the credit card companies actually work, what we pay and why, or where this escalating debt might eventually lead us, one thing is obvious. Today, credit cards are far more than just a convenience. They pave the roads to our financial salvation and, too often, our financial demise. The fantastic plastic has become an integral cog in the vehicles propelling us—increasingly toward financial breakdown—through our educated professional middle-class lives.

THE BUSINESS OF CREDIT: THE INSIDE STORY

The rapid rise of credit card use in the United States since the 1980s has been neither accidental nor haphazard. The credit card industry has benefited enormously from the post–industrial revolution, that societal shift from economic emphasis on manufacturing and production to emphasis on consumer services. As banks realigned their priorities to adjust to the deregulation of the 1980s, and as inflation and job loss contributed to the rising financial insecurity of the middle class, exploiting the population's need and desire for readily available consumer debt proved a moneymaking slam dunk.

Today, credit cards have become the most profitable sector of banking, reporting profit margins three and four times those of other sectors of the financial-services area. The credit card industry takes in $2.5 billion in profits a month. And if it seems as if payments on your panoply of cards—whether the issuer is an airline, a university, or a department store—go to the same bank, you're right. The power of the card industry is concentrated into relatively few hands, with the top ten card companies owning 90 percent of consumer accounts.[19] But there is little evidence that the industry intends to let any of that increasing wealth trickle down to their customers. Drops in the federal interest rate are rarely accompanied by corresponding drops in consumer APRs. Instead, CEO packages climb alongside fees, penalties, and interest rates. Profits are channeled toward mergers and acquisitions—we've gone from 14,600 FDIC-insured banks in 1975 to fewer than 9,000 in 2000—and toward ensuring high dividends to stockholders.[20]

The simple truth is that banks and credit card companies don't want to make it any easier for you pay off your debts. They make more money when you don't have enough. In industry parlance, those who settle their cards every month are called deadbeats. The ideal customer, the one most actively courted, is the one who pays some each month but keeps a balance and may be late or even miss a payment from time to time. I've certainly noticed that the higher I let my balance climb, the more card solicitations start pouring through my mailbox. Like the health-care and student-loan industries, credit card companies traffic heavily in confusion. Credit card contracts are rife with small print, enough legalese to baffle F. Lee Bailey let alone your average consumer. Yes, the banking industry is providing us with the opportunity to live a lifestyle we couldn't otherwise afford, but buried in that small print you find near-criminal strings attached.

If you look at the return address on your statement, chances are your card company is located in a state such as South Dakota or Delaware. These are the states with either weak or nonexistent usury laws; there is no cap on the interest rate a company based there is allowed to charge. Usury laws preventing exorbitant interest rates are nearly as old as the written word itself. The clay tablets containing the legal code of Hammurabi, dating back to 1750 BC, included rules limiting the amount of interest that could be charged on the purchase of grain or silver. The Old Testament is rife with warnings against the dangers of usurious lending.[21] At one time, the U.S. government had national usury laws dictating the amount of interest that could legally be charged on a loan. But such laws were repealed after the Depression to aid the faltering banking industry, and some states never put new laws in place. Credit card companies located in those states—and nearly all of them are—can raise your APR to 20, 30, even 40 percent, all within completely legal boundaries.

Most of us don't know that our card companies reserve the right to raise our APRs at any time, for any reason, as long as they give us fifteen days' notice. If you drop behind in your payments, even by a single hour, they also reserve the right to charge whatever late fees they decide. We don't realize that if we take out a small cash advance we must repay that advance at a higher APR and that we have to pay off our entire balance before we're allowed to chip into the cash-advance amount. Or that our minimum balance is carefully calculated to ensure that it will take us years to pay off the full amount, if we ever do. And we certainly don't know about one of the card company's most invasive creations, the notion of universal default. Even if you pay your credit card bills on time, the bank can raise your interest rate automatically if you're late on payments for another bill, such as a cell phone, car, or house payment, or if they simply feel that you have taken on too much debt. The logic behind universal default is that a customer who can't repay other financial commitments has automatically become a higher credit risk and the card company is entitled to collect on that increased risk. Why they think a customer who's having trouble repaying other bills will suddenly have more money to pay off this particular card goes, like so much else, basically unaddressed.

For the most part, consumers have their hands tied when it comes to fighting such unfair policies. They can attempt to call the card company and bargain down their APR or extend their credit limit, but beyond that there's little recourse. Congress is responsible for regulating the card industry—they've stripped the states of their power to enact stronger laws—but beyond the occasional hearing they don't do much. The banking industry is simply too strong a political power. Each credit card and banking association has its own lobbyist and political action committee. In the 2004 election cycle, the finance and credit companies curried political favor by making close to \$8 million in campaign contributions.[22]

On the other end, we find mostly nonprofit advocacy groups that are committed to standing up for the consumer but that have few funds to sway political influence. No overarching government entity is responsible for monitoring the credit card industry, despite its size and scope. The Office of the Comptroller of the Currency (OCC), charged with regulating the national banking system and funded by fees and assessments charged to those same banks, is responsible for monitoring some, but not all, providers. But aside from a periodic issuing of optional guidelines, it has remained a small and largely inactive presence in industry regulation. Other card companies are monitored by other agencies—the FDIC (Federal Deposit Insurance Corporation), the OTS (Office of Thrift Supervision), the FCUA (Federal Credit Union Agency), and the Federal Reserve—none of which evince much interest in taking an active role in protecting consumer rights. Once again, we're reduced to the notion of personal responsibility. If you have a problem with your credit cards or the credit card industry, figure out a way to take care of it on your own.[23]

No one I interviewed claimed to have found a solution to handling their credit card debt, except to do their level best not to acquire too much of it. Nearly all of those who weren't carrying card debt when we spoke had done so in the past. They weren't the more sensible spenders, the debt-averse, the ones who had figured out the magical secret to managing their money. They were the lucky few who'd gotten their heads back above water and knew how easy it would be to go down again. They weren't savvier, just more heavily scarred.

A few people had turned to debt-consolidation companies for help in getting things under control, in essence paying someone to help them pay off their debt. Others had reached the point where they just ignored their credit card bills because there was no possible way they could pay. But most people swam somewhere in the middle, paying off a little when they could and trying not to let the numbers skyrocket. They weren't pleased with this situation, but they didn't know what else to do.

It's hard to know what sort of answer to look for when it comes to dealing with our personal and collective debt. It's grown as invasive and unrelenting as any modern plague. The card companies could become less usurious, at least giving us a chance to someday pay off what we owe. In March 2007, Congress held a new round of hearings looking into stronger legislation to prevent credit card companies from employing practices like universal default and charging cardholders outrageous late fees and other penalties. Industry heavyweights including Chase, Citigroup, and Bank of America were represented at the hearings. Already such political attention has pushed Citigroup to end its universal-default policy and withdraw the right to raise APRs at any time without notice. Chase has revised its policy on charging over-the-limit penalties to its customers. With such action stemming from a simple appearance before a Senate subcommittee, we may be optimistic that Congress does have it in its power to truly force the card companies to enact change.[24]

We could also emphasize a shift in cultural values, away from buying and spending and accumulating stuff and toward less tangible human assets. But even this doesn't seem enough. Excluding some unexpected financial windfall, as we get older and our lives fill with families and responsibilities, it's hard to envision our household expenses decreasing, no matter how much we attempt to cut back. Given the state of the economy and the increasing polarization of wealth, counting on wages rising faster than the cost of living seems equally dubious.

If escalating consumer debt truly has become the default system, it leaves us with a host of troubling questions about our future. Where does this seemingly endless supply of credit really end? What if we all still owe into our sixties and seventies, if we wind up saddling our children with such debt instead of helping them out the way some of our parents have done for us? What wisdom will we pass on to future generations about the connection between saving and spending, the difference between want and need? And how will we prepare them to make their way in a society with such high consumer expectations and such ready acceptance of financial instability as part of everyday life?

8

A QUESTION OF EQUITY

Rent Rich or House Poor

Denise and her husband, Evan, knew they wanted to own a home just as soon as they got married in their late twenties.

"We wanted the tax break," she explains. "We were tired of just throwing away rent money every month. But even more than that, we loved the idea of our own space. We wanted to be able to paint the outside of our house whatever color we chose, to be able to play music as loud as we wanted, and walk around naked whenever we felt like it. You can't do that in a rental place."

Though they saved enough to buy a small two-bedroom home in a middle-class Maryland suburb, they wound up staying there only a year. When Evan decided he wanted to apply for the police force in the Virginia neighborhood where he grew up, they had to move to become residents of the state.

"We sold the house and started renting again. It did feel like a step backwards, but at that time it was no big deal. To be honest, we hated the house and the neighborhood. We figured we'd just save our money and start over again. This time we'd find something we really loved."

It took years of saving and living in a rental apartment but, two years after the birth of their first child, Denise and Evan found a three-bedroom freestanding house they loved, easy commuting distance for both of them, with a big yard for their son and the new baby Denise was expecting. Even better, it was just ten minutes from the Eastern Shore town where Evan had grown up. The only catch was the $450,000 asking price, a huge stretch but one they decided they could just manage.

"Everyone told us we would regret stretching ourselves that thin," Denise recalls. "Our lawyer warned us. My parents warned us. But we loved that house like crazy. It was in great shape so we would barely have to do any work to it. It just felt like the right place to raise a family. So we decided to take the risk."

Evan was making close to $90,000 a year as a heating-and-cooling engineer, and he'd decided to drop his law-enforcement dreams in favor of this more lucrative, unionized occupation, one he'd taken up when he dropped out of college at twenty. Denise worked as a graphic designer for a national chain of retail stores, earning $50,000. They took out an 80/15/5 split on the mortgage— 80 percent in a thirty-year fixed-rate jumbo loan of over $300,000 at 6 percent interest, 15 percent in a second mortgage, and 5 percent down payment—borrowing from Denise's 401(k) to cover the $25,000 down payment. With nearly all the selling price provided by bank loans, the combined monthly mortgage payments wound up at a hefty $3,700 a month.

"We were just barely making it, but we were making it," Denise recalls. "And once we started living there, we loved the house even more. It really felt like we'd made the right choice."

Finances were tight, with little room for vacations, meals out, or other luxuries, but—with two children, a beautiful house, two cars in the garage, and a pair of solid jobs—for the most part Denise and Evan felt like they were making a legitimate stab at chasing the middle-class American dream.

Only one thing really nagged at Denise as she scrambled to balance work and home life with two small children. Her daughter Lily had experienced developmental problems from an early age and they seemed to be getting worse, not better. At first doctors brushed off Denise as an overconcerned parent, but over time it became clear that there was something seriously wrong. Finally, after over a year of toting her to various pediatric and child-development experts, a number of whom weren't providers recognized by the health plan Evan got through his union, Lily was diagnosed with a rare form of mental retardation. Suddenly everything changed.

With a firm diagnosis in hand, Evan and Denise dedicated themselves to getting Lily the best care possible. Her disability made her eligible for Medicare waivers that covered doctor's visits and regular speech and occupational therapy, but Denise also sought out the best child-development doctors in the area and took Lily to them for regular evaluation, despite the fact that most of them didn't accept any health insurance at all.

Denise did her best to keep up with her job, staying late and working at home to make up for the face time she missed while taking Lily to and from appointments. But eventually her boss became frustrated with her missing so much work. He fired her on her thirty-fifth birthday, offering her just two weeks' notice and no severance pay.

"I figure that's a perfect illustration of corporate compassion," offers Denise with a wry laugh. "They just said it's clear you can no longer do your job so you'd better leave."

Given all the time and energy Lily demanded, Denise knew there was no way she could look for another job, at least not until several years down the road when Lily was in school and their son, now five, was a little older. They were just going to have to figure out a way to get by on Evan's income, including absorbing all the added expenses that came with Lily's diagnosis.

"The first thing we lost was the house," Denise recalls. "It was heartbreaking. We tried everything we could to keep it. But there was just no way we could make those kind of payments on Evan's salary alone. That first winter we realized we couldn't even afford to buy oil to heat the place."

Fortunately, they found a buyer fairly quickly, and were lucky enough that one of Lily's doctors had an aunt looking to rent her four-bedroom house only ten miles from where they'd been living. Now instead of paying $3,700 in mortgage, they write a $2,000 rent check and their landlord takes care of everything else. After selling the house, paying off their mortgage, and paying down their debt, they even had $20,000 left over to invest in Denise's 401(k).

Life with Lily has taught them a great deal about acceptance and gratitude, but Denise admits it's still hard for her to wake up every morning in a house that isn't hers.

"I keep telling myself I'd better get used to it," she says. Given the high housing prices in Virginia, she figures it will be at least eight to ten years before she and Evan can even come close to affording to buy again.

"I went to high school at a very fancy boarding school and I remember spring break all the other girls would be going off to the Virgin Islands and I kept saying to my mom, I want to do that, I want to go there. Finally one year she broke down the costs of going to school for me, item by item, down to every last book and pencil and train ride home. Just so I'd understand where all the money went. Now she's the one who doesn't understand why we can't afford a house on Evan's salary. And I want to do the same thing for her. I want to break it down item by item, just so she can see where all the money goes. The rent, the food, the clothes, all the extra expense involved in Lily's care. We have to buy toys, videos, coinsurance on equipment, books, seminars, modifications to the house. I have no problem believing it when they say that families of a special-needs child can see their expenses go up as much as 50 percent."

Denise thinks constantly about when and how she might go back to work. She hates not contributing to the household, hates feeling like she has to ask Evan permission to spend anything, even if it's just to buy groceries. She tried freelancing for a while right after she lost her job but the clients demanded too much face time and she couldn't spend so many hours away from Lily. Now she's thinking she might transition to something in the social services field, given all she's learning going through the system herself. Of course, that would probably require going back to school, requiring time and money they don't have.

Evan has been extremely supportive, but he too has been pressuring Denise to find a way to start bringing in some income again.

"It's tough having all that provider stuff resting on his shoulders. He works so hard and we still struggle. He wants a home that's ours. He wants a financial cushion. And I understand how he feels. I have a college education. Evan and I both had good jobs. Looking back I can say we should've bought a house earlier, or we shouldn't have stretched ourselves so far. But how could we have known? Dealing with finances was always like spinning plates. One unexpected thing thrown in the mix and suddenly it all goes tumbling."

Even for professional middle-class families like Denise and Evan's, those who earn enough to pay their bills on time and even save up money for something more, affording big-ticket items like a house means walking the financial edge, a place where one unforeseen development—a health crisis, job loss, the arrival of another child—can pull that sense of security provided by home ownership right out from under you. To be middle class has always meant owning one's own home, a comfort not generally granted the working poor. But today, too often, it's only those at the upper end of the middle-class income scale who can avail themselves of such security without risking their entire financial futures, and even for them it's become a stretch. Especially for those living in urban areas, it's growing harder to afford homes—to buy them, pay them off, maintain them, and hang on to them—meaning that we risk losing what is supposed to be our major financial asset, not to mention a cornerstone of any middle-class dream.

Americans spend significantly more to own a home than they did thirty years ago, with the average home price rising from $130,524 in 1975 to $219,000 in 2005.[1] Nor is the phenomenon exclusive to high-profile cities like New York and Los Angeles. It stretches from the Eastern Shore of Virginia, across the urban and suburban Midwest, through the South and the Southwest. The 2005 Census showed the largest increase in the population paying at least 30 percent of their income in rent came not in Manhattan or the tony suburbs of Los Angeles, but in Olanthe, just outside Kansas City, Kansas, where the average price for a new home has doubled in the past five years.[2]

Our housing problems stem from a combination of factors, which grouped together can easily lead to families like Evan and Denise's stretching to the breaking point to grab this slice of the middle-class dream. On the one hand, housing prices have skyrocketed since 2000, outstripping the growth in incomes more than sixfold.[3] If you want to buy a home in a good school district with enough room for a family, if you want to own a condominium in a safe neighborhood within commuting distance to and from your job, you'll have to pay more than most educated professionals have available. Single people are discovering that they can't afford houses without a partner. Some families I spoke to reported struggling to choose between home ownership and having children, whereas once the two were assumed to go hand in hand.

Home ownership has featured high on the American desirables list since the 1950s, when the combination of government housing subsidies and rapid suburbanization first made "home sweet home" a widespread middle-class reality. Back then the luxury of available land was generating the first wave of suburban sprawl, bringing with it a proliferation of low-cost housing. But fifty years later, Americans are now coming face-to-face with the financial impact of our limited natural resources. Land, that endless American bounty, has finally tapped itself out. Alongside the decreasing availability of physical space, we're also facing a rise in the cost of building materials like timber, copper, and nickel as we continue to drain those resources as well.

On the other hand, members of the middle class are grappling with the real need for a house as a future source of equity, perhaps the only resource they will have to fund their children's educations or see themselves into retirement. Despite the rising costs, housing today remains our prime source of wealth and our most reliable appreciating asset. Most middle-class households have the bulk of their assets not in stocks and bonds but in housing equity. Acquiring equity can be crucial to affording retirement. Selling that home is what's supposed to sustain us in our old age.[4]

In addition, we've been living in a hyper-debt-friendly era characterized by the mass availability of mortgages to almost anyone who asks. If you want to buy a house you really can't afford, chances are there are plenty of lenders willing to help you—at astronomical interest rates. In early 2007, using several online mortgage calculators, I was assured that on a $40,000 income and with no outstanding debt, my fictional household could afford to buy a $200,000 home. My gut reaction is that surely, at this point and on that income, I can't afford a house at all.[5] Though the ready availability of high-risk mortgages may shift, given the financial turmoil in the mortgage lending industry that had begun to unfold by the later part of 2007, much of this upset revolved around subprime loans offered to members of the working poor and missing class. It's likely many middle-class families will continue to have access to homes and mortgages they can't quite comfortably afford.

Combine all the above with the emotional considerations, that desire for a "home of one's own" whatever the financial cost—whether it's because we yearn to nest, want to paint the outside cobalt blue, or hope to prove our material success to ourselves and the world—and you have a clear recipe for financial trouble.

On a practical level, owning a home before you can truly afford one doesn't make much sense. Between taxes, heating, home repairs, and all the costs associated with the purchase, you might as well just hook up a hose to your bank account and turn on the faucet. But psychologically, home ownership gives us a sense of security that, in this uncertain age, many people are willing to purchase at almost any price. In a *New York Times* poll, owning a home featured above everything—even a fat bank account—as an indicator of wealth and status in our society.[6] A house feels steady and true, less volatile than almost any other investment, even our jobs and salaries. It's one of the precious few things we can fall back on when times get tough. Home ownership is beyond just typical Americana. It's iconic. Every real American family has had one, from the Finches to the Cleavers, the Cosbys to the Simpsons. So it's understandable why—no matter what their debt level or financial prospects—members of today's educated professional middle class are willing to push themselves to the breaking point to possess one as soon as they can.

RENT RICH: STUCK IN THE SAVING ZONE

The transition from renter to owner is nearly as significant a rite of passage into middle-class adulthood as the first paycheck, the first promotion, or the first child. Renting equals temporary, insecure, still climbing. Owning means established, successful, and provided for.

But though it certainly requires far less money up front, in the long run renting a house or apartment these days is not necessarily an easier alternative to buying, especially for those doing so in the hopes of someday saving up for a house. Far from providing a temporary savings zone on the road to home ownership, renting today can be a serious money drain. Apartment rents across the country were expected to rise 5.3 percent in 2007 alone, the largest jump since 2000.[7] Lack of space, a glut of people, the desire to wait out the sky-rocketing housing industry before buying, and the polarization of in-comes—the wealthy can and do pay enormous amounts to rent in desirable neighborhoods—are driving the middle and lower classes to the fringes of the rental market and making it harder for them to rent and save at the same time.

With the jump in housing prices, landlords are increasingly con-verting rental properties to more lucrative condominiums for sale or choosing to build fewer rental properties in the first place. In 2005 alone, one out of three apartment buildings sold were converted to condos, taking over 190,000 rental apartments off the market.[8] In suburban areas, zoning codes restricting or preventing the rental of above-garage and basement apartments in residential neighborhoods often limit affordable rental housing. Publicly cited are worries about traffic, parking, and strain on public services, particularly schools. Unspoken but ever-present is a further polarizing "us versus them" attitude centering on what will become of a neighborhood once the less affluent, less white, less homogenous segment of the middle class is ushered in.[9]

As more people are reluctant or simply unable to buy in this bloated market, landlords gain the upper hand and up go the rents. Paying a monthly rent becomes no cheaper than paying a mortgage. And as housing prices remain high in many areas, those areas are flooded with a higher income level of renters who can't afford to buy yet or who want to wait until prices lower, jacking up the cost for ev-eryone else. As of the final quarter of 2005, the average rent in New York City was $2,400; in Los Angeles, $1,421; in Boston, $1,216; and in Washington, D.C., $1,160. Nevertheless, it's estimated that housing prices would have to rise 4 to 5 percent in the next five years for buyers in any of those markets to do better than renters.[10]

"We want to buy," says Kayla, thirty-eight, an alternative health practitioner. Together she and her husband, a research scientist, make over $100,000 a year, yet they still live in a rented apartment in Brooklyn. "We should buy. But it's hard to know what to do. Does it make sense to go even deeper in debt for some tiny one-bedroom in Brooklyn? Should we keep renting here and look for a real house up-state instead? When you factor in our student loan debt and the crazy housing prices, I'm not so sure we can afford to become home owners after all."

For many educated middle-class professionals who've chosen lower-income creative or service careers, life risks getting stuck at a permanent college-dorm level. Especially in large urban centers, you find a proliferation of single people still living with roommates. Not only those in their twenties just starting out, but full-on adults in their thirties and forties who have active careers but who haven't partnered up and still need help in defraying expenses. In Manhattan, an average five-hundred-square-foot studio apartment rents for $2,200 to $2,600 a month. Even if you're willing and able to spend half your income on rent, you'd need to make over $50,000 to afford it, considerably more than the $43,277 average per capita income for the New York area. The recommended maximum, however, is 30 percent of your income. To pay that you'd need to be earning $70,000.[11]

Initially, sharing space with a roommate may teach valuable life lessons about taking responsibility for cleaning the bathroom or divvying up the refrigerator shelf space and sharing the remote control. But over time, roommate living can make it trickier to form serious relationships and to think in terms of long-term savings and investments. When rent and bills eat up the bulk of our income, we might cling to any lifestyle that makes it easy to put off the financial and emotional decisions of adulthood, whether that be getting married or contributing to a 401(k).

For others attempting to prepare for the financial leap to ownership, reversion can be even more pronounced. In today's expensive housing market, moving back in with their parents may be the only way for many individuals and even families to save enough money to permanently move out. Though this might make sense in practical terms, living at home when you're in your thirties and forties can take a serious emotional toll. Our culture places a stigma on adults who still live with their parents. No matter what your profession, no matter what your circumstances, the kind of home you do or don't possess is a prime measure of success, a clear outward sign you have or haven't made it.

"Financially, I keep telling myself it makes a lot of sense," says Rachel, forty-two, a single high school teacher who shares her apartment on Manhattan's Upper East Side with her mother. "But it puts a real crimp in your social life. It's embarrassing. I'm afraid to bring anyone I date back to my apartment because I don't want them to know I share it with my mother. What are they going to think? That I'm still thirteen years old?"

For those of us stuck anywhere in the rental loop, it's hard to know when it's finally safe to attempt the shift from renting to owning. If you wait until you feel financially secure, you could be in your mother's back bedroom until you're ninety. If you wait until someone's willing to offer you a mortgage, well, then, you can have that three-bedroom Victorian today, though you may lose it in a year. There are real dangers to both sides of the equation. Wait too long and you won't have enough housing equity to help you out in your retirement years. Move too soon, and you'll wind up so deep in debt you wind up losing that house you worked so hard to acquire. In these financially volatile times, when job loss and income drops are an uncontrollable fact of middle-class life, those contemplating buying face the legitimate fear that even if they can put aside enough money for a down payment, there could easily come a time when they won't be able to afford the mortgage or taxes or home repairs.

Olivia, thirty-three, makes $80,000 a year as a project manager for an Internet company in the San Francisco Bay Area. Though she once had dreams of becoming a writer, she went into the tech industry because it felt more financially secure and because the comfort of eventually owning a home and filling a retirement account were important to her. She's been saving up to buy her own place since her midtwenties, bartending on weekends to supplement her income, and now has $80,000 in the bank, enough for a down payment on an apartment even in the explosive Bay Area real estate market. But knowing that, as a single woman, she'll be solely responsible for making every payment, she's still hesitant to take the plunge.

"It's scary. I have no idea what I can afford. Yes, I have enough for a down payment, but what about mortgage and taxes and everything else? What if I lost my job?" she asks, still gun-shy from two previous layoffs earlier in her career. "Then there's the fact that if I buy something, I won't be able to afford any of the other things I enjoy. No vacations. No eating out. My life will become just me and my apartment. Is that really what I want? These are hard questions. I'm really in kind of a financial panic about it all. Do I really make enough money to do this? How do I know?"

HOUSE POOR: FINANCING THE LEAP

Though most educated middle-class professionals may share Olivia's reticence, they also feel Denise and Evan's hunger to purchase a home as soon as possible, even if it's not necessarily the most sensible financial choice. And that hunger is largely winning out. Despite the obstacles, home buying in America is on the rise. Today, nearly 70 percent of households own their own homes, up from 66 percent in 2000.[12]

How is this possible, given our worsening financial straits? It's possible because ownership has become a slippery concept. Though more of us may own homes, we actually own less of them. The current rise in home ownership in America has come accompanied by a serious spike in household-related debt, with mortgages alone escalating from 19.7 percent of disposable income in 1949 to 66 percent in 2000 to 96 percent in 2005. The same number of people have debt against a primary residence as have credit card debt, more if you count those with debt secured against any residential property.[13]

Though they have consistently higher incomes than single buyers, married couples are also most likely to take out a mortgage to buy a home.[14] Marriage is when many educated professionals first really start to worry about permanence and stability—the twin ties of kids and commitment—and owning a house is key to their image of security and success, no matter how far finances need to be stretched.

"Buying a house was the top of the agenda once we got married," explains Luanne, twenty-eight. Though she and her husband, Hugo, have a combined income of only $60,000—she's a graphic designer for a financial planning company, he works in facilities maintenance for the county—and though Hugo's significant credit card debt meant that his credit was nearly shot, the couple began looking for a house in the Fort Lauderdale area, where they'd both grown up, practically the day they tied the knot.

"The security of owning a house was really important to me," says Luanne, who grew up in a working-class family with never-ending financial troubles. "My father worked as a welder and he was always being laid off. My parents went through bankruptcy and more than once we had to sell our house to avoid foreclosure. I don't want that kind of a life for me or my family."

Luanne sought security in marrying young, in relegating her love of fine art to hobby status and choosing a more practical career, but also in making sure that she and Hugo invested in a house before they even considered the prospect of starting a family. After nearly a year of searching, saving, and adjusting expectations, they settled on a $180,000 fixer-upper townhouse on the outskirts of Fort Lauderdale.

In early 2006, they put together what just a few years ago would have been an impossibly sweet deal, especially given Hugo's credit history. It included no down payment at all and an 80/20 split on a first and second mortgage—divided in two so they could avoid having to pay mortgage insurance—which covered the full cost of the house. It's an adjustable-rate mortgage, which means that the interest rate and thus payments will take a significant upward leap in three years time, but Luanne and Hugo are hoping they can either refinance or sell the house at a profit before that kicks in. To cover the closing costs, both sets of parents pitched in a little money. Aside from their current $1,300 mortgage payments, Luanne and Hugo have essentially put forth no money at all.

But despite receiving such generous financing, home ownership has put the couple in a far more financially precarious position than they were before. They owe everything on the house and own almost none of it. If real estate values in their neighborhood drop before their mortgage adjusts upward, they will be essentially trapped in a home they can't afford. They have no additional financial cushion —meaning that if they encounter an unexpected financial blow, such as job loss or a medical crisis, the house will be one of the first things to go.

So far, home ownership has brought with it more increased debt than increased stability. Aside from the mortgage and the money they borrowed from both sets of in-laws, they've had to turn to credit cards to get started on the extensive renovations needed to make the house livable and increase its resale value.

"I've just accepted that for the foreseeable future, every financial decision we make will revolve around the house," Luanne tells me. "We're already planning to refinance next year, so we can afford to pay for more repairs and increase the resale value. Sure we'll owe more, but in the long run it's worth it. As long as we keep investing in the house it will pay us back somewhere down the line. It's debt, but it's debt toward the future. I just kind of have to believe it will all work out."

Luanne and Hugo are far from unusual in owing more on their house than they own of it. In today's financially strapped times, owning a home gives us a sense of security not just because it's a concrete place to hang our hats or an asset that might see us into retirement, but because it gives us something to borrow against in the here and now. The ready availability of household credit means that more and more Americans are using their homes—refinancing via second mortgages, home equity loans, and lines of credit—to cover their living expenses, fund home repairs, and pay off their higher-interest debts.

By 2004, 45 percent of home owners with first-lien mortgages had refinanced those mortgages over the previous three years, extracting an average of $20,000 extra dollars apiece. In addition, 17.8 percent of home owners had taken out home equity lines of credit—up from just 11.2 percent in 2001—and 12.4 percent were borrowing against those credit lines, depleting their household equity to the tune of an additional $22,000. Outstanding debt on home equity loans and lines of credit has shot upward since the '90s, reaching roughly a trillion dollars by the fourth quarter of 2003.[15]

Many of the home owners I spoke to treated their houses, apartments, and condominiums less as investments than as a source of ready, much needed cash. They'd looped other debt—student loans, car payments, credit cards—into their mortgages, so that their entire financial lives hinged on that property. Like Luanne and Hugo, many people are borrowing against their homes to pay for their homes. Forty-three percent of those with home-secured debt took out that debt for home-improvement purposes, with debt consolidation the other most prevalent reason.[16]

Of course, carrying debt on a house is not necessarily a problem, provided you can manage to pay it. If the only sensible way to purchase a home was to write a $180,000 check and be done with it, most of us would be relegated to rental status for the rest of our lives. But that line between acceptable household debt and detrimental household debt is growing increasingly blurred. Like ownership, affordability has become a slippery concept. Today more and more middle-class home owners are discovering that—despite the hard sell they got from their bank or mortgage lender—stretching to buy a home can put them in an exceedingly tight financial state.

It used to be a fairly safe rule of thumb that if the bank was willing to offer you a mortgage, no matter what your circumstances, you could probably afford it. Taking out a mortgage was a straightforward endeavor. Your income and credit history were vetted by the local bank or savings and loan, you signed up for a fifteen- or thirty-year fixed-rate mortgage, then you made your monthly payments like clockwork until one glorious day you woke up debt-free. Beyond choosing whether to pay ahead of schedule or take the full span of years to own your house free and clear, there really wasn't too much choice involved.

Shifts in the mortgage and lending industries over the past twenty-five years mean that today it's become much easier to buy a house, but much harder to hold on to one. In 2006, a full 50 percent of home buyers put down 5 percent or less of the sale price for a down payment, a mortgage option available to only those with near perfect credit as recently as three to five years ago. In the 1970s, first-time buyers typically put down 18 percent on a home. By 2002, that average had dipped to just 3 percent. The rest of that purchase price is caught up in decades worth of mortgage payments, refinancing, and spiraling household debt.[17]

For those who can't afford a traditional fixed-rate mortgage, there are an increasing number of nontraditional options available, interest-only loans and adjustable-rate mortgages being two of the most popular. These mortgages work like credit cards, with attractively low rates to begin with, then an adjustment upward, usually after a period of three to five years, that's accompanied by a steep rise in interest rates and monthly payments. At that point the borrower must suddenly come up with as much as twice the money each month or refinance the mortgage, often with another adjustable-rate loan that will put off the day of reckoning a few more years.

In 2005, 26.7 percent of all housing loans were interest-only, and an additional 15.3 percent of borrowers took on adjustable-rate loans. In areas of the country where housing prices had soared, including cities like Denver, Phoenix, and Seattle, the rate of interest-only loans had climbed as high as 40 percent. In addition, an increasing number of home buyers—roughly 22 percent in 2005—take out piggyback loans that allow them to also borrow money for the down payment; thus they become "home owners" while actually putting next to no money down on their new homes.[18]

These changes in available financing reflect a broad shift in the mortgage industry that began during the financial free-for-all of the 1980s. Seeing the amount of money poured into home mortgages as a possibly lucrative source of investment, Wall Street bankers began pooling tens of thousands of individual mortgages into single entities that could then be sold off to pension funds, corporations, or foreign investors. They pressed for the creation of two government facilities, Freddie Mac and Fannie Mae, both of which were given the power to guarantee such mortgages, in essence turning them into government-backed bonds.[19]

By 2003, 76.6 percent of home loans passed through the hands of just twenty-five major banks and mortgage lenders, up from 28.4 percent in 1990. Though the number of mortgage brokers has skyrocketed—ninety thousand new since 2000—these smaller operations simply bundle and sell their loans to the larger banks and brokerage firms that then repackage them and offer them as securities to investors. These days, nearly 70 percent of mortgages are securitized and sold on the secondary market. In fact, many adjustable-rate loans include prepayment penalties that prevent borrowers from getting out of the mortgage early, penalties established so investors can know exactly when they'll cash in.[20]

Loan terms grew more liberal because individual brokers no longer suffered consequences if a few borrowers defaulted. If one loan went bad, the effect was diluted by all the others that didn't. Lenders were compensated on the basis of how many clients they signed up, not how many could successfully pay off, making them more likely to lend to higher-risk individuals. The lending industry grew so competitive that applicants could undergo little or no income verification, especially since lenders got bonuses for pushing the sort of higher-interest loans that don't require such verification. To boost volume, lenders started providing loans at 100 percent financing and with little or no income documentation.[21]

All this rapid-fire mortgaging and refinancing became a gold mine for the banking industry, including investment banks, brokers, mortgage companies, and Wall Street. Even the government benefited, since those paying less up front for homes have more disposable income, which keeps the consumer spending rates from dropping, therefore maintaining the guise of a healthy economy. But in the long run they can be extremely damaging to the home owners themselves. Foreclosure rates are rising at a frightening pace—jumping 43 percent from 2005 to 2006—with 2 million households estimated to face foreclosure in the next two and a half years.[22] By mid-2007, the mortgage industry itself had begun to suffer a backlash against the high volume of loans offered under such liberal terms. Increasing foreclosures caused several major subprime-mortgage lenders to shut down or file for bankruptcy, and generated a credit crunch severe enough to threaten the solvency of other financial institutions. The longer-term effects on current and potential home owners remain uncertain, but it seems clear that the real estate industry will remain volatile for a number of years to come.

Minorities have served as particular targets for mortgages with poor terms. Home ownership for minorities has risen along with the tide, but it still lags behind whites. While 70 percent of the overall population own homes, only 46 percent of Hispanics and 48 percent of blacks do.[23] Minorities who do manage to purchase are less likely to be given the option to refinance, shutting down a key path for obtaining liquid assets or freeing up income at a lower interest rate. The Joint Center for Housing Studies at Harvard estimates that the collective population of black home owners may overpay as much as $22 billion over the course of thirty years—the typical length of a mortgage—because of missed, or unavailable, refinancing opportunities.[24]

Minorities are also far more likely to be given subprime loans, targeted toward those with low incomes or bad credit and offered at exorbitant interest rates. Roughly 50 percent of home loans to black and Hispanic households are subprime, compared to less than one-fifth of those issued to white borrowers. This racial gap between subprime and prime lending persists even after controlling for borrower income. A white borrower with an income of *less than* 80 percent of area median has about the same likelihood of obtaining a prime mortgage as an African American borrower with an income *in excess of* 120 percent of area median. Banks and lenders are more likely to push subprime loans to middle-class black families, most of whom would qualify for a conventional mortgage, than to low-income whites.[25]

Do any of these looser lending policies help individual home buyers? Without question, they get us into homes we couldn't have afforded thirty years ago. But they also contribute to the rising percentage of the population who pay over 30 percent of their income toward housing, making them officially "house poor." The 2005 Census showed strong increases in the number of house poor, not just in major urban centers like New York and Los Angeles but in places like Wyoming, Michigan, Round Rock, Texas, and Plymouth, Minnesota.[26] Though the bulk of this country's house poor remain low income, affordability pressures are moving up the income ladder. The number of house-poor middle-class families more than quadrupled between 1975 and 2001, and the number of middle-income households with severe housing-cost burdens—those paying more than half their income for housing—went up by 707,000 between 2001 and 2004, to a total of 3.1 million. If you add in those who are below middle-income, the figure becomes truly staggering, 15.8 million home owners facing a severe housing burden.[27]

It seems the key lesson to take into the home-buying arena today is twofold. First, despite the promises made by college educations, steady jobs, and the American dream, it is possible for a house to be a poor investment, a liability rather than an asset.

Second, when it comes to figuring out whether you can afford a house at all, the bank is not necessarily your friend. Banks have been caught pushing subprime mortgages to those who would still qualify for a regular mortgage, and deliberately issuing mortgages to families they knew couldn't afford to pay them, with the intention of foreclosing then reselling the property.[28] One of the best things we can do to protect our interests is to educate ourselves on what the various mortgage options mean and the kind of long-term debt we're actually taking on when we sign that dotted line. We need to examine what sort of income we'll require not just now but also five, fifteen, thirty years into the future to sustain this fixed and perhaps even escalating debt. And we must take into consideration what would happen if, somewhere down the line, we encountered the very real possibility of changed financial circumstances.

OWNERSHIP: FEEDING THE MONSTER

For those who do manage to successfully navigate the mortgage maze and acquire some equity in the form of a house, condo, or apartment, the ramifications of that purchase can become the sole focus, not to mention an overwhelming stressor, of their financial lives.

Nate, an Ivy League graduate with a master's degree in journalism, works as a TV producer for a financial show at a major cable network. He earns close to $100,000 a year by supplementing his base salary with teaching and writing gigs. Two years ago, after the birth of their daughter, he and his wife bought a three-bedroom home in a modest section of Long Island, New York. Though they knew they couldn't afford the move, they felt anxious about the ballooning housing market and feared if they didn't buy then, it might never happen.

In order to swing things financially, they took out a five-year adjustable-rate mortgage at 4.25 percent and a home equity line of credit, which they've needed to tap several times in the past year to cover home-repair costs and which they plan to use to help pay their daughter's preschool tuition. Their credit line opened at a quarter below the prime index, but it adjusted higher with each federal rate hike.

"Everything we have is in that house," Nate tells me. "No question, we are playing heavily against the future. It makes me very nervous. I hate that we have to spread ourselves so thin. I know my parents never would've done that."

Nate grew up in a household that emphasized tending to mind and spirit over financial gain. His father was a rabbi and a college professor. His mother worked as a therapist and guidance counselor. The family was always financially sound, managing to set aside enough to send Nate to private Jewish day schools and pay for his undergraduate education.

For Nate and his family, there's no similar sense of security. He's already feeling the pressure to find a higher-paying job by the time their mortgage adjusts three years from now. If he doesn't, there's a good chance they'll lose the house.

"We have very little in savings," he explains, "and we never manage to add to it. Yes, we have assets, but those assets also mean we have further to fall. Basically, we're stretched about as far as one family can stretch."

The small amount of money his wife makes working two days a week in her father's ophthalmology office helps to bridge the gaps, but nothing more. The couple looked into the possibility of her going back to work full-time, but the cost of child care would've negated any extra income she brought in.

Nate worries constantly about both their immediate and more distant financial future. If he lost his job—and given that there have been company layoffs each of the past four years, this is by no means out of the question—they would have at most a two-month cushion. Since the house will probably be their only large-scale investment for a long while, he sees it doubling as their retirement fund. He does have a 401(k), but anticipates using that to pay his daughter's college tuition. He admits it's not the wisest money choice—the financial show he produces would never advise such a thing—but he considers her education more important than his own financial security.

"I know we could've been financially comfortable if I'd made different choices," Nate offers. "And sometimes that does get to me. I make less than half of most of my college friends who went into big-time corporate jobs. But most of them are miserable. At least I can say I enjoy what I do. That's important to me, and it's an important message to pass down to my daughter. I don't know what the future will hold financially—we've sunk everything into that house but if we have to sell we have to sell—but I do know my child won't grow up in a home full of unhappy, money-driven people. It's not a pretty choice, but there's no doubt in my mind it was the right choice to make."

For many middle-class families like Nate's, the decision to take the financial leap into home ownership is just the beginning of the anxiety roller coaster. As one forty-four-year-old IT specialist put it, in describing why he'd chosen to put off buying a house for at least another five years: "If you build a monster you have to feed a monster."

Most young middle-class professionals emerge from their educational cocoons still swathed in the myth that a house is the most secure and stable asset out there. You can see it, you can sit in it, it provides you with a steady cushion to borrow against and fall back on, meaning that if you can just stretch far enough to make that purchase, you won't have to worry anymore. As a result, some middle-class professionals are making illogical, and occasionally bizarre, choices, from counting on finding a new higher-paying job in five years to—according to one *USA Today* article—women selling their eggs (a process that requires extensive hormone treatments) at thousands of dollars a pop, just to afford to get into a home of their own.[29]

But once we have that home, we can quickly discover that household equity is not the security slam dunk we assumed it would be. Buying a home is not a onetime expense but a long-term financial commitment that requires something increasingly elusive to today's economically volatile middle class—financial steadiness over time. You can't just save up for a down payment, scrape together that monthly mortgage, and then kick back in your new living room. You have to furnish that living room, and all the other rooms surrounding it. You have to maintain the yard. You have to cover home repair, heating and cooling, property taxes, and home owner's insurance— which rose 62 percent between 1995 and 2005—every month and every year, year in, year out. Far from buying us freedom, the incessant costs related to ownership can leave us feeling under the financial gun for the rest of our home-owning lives.[30]

For many buyers, once they figure out the financing and sign the dotted lines, the perils of home ownership have just begun. First there are the everyday practicalities. Roofs fall in, furnaces conk out. Weekends are suddenly spent at the hardware store scanning the aisles for caulk, bathroom faucets, and fertilizer for the front lawn. Even if you do get a great deal on a house, the expense of maintaining it can be paralyzing.

"I had to eat PB&J to buy my house, then I had to eat PB&J to stay there," says Desiree, thirty-five, a hospital lab tech who makes $53,000, explaining her decision to sell her lakefront bungalow after six years. "The house was a great deal. I bought it back in 1999, right ahead of the real estate curve. But once I owned it, I still had to pay the electric bill, the yard care, the property taxes—which went way up—and the constant repairs. All my time and money were channeled straight into Home Depot. It wasn't worth it. I was so worried about paying the bills, I couldn't even enjoy the life I had while I lived there."

Even if you're lucky enough to score a deal in an up-and-coming neighborhood like Desiree did, as the caliber of homes and home owners rise, you can find your property taxes going through that new slate-shingled roof. True, your home value increases, but if prices rise too rapidly, two, three, or five years down the line you can find yourself trapped in a neighborhood where you couldn't afford to buy again and can't afford to stay. You're stuck unless you can find another up-and-coming area with good deals to be had—and with the rapid rate of gentrification in many urban areas these are increasingly rare—because though you may be able to make a profit selling your house, chances are it won't be enough to rebuy on the same street.

"I did really well on the sale," says Desiree. But she's crystal clear that her future plans do not include overextending herself on another home purchase. "I couldn't afford to buy back in that same neighborhood even if I wanted to. Anyway, there's no way I'm plowing that money back into another house I can't afford. I learned my lesson. I figure I have enough for a nice little condo with maybe a little left over in savings. I see this as a sign of financial maturity. I have a much clearer sense of what I can realistically manage now."

Many people take out aggressive mortgages to buy houses they can't afford because they envision an outcome like Desiree's. They're staking their financial futures on the fact that property values will rise. They take out home equity loans and rack up credit card debt funding home improvements, assuming they can always sell if they get in too much trouble. But it's far from a risk-free strategy, especially for those for whom that home is their primary or only financial asset. What happens if the housing market drops in their area? Given the inflated prices of the past five years and the slumps that have already hit well-populated areas in states like California, Nevada, Arizona, and Florida, it's a legitimate concern.[31]

The exact status of the market in a given area can be hard to track, as sellers grow more anxious to broker any sort of deal and realtors scramble to maintain at least the guise of a healthy industry. Sellers have begun to artificially inflate prices by throwing in perks ranging from paying the buyers' commission to giving them new cars, new granite countertops, vacation timeshares, and cash rebates.[32] So not only is it getting costlier to buy a house, it's also getting costlier to sell one. As the housing market levels off or even dips in many areas, people risk getting stuck in houses they can't afford to keep and now can't get rid of. They run the danger of owing more on the house than it's worth, what's known as being "upside down" in a house. Far from creating a sense of financial security, these are the desperate situations that can easily lead to middle-class bankruptcies and foreclosures.[33]

The financial knots we're tying ourselves into now, as we scramble to purchase homes and wind up owning less of them, can have serious long-term ramifications. Because today's overall tighter finances often necessitate putting off major purchases, many adults—like Nate—don't buy their first home until they're well into their thirties or even forties. As a result, those thirty-year mortgage payments follow us right into retirement, hanging around even as rising health care and tuition expenses for college-aged children begin to spike. As a result, we discover too late that the asset we gambled everything to acquire because it was going to see us through retirement is instead pushing that retirement further and further away. Already, an increasing number of seniors are borrowing against their homes, accumulating more debt just at the time when they're supposed to be shaking themselves free. In 1983 only 15.7 percent of households headed by someone age sixty-five to seventy-four had debt on a primary residence, and only 3.7 percent of those age seventy-five and older. By 2004, those numbers had risen to 32.1 percent and 18.7 percent respectively. Given the inflated housing market of recent years and the deep debt we're generating today by taking on homes we can't afford, by the time we reach our sixties and seventies we run a serious risk of still owing too much on our homes for them to provide anything but an additional burden in our waning years.[34]

Even for those members of the educated middle class who've avoided pricier urban and upscale suburban areas, the volatile real estate market is having its impact. As major cities become less and less affordable, aspiring home owners are looking for more creative ways to build equity. I talked to a handful of people who lived in the most expensive markets like New York, Boston, and San Francisco who, unable to buy locally had chosen to purchase homes in smaller towns just because it was the only way they could foresee having any real estate equity at all. They treated such assets as rental properties and perhaps future homes, but with their higher incomes adjusted to living in areas with a higher cost of living, they were also helping to drive up real estate prices in those less affluent neighborhoods.

As incomes stagnate and expenses rise across the country, housing pressures, too, inevitably spread. The compromises we once made to create a more stable life for our families—moving away from the city, searching out emerging neighborhoods, trading in excitement and adventure for some peaceful quality of life—can no longer be taken for granted.

OUR CHANGING COMMUNITIES

Four years ago when Jamie and her husband, Keith, moved themselves and their three children from Washington, D.C., to a small northeastern college town, they had a definite life adjustment in mind. Gone would be the days of paying $15,000 a year for child care and juggling out-of-control credit card debt. In a town that valued life balance over ambition and creating a family over making money, Jamie would take a few years off to be a stay-at-home mom and Keith would find a rewarding job in the nonprofit sector. They would make enough on the sale of their D.C. house to buy a comfortable new home plus establish a healthy savings cushion. They'd picked their new hometown carefully, ensuring it was within driving distance of Keith's parents and had high-quality schools and plenty of cultural opportunities for their children.

"We loved D.C.," Jamie offers, "but the expense of living there had just gotten too stressful. We were dragging ourselves into debt so deep we couldn't foresee ever getting out again. This move was supposed to be the answer to our prayers."

But the reality of life in their new hometown turned out to be not quite as idyllic as they'd hoped. Apparently Jamie and Keith weren't the only family to come up with the "downsizing to a better quality of life" concept, and local housing costs—boosted by other big-city refugees and retirees looking for a town that contained the perfect combination of intellectual stimulation and peace of mind—ran much higher than they'd bargained for.

"Little did we know that because of the quality of the local schools, we were actually moving into the most expensive housing market in the area. We thought about going someplace cheaper, but my son is dyslexic and it was really important that he be in a school that could deal with his special needs."

They'd originally hoped to rent a home for a little while, but given the influx of new residents, the local rental market was prohibitively tight. Instead they found a small house right in town for $350,000, a little cramped for their large family but close to schools, shops, and the local college campus. The $2,500 monthly mortgage was more than they'd intended to spend but they decided they'd just figure out a way.

Keith loved his new job as a director of a nonprofit children's organization, but it turned out that the $50,000-a-year salary was hardly enough to support a family, about to expand to six, no matter how much they scrimped and saved. In addition, the job offered no benefits, which meant that unless Jamie went back to work they would have to find a way to pay for health insurance out of pocket for themselves and all four kids. So Jamie scrapped her plan to stay home and took a part-time telecommuting job, including benefits, with the same pharmaceutical company she'd worked for in D.C. It was hardly a career she felt passionate about, but the extra $50,000 a year would be enough to ensure the family could get by.

"Emotionally it's been very difficult to adjust to the fact that staying home, even for a year or two, is never going to be an option," Jamie admits. "I don't know if I'll ever get over that. I would've given up almost anything to do it, but there was nothing left to give up."

Today they have a new financial plan, one that involves buying and renovating houses in the hopes of earning enough money to help their kids pay for college. They recently purchased a second home, which they're in the process of fixing up. Every night after work Keith goes directly to the new house and spends a few hours gutting and rebuilding. It means the kids don't see much of their father, but Jaime hopes the imbalance—all work, no family, reminiscent of their harried life in D.C.—is only temporary. That savings cushion they'd hoped to establish never materialized; they currently have about $5,000 in the bank, and until they can refinance both homes their financial existence remains every bit as precarious as when they lived in the big city.

"In terms of quality of life, fresh air and all that, moving here has been a big improvement," Jamie tells me. "But I can't really say it's eased the financial pressure in the least. Keith and I are both very creative people. We've worked hard to set up a life outside the conventional ideas of how you're supposed to do things. I don't regret that for a second. But with that comes a great deal of stress about how to pay bills and the kids' college tuitions and worrying if we'll ever be able to retire. It feels like we're living just a breath away from financial catastrophe. Everybody I know feels the same way, my old friends in D.C. and the new people I've met here. The pressure is driving every last one of us crazy. It seems like today, if you want to create any kind of meaningful, non-money-driven life, those worries will follow you wherever you go."

The decisions we make about where, when, and how to rent or own our homes encompass more than just individual choice. They have a huge impact on our communities. With the increasing polarization between the wealthy and everyone else, we need to begin looking seriously at how escalating housing costs and financial stresses affect the topographical map of the country.

Today the educated professional middle class is being squeezed out of urban centers that once served as the hubs of creative and service work. I spoke to a number of individuals and families like Jamie's who either already had or were seriously considering picking up and moving, changing jobs, deserting these creative centers because the financial drain was so heavy they could no longer appreciate or take advantage of what such cities had to offer. The wealthy upper strata are driving up the prices for everything from housing to day care, making it impossible for the educated professional middle class, not to mention the working class, to compete.

As a result of this economic shift, middle-class urban neighborhoods have become an endangered species. According to a study of major metropolitan areas conducted by the Brookings Institution in 2006, middle-income neighborhoods are disappearing even faster than the proportion of people earning those middle incomes, dropping from 58 percent of metro neighborhoods in 1970 to just 41 percent in 2000. (Middle income in this case is defined as between 80 and 120 percent of the median income for a given area.) In Los Angeles, such middle-income neighborhoods comprise just 28 percent of the city, a 24 percent decline since 1970. Major metropolitan areas ranging from New York to Memphis, Tucson to Atlanta, Chicago to Honolulu, have suffered similar fates. In the process, the diversity that's always given such cities their vibrancy is being sucked away.[35]

"These days in many larger cities there are fewer and fewer 'zones of emergence,' neighborhoods in transition where middle-class families can afford to buy," explains Alexander Von Hoffman, senior research fellow at Harvard's Joint Center for Housing Studies. "When that happens, it gives such families little choice but to leave."[36]

Once the variety and creative energy generated by a diverse urban population begin to draw a higher income group, those who created such energy can no longer afford to stay. They're pushed into outlying neighborhoods and then pushed again, until suddenly they find they're not living in the city they came to live in at all. As a result, those cities so prized for their diversity and cutting-edge appeal are becoming more economically stratified and homogeneous. In an age when a starting-level teacher's salary can be $100,000 less than that of a first-year lawyer, even those with the finest educations who've elected a life of public service discover there's no affordable room— let alone rooms—left for them in these urban hubs. As the middle stream out in search of a more comfortable life, we're left a population that falls into in a sort of modern-day Dickensian model, comprised of only the very rich who can afford to stay and the very poor who can't afford to leave.

It's telling that today one of the healthiest real estate trends we're seeing in major urban areas is the jump in sales of million-dollar-plus homes. That 31 percent of such buyers pay cash rather than seeking financing, that they are disproportionately white, and that they mainly work as corporate executives, business owners, doctors, and lawyers all speaks eloquently to the changing face of our cities.[37] Today Manhattan, which for centuries has reveled in its reputation as a hub of opportunity and round-the-clock vibrancy, is only 8 percent middle income, versus 40 percent low income and 51 percent high. The city has become increasingly white, wealthy, and unaffordable— particularly for families—with rent on the average studio apartment running over $2,000.[38]

This rise in income inequality, with no buffer provided by the disappearing and displaced middle class, inevitably leads to increase in tensions between haves and have-nots. Perhaps it's no surprise that this division is particularly pronounced in cities like Boston, Seattle, and Austin, which have risen to prominence on the heels of tech-industry wealth. Though these cities ostensibly provide the cutting edge in creativity and innovation, they're also rife with large influxes of the obscenely loaded, such as those in on the ground floor of companies like Microsoft or Dell.

Seattle, birthplace of Microsoft—and my hometown—has seen the income gap between richest and poorest climb 45 percent since 1980, while the gap between the middle 20 percent and wealthiest 20 percent has grown 16 percent. City homes that in the '60s and '70s were owned by teachers, carpenters, and mechanics now go to tech-boom beneficiaries for over a million dollars apiece. Median housing prices are around $430,000, requiring a household income of close to $100,000 if you also plan on affording food, clothes, a car, and maybe a night or two out on the town.

I can see the stratification growing more pronounced each year I go back. The small neighborhood private school I attended now draws children from the wealthiest families in the city able to pay $14,000 a year to educate their six-year-olds. Those friends of mine who've stayed mainly work as high-end doctors and lawyers, entered the biotech field, work for Microsoft, and/or come from inherited wealth. And even they are having trouble affording homes in the middle- and upper-middle-class neighborhoods we all grew up in. A few less corporate types, mostly the ones without families, still rent studio apartments or tiny bungalows on the far outskirts of the city—which is getting farther out all the time—and manage to patch together a living, though they have very little in the way of savings. The ever-increasing cost of living, primarily housing, makes them doubtful about whether they can stay long-term. Most new housing rising up around the still-booming city center consists of luxury condominiums designed for the high-income and high-net-worth portion of the population. The limited government and nonprofit housing money available is reserved to help those at the poverty level. On the lip of a legitimate housing crisis, one that threatens to change the shape of the city itself, an increasingly strapped middle class is finding itself left to sink or swim on its own.[39]

In order to create any chance at a comfortable lifestyle, to be able to pay their bills, afford a house, and manage to spend any time at all with their families without going into massive debt, members of the educated professional middle class are fleeing cities like Seattle, Washington, D.C., Los Angeles, and New York and seeking solace in fraying older suburbs and small college towns.

Yet like Jamie and Keith, these urban refugees often find that smaller towns do not provide the economic or social havens they expected. Many financial burdens remain identical, from gas and heating costs to health insurance and income taxes. Though the overall cost of living may be lower, that dip is usually offset by an accompanying dip in local salaries. In exchange, we can find ourselves making huge sacrifices when it comes to ethnic, cultural, sexual orientation, and class diversity.

In a big city, however polarized, the concentration of population makes it hard for any economic or racial group to achieve true isolation. But in the suburbs, cutting oneself off from those of a different background or economic status has been honed to a fine art. From gated community to air-conditioned SUV to school or office and then home again, a safe, protected, and homogeneous existence is all too easy to achieve. Echoing big-city trends, the number of suburban middle-class neighborhoods dropped 20 percent between 1970 and 2000. Instead, census reports show a rising number of upper-income suburban families shutting themselves off from the surrounding community in McMansions and upscale housing developments, in essence creating a world of their own.[40]

Moving to outlying areas also puts pressure on another big-ticket item, a car or cars and money spent on gas, insurance, and repairs. When you move far from the city, this major expense becomes an absolute necessity. With two people in the workforce, most families who don't live in areas with good public transportation need a second car and that car, too, no matter how utilitarian, requires maintenance to keep it running and fuel to get you where you need to go. With gas prices regularly topping $3 a gallon, taking on a long-distance commute can be a serious drain on the budget.

Of course, there's always the theory that the market dictates the shape of a community and that America remains a big and in some sense still-underexplored country. Uprooted middle-class families are capable of moving even farther out, to underpopulated rural areas like the town of Ellsworth, Kansas—population 2,900—that in 2004 was offering free parcels of land to anyone willing to move there.[41] But there's understandable difficulty in getting people to latch on to such a theory. Even if you can find a job with a livable salary, small-town and rural living offer plenty of other obstacles to the sort of existence educated middle-class professionals desire. The young or single usually find few career opportunities and less culture and diversity in rural communities than in urban centers, which explains why the younger generations tend to pour out of such communities. Families must deal with the often poor quality of local schools and the distance from other cultural influences like museums, theater, and music. And biracial, minority, or LGBT individuals and couples often feel safer and more comfortable in a diverse urban environment.

"Even if financially it makes sense for me to leave, I wouldn't," explains Geeta, a Boston-based editor. "As a lesbian, I've felt at risk in nonurban environments and refuse to compromise on my physical safety or my psychological well-being."

Increasingly, educated professional individuals and families are being forced to choose between affordability and access to diversity and intellectual and cultural stimulation. Like so many other choices we're facing today, it's one few of us were prepared to make.

In her classic 1961 indictment of contemporary urban planning, *The Death and Life of Great American Cities,* author Jane Jacobs laid out a template for healthy, thriving cities that included networks of mixed-income and mixed-use areas, high-density neighborhoods, regular street and sidewalk traffic, and a blend of cultures, classes, races, and backgrounds among its citizens. Though her original model was her home on Hudson Street in the heart of Manhattan's Greenwich Village, the formula she set out is applicable to any urban area.

Jacobs's is a widely cited template, one that today we're in the process of bludgeoning to smithereens. As she foresaw decades ago, when cities shrug off aspiring to diversity in favor of becoming the domain of only the wealthy and the poor, the whole society suffers. For members of the educated professional middle class, leaving major urban centers means exiting the healthiest, most innovative job markets, not to mention the hubs of people, ideas, and diversity that tend to feed those engaged in creative or intellectual pursuits. But those who stay behind wind up sacrificing, too, in terms of loss of texture and economic diversity, and political and community investment.

The answer isn't to stand at the city gates and wave heartily as the middle class leave in droves, which all too many metropolitan areas seem to be doing now. If we're to save our middle class, and our communities, we must consider how to make those cities, large and small, more affordable to those in the middle.

Back in the 1960s, Jacobs chastised city planners for their shortsighted concept of urban improvements:

> Look at what we've built ... Low-income projects that become worse centers of delinquency, vandalism and general social hopelessness than the slums they were supposed to replace. Middle-income housing projects which are truly models of dullness and regimentation, sealed against any buoyancy or vitality of city life. Luxury housing projects that mitigate their inanity, or try to, with a vapid vulgarity. Cultural centers that are unable to support a good bookstore. Civic centers that are avoided by everyone but bums, who have fewer choices of loitering place than others. Commercial centers that are lackluster imitations of standardized suburban chain-store shopping. Promenades that go from no place to nowhere and have no promenaders. Expressways that eviscerate great cities. This is not the rebuilding of cities. This is the sacking of cities.[42]

Forty years later, her description still seems terrifyingly on the mark. It's not enough to just spend money. We must think about preserving character and balance within the cities themselves. Creating more middle- or low-income housing doesn't mean creating "projects," offering a drab, homogenized, shut-away way of living that separates residents from their wealthier and poorer peers. This is not what people come to cities for. There's a crucial difference between truly mixed housing and neighborhoods—single buildings or collections of buildings that contain a mix of incomes—and isolated middle- and low-income housing. As we press for change, we must be conscious to do everything in our power not to create an even more segregated society than the one we have now.

Making our cities and towns more affordable and economically diverse won't just benefit the middle class. It will quite possibly save the cities themselves. Without economic and cultural diversity, even the richest and most powerful big city risks turning into a glorified upscale housing development. The sort of innovation that stems from a clash in backgrounds, ideas, and experiences will fade, stripping such cities of those very qualities that made their grand and glorious reputations in the first place. The young and hungry won't stop coming but they will stop caring, stop investing long-term in their surroundings and focus only on tending to themselves.

I remember, when I was in my early thirties, flyers coming around my Greenwich Village apartment, just ten minutes walk from Jacobs's own, detailing community issues and inviting residents to come to town meetings and join the community board. "You've got to be kidding," I thought, pitching them into the trash alongside envelopes that had contained rent, electric, cable, phone, and cell phone bills. "I don't have time for this. I could never stay here. This is all transitory. I have to live like I could leave tomorrow."

I stayed in that apartment for six and a half years and never once ventured near anything that could tag me as part of the community. I was scraping and struggling, cringing with every yearly rent hike and my all too stagnant writer's income, as the clock ticked on how long I could afford to stay. Never once did the neighborhood settle around me in a way that it truly felt like mine.

Research shows that those who can comfortably afford to own property in a community tend to have a greater stake in its political and moral constitution. They vote, involve themselves in local politics, invest in the community, and overall have a healthier sense of collective responsibility. Meanwhile, those living under financial stress have less community, civic, and social interaction. They reach out less to friends and neighbors and invest less in the health of their neighborhoods. Their worlds narrow to the struggle to simply take care of themselves.[43]

Neighborhoods change in long sweeps—twenty to thirty years, not three to five. The seeds of the shifts we're seeing today were planted with the increase in economic inequality that started back in the '80s. It will take an equally long time for such trends to swing back and for more of a class spread to be reinstated. It's critical that we start that reversal process now.

When downtown Manhattan's Stuyvesant Town and Peter Cooper Village, two stalwarts of middle-income housing in existence since 1947, were put on the block in August 2006 for a record-setting $5.4 billion, the potential sale launched a flurry of speculation about the changing landscape of the city itself, with more and more of its working- and middle-class inhabitants being edged out by the rich. The buildings' tenants teamed together and managed to put forward a $4.5 billion bid for the property, despite receiving no help from the city. In the end, they lost out to a high-powered global real estate developer backed by an investment bank. Though the tenant bid was unsuccessful, it did provide a powerful example of how individual citizens may think about coming together to generate change.[44]

Instead of standing by or moving out, we must pressure local and federal government to incentivize building middle- and low-income housing by providing builders with subsidies and tax breaks. The introduction of such housing—whether by construction or legislation—has to outpace the selling off of existing properties, a real problem in cities where the market for high-end residences seems to be permanently hot. For those who claim land and construction prices are simply too high, there's evidence slowly popping up all over the country to prove otherwise.

For example, one of the nation's largest privately owned homebuilding companies, Kimball Hill Homes, recently formed a new division to focus on inner-city development and embarked on four projects—three in downtown Chicago and one in Detroit—dedicated to affordable housing. The $2 billion investment will create six thousand new units, split among market-rate, affordable, and public housing. Kimball Hill isn't operating alone. They've teamed up with other local developers and City View, a company chaired by former Clinton-era housing secretary Henry Cisneros that specializes in financing affordable housing nationwide. They've also employed local minority-owned construction companies and other nonprofits to facilitate the building process. A percentage of market-rate units in each building, plus state and city funding, Chicago Housing Authority grant funding, and various low-income mortgage programs have all worked together to make the buildings possible. In the process, they're creating a positive, exciting, and imitable model for housing that can support the mix of cultures and socioeconomic backgrounds that will keep our urban areas vibrant and alive.[45]

9

FROM RIPPLES TO REVOLUTION

Changing the System, Changing Ourselves

So many of the people I interviewed asked me: "Are you going to tell us how to fix our financial problems?" The answer to that question is no. I can indicate why the educated professional middle class is in such a precarious financial position and assure you that you aren't alone. I can tell you about those who've found a sense of financial peace or focus or direction. But there aren't any easy ways out of this web of burdens, risks, and expectations. While I can't tell you how to fix things, I can tell you how to start.

First, being angry is not nearly enough. We need to act. We need to examine what we can do both as individuals and as a society to stop this downward spiral and reignite a sense of social responsibility—from improving government-backed education, health-, and child-care programs to initiating a shift in values so that our self-worth is no longer defined by the size of our bank account. As I hope is obvious by now, this isn't a financial planning book. It's about understanding and changing a system that no longer works for the majority of its members.

Though we can certainly feel isolated in our individual financially stressed bubbles, the good news is that the economic struggles of the professional middle class aren't being ignored. There are numerous progressive economists, activists, and institutions out there formulating plans to improve problems ranging from the cost of education to the lack of health care and retirement options to increasing levels of credit card and household debt. Liberal organizations and think tanks like the Center for Economic Policy Research, Demos, the Economic Policy Institute, and the Hamilton Project at the Brookings

Institution have all published scores of papers that outline the economic stress placed on today's middle class and suggest paths toward
change. It's exciting to see that, within the progressive end of the system, a very active dialogue is currently taking place.[1]

The problem isn't that new ideas don't exist, but that we seem to
be getting caught someplace between conversation and implementa-
tion. Economists and academics can attend endless conferences, but
until these ideas filter down to the middle-class masses, until we not
only begin hearing about them but also come to understand that we
have the power to do something about them, nothing will change.
We have to get these progressive ideas out of academia and think
tanks and into the mainstream, build a bridge from the ivory tower
to the city streets. In part the burden of responsibility is on those
thinkers behind these as yet still largely theoretical ideas. But the
onus is also on us, the lay population. We have to be curious. We
have to care enough. In a society as deeply rooted in individualism as
ours, it's tough to accept that our financial inadequacies might result
from a systemic flaw over which we have little control rather than
from our own personal failure to thrive. But the evidence seems
pretty clear. It's not that we're all "doing it wrong" but that, given
the expenses most individuals and families shoulder these days, you
simply can't make a decent living in a slew of what were once respectable and rewarding middle-class jobs.

In 1926, two years before he took office as governor of New York,
Franklin Delano Roosevelt observed that: "In government, in science, in industry, in the arts, inaction and apathy are the most potent
foes." In the coming decade, he would go on to prove what can happen in a country that refuses to bow down to such foes.[2]

A key first step toward change occurs in our minds. We need to resist an encroaching fatalism, the sense that our current economic
straits are generated by forces too powerful and too firmly rooted in
our government and national values for us to alter them. Social
change is as much a part of our history as opportunity, individualism, and the American dream. In fact, it is the American way.

The New Deal was a time of formidable change that might form a
model for what we can achieve today. It left a lasting social legacy in
the form of Social Security, child labor and minimum-wage legisla-

tion, as well as banking and security legislation. It brought electrical power to thousands of rural poor, boosted the banking industry via federal deposit insurance, and stimulated private home ownership. But the New Deal was as important for what it stood for as for what it achieved. It sent a message to every citizen that we were a country that valued social equity, widespread financial security, and a permanent improvement in the American standard of living. The New Deal aspired to social equity but it was not socialism; it worked to modulate market competition, not destroy it. Its goal wasn't to end capitalism, but to figure out how to distribute those benefits wrought by capitalism more equally.

Politics in the 1930s weren't all that different from politics today. The New Deal didn't stem from an isolated sense of public service that germinated from the saintly mind of FDR. It was the product of political pressure, a real public unrest rising from a country enduring severe economic hardship and surrounded by a business culture it saw as unregulated and rotten. Liberal voices like Louisiana senator and populist Huey Long and radio preacher Father Coughlin stirred public anger about social inequality and corporate corruption to a dangerous pitch. A similar pattern unfolded decades later in the 1960s when the collective uproar generated by activists including Martin Luther King and Malcolm X spurred President Johnson to take action regarding civil rights and the war on poverty. In each case, the laws were signed by the politicians but the push came from the people.

This spirit of activism, this popular "can change" wave that radicalized the '30s and the '60s is the glue that sticks the policies to the citizens. But today, that public force seems to have dissipated. It's been channeled into the workplace, trapping most of what's creative and generative inside the corporate, financial, and industrial world. That activist energy needs to find its way back onto the streets. Fighting back requires two things: imagination and a strong sense of social responsibility. It requires asking ourselves, on a moral and ethical level, what sort of country we want to live in and what we want our children to inherit.

One of the key questions we face as Americans today is how to find a balance between a market-driven economy fueled by indi-

vidual opportunity and a sense of mutual responsibility and compassion. It's a line we, as a capitalist culture, should always be monitoring and revising. But in recent years, things have gotten seriously
out of whack. We've been consumed by the principle of market fun-
damentalism, putting protection of the free market above all else. But
economics cannot be divorced from values—is this the value system
we want to embody?

As individuals within this system, we're allowed to believe differently. We can say that we don't want to be a work culture, a business
culture, or a corporate culture. That we don't want to be defined by
how much money we make, or even by what we do to make it. We
can resist there being just one definition of the good life. This is not a
question of personal net gain or net loss, but of priorities. There's a
clear message delivered by a government that, in 2007, can find over
$400 billion dollars to back the war in Iraq, but can't scrounge up
any more than one-eighth of that to fund federal child care.[3]

Our college experiences instilled aspirations to a comfortable and
successful lifestyle that many of us have failed to achieve. But our expensive educations instilled us with other self-sufficient qualities as
well. They provided us with a sense of autonomy and activism. They
gave us the cultural savvy and analytical tools to understand that social justice involves digging your heels in, risking something, sometimes risking everything, to accomplish core-level change. We are an
educated, smart, organized, generous, frustrated, and frightened
population. What better ingredients to start a revolution?

There's an idea in some social-change literature that only when
life gets truly uncomfortable do people take the necessary steps—
from ripples to revolution—to upend their world. The malaise of
privilege is supposedly the enemy of change. So it's time we began asking ourselves what it would take to make us feel "truly uncomfortable" today. In a 2005 *New York Times* poll, the bulk of respondents reported that achieving the American dream meant three
things—financial security, freedom, and contentment. Yet in that
same poll, only 32 percent felt they'd already attained these things.[4]

So what line needs to be crossed before we start objecting? Are we
content enough, free enough, secure enough that we'd really prefer to
just sit tight? Look around and ask yourself: What sort of society do

I really want to live in? What sort of society do I want to pass on to coming generations?

The choice is there.

PERSONAL RESPONSIBILITY

As individuals, one of the biggest mistakes we can make is resigning ourselves to what we consider to be our fate. How many times do we hear ourselves saying *This sucks, but this is just how it is if you want to be a [insert: teacher, environmental scientist, social worker, journalist], if you want to focus on priorities other than making money, or if you want to spend more time with your family, your community?* If we're going to act collectively to change things, one of our first steps is to reclaim and redefine the notion of personal responsibility.

We can begin by refusing to believe that the options being handed to us truly are the only ones available. Most corporate entities don't want to help the educated middle class or the working poor find more balance and economic stability in their lives. They're not looking to reestablish ethical modes of doing business, more equitably redistribute their profits, provide employees with better benefits, or make other strides that might reduce their profits. In fact, they're making a push to roll back those laws and regulations put in place by the Sarbanes-Oxley Act in 2002—enacted in the wake of Enron and other corporate scandals to more tightly regulate financial practices and corporate governance—in an effort to protect themselves from criminal and civil lawsuits filed by those who've fallen victim to their corrupt practices. They're far more concerned with protecting themselves than protecting their employees.[5]

Nor is it effective to expect government economic experts to lead the charge toward change. Those experts realize that our spending habits will shift if they in any way reinforce this sense that we're teetering. If consumer spending goes down, they fear it will endanger the economy. Their reassurances that the economy is thriving—even when on our streets and in our pocketbooks it feels like anything but—encourage people to spend beyond their means. That's the point. We should be paying attention to what's happening with our own bank accounts, paychecks, bills, and daily financial lives, not what we hear about the health of the general economy, because those figures can easily be skewed by the continued swelling of a wealthy elite. And we should act accordingly.

Instead of relying on others to inform us about our financial state, we need to become personally responsible for educating ourselves. We need to learn how the mortgage industry and credit card companies truly work. We need to look at what we're paying to purchase our homes, cars, and educations and how long it will take us to pay off things like private student loans and interest-only mortgages. We can't wait for the banks and lenders to explain it to us. It's in their best interests that we don't understand. Ask questions. Opt for the simplest, most straightforward financing options. Don't take on expenses you can't shoulder except when there truly is no other choice. Don't count on huge raises and bonuses or the prospect of finding a higher-paying job when you make major money decisions. Factor economic volatility into your financial plans.

And don't just take personal responsibility for educating yourself. Educate your children. Inject them with equal doses of idealism and economic reality. Time and again, the people I interviewed told me, "I wish I knew more about money." Looking back, they wondered whether, if they'd truly understood the impact of the financial choices they made in college and their early twenties, they might have acted differently. The foolish mistakes we make early on are no longer just foolish mistakes. They can have lifelong ramifications. Financial literacy isn't more important than social or psychological literacy, but we can't afford to ignore it, either. As parents and educators, we can see to it that a high school and college education includes teaching students about handling their money and instills in them realistic expectations about the kinds of salaries and lifestyles they can anticipate.

We also need to take the very personal step of lowering some of our material expectations and becoming more responsible about spending and debt. This is a value shift, too. We have to take it upon ourselves not to get sucked into lifestyles we can't support—no matter what sort of credit or mortgages or loans we're being offered. Know your financial reality. Know the line beyond which you'll be in over your head.

Becoming personally responsible means avoiding debt whenever possible, even if that means living beneath what you had always hoped and intended would be your means. Having to curtail your expectations doesn't mean you've failed. It means that economic circumstances beyond your control have changed and that, until they begin to shift back again, your material life will reflect those changes.

Do all you can to diminish the confusion factor when it comes to student loans, health insurance, credit card bills, home-secured debt, and retirement plans. Keep clear track of what you owe and what you're being charged. Make sure education loans, mortgages, and any financial consolidating or refinancing are explained to you and that you truly understand what you're signing up for before you commit—even if that means having three different managers explain it to you fourteen different times.

Make a budget and stick to it. Learn to differentiate between want and need. Understand and accept the financial pressures you're under, and if that pressure is more than you can manage, ask for help. Don't be afraid to seek advice on how to best afford college, save for retirement, get the mortgage that fits your income, or most sensibly refinance. If you're unsure of your options, use a financial planner. In addition, shed any shame you might feel about your financial ignorance or limitations, and ask friends who seem to be managing if they have any tips. Or spend an afternoon browsing the financial shelves at the bookstore or the library. Cherry-pick advice from some of the more practical financial-planning books, not the kind that promise to make you a millionaire in under a year but the kind that tell you where to save and where to spend when money is tight, that can explain different retirement and investment options in a down-to-earth and comprehensible way.

Most important of all, don't buy into the "you are what you make" value system. If you're to find any financial peace, it's essential you truly believe that you, your family, and your future are all worth something more.

RECLAIMING THE MEDIA

As trapped as many of us might feel, we members of the educated professional middle class are not helpless victims of our plight. We have a public voice if we choose to use it and I like to think that we're too smart, too resourceful, and too proactive to let this widening inequality gap continue to grow unchecked. We have alumni networks, community and school ties. Unlike the poor and the working class, in many cases we do have direct or indirect access to the wealthy decision makers. It's time we began plumbing that access for all it's worth, not just for ourselves but for the greater good of all members of society.

Print, television, and radio journalists seem to have treated the problems of the educated professional middle class with a collective shrug. This is particularly curious given the fact that the majority of reporters, editors, and producers occupy this precarious middle-class financial edge. Nearly every reporter, writer, artist, actor, and documentary filmmaker I've ever met knows what it's like to be in tight financial straits. This is our story. We need to let the economic news finally reflect the true economic state of America.

Beyond just the news media, contemporary films, books, and TV shows rarely depict struggling members of the educated professional middle class. Here again there's ample room for us to step up. The bulk of novelists, independent filmmakers, playwrights, and screenwriters tend to sit squarely within the confines of the creative but struggling middle class. So where's the TV show that crosses *Roseanne* with *thirtysomething?* The fictional marriage of Richard Price and Jonathan Franzen, the Paul Anderson/Todd Solondz/Mike Leigh production? It's time for the creative element of the educated professional middle class to stop suffering in martyred silence and make themselves heard.

POLITICAL PRESSURE

Members of the educated professional middle class also have a political voice. It's true that politicians care about what those with the most money for political contributions care about. But they also care about getting reelected, and that means pleasing the loudest and most organized and insistent set of voters. As intelligent, articulate members of the political system, we are in a position to demand more federal support for education, child care, health care, and retirement. We are in a position to demand change in any or all of the areas I've discussed—health care, pensions, student-loan reform, mortgage-industry regulation, and government-backed child care and parental leave. We are in a position to say that this is far more than just a financial issue, it's a moral issue about the shifting values and priorities of a country where a staggering number of people cannot manage to get by.

Despite their college degrees and middle-class rhetoric, most members of Congress are not living a middle-class life. In 2006, at least forty-six out of our one hundred senators were millionaires; as such they are most likely out of touch with not only the working class but with the educated professional middle-class experience as well.[6] But their aides, assistants, younger staffers—plus often those local politicians holding lower-level offices—are not. Think about how to begin targeting them instead. (Hint: They are the ones you went to high school and college with. They're also the ones who answer the phones.) If you tell pollsters, aides, office staff, and council people that the economy is the central issue on your mind, they will listen and pass that message on.

We can also begin to think smaller, focusing on local government rather than marching straight to the doors of our Congress members. Often state and local governments are the first to act when it comes to remedying social problems that have gotten bogged down in federal bureaucracy. We see this in Massachusetts and California, where the state governments have taken on health-care reform, or in New York attorney general Andrew Cuomo's cracking down on corruption and fraud in the student-loan industry. One of the few times the federal government has actually censured the credit card industry, fining the card company Providian for false marketing, was initiated not by the Office of the Comptroller of the Currency but by the San Francisco District Attorney's Office. So take the time to familiarize yourself with your local politicians and their stands on these issues, pressuring them whenever possible to act in ways that may ease the burden on the working poor, the missing class, and the middle class.

Of course, enhancing government spending on education, health care, and other social services costs money, and a common political retort is that, with our debt-strapped national budget, we simply don't have any to spare. One obvious way around this is through tax reform. In America today, it's not hard to figure out where the money is. It lies with the top 1 percent of the population, those making over $348,000 a year, who now receive their largest share of national income since 1928.[7] One of the most effective moves the educated professional middle class could make would be to push hard for more progressive tax laws, milking an increased percentage out of the wealthy so there's more to go into the discretionary spending pot. Eliminating just a quarter of the tax subsidies provided by the current tax code would free up $180 billion a year that could be directed to improving education, expanding health care, or any of the numerous other areas where middle- and low-income families now struggle.[8]

One of the great financial equalizers beginning in the 1930s and stretching through the '70s was progressive taxation. If you look at a graph charting income inequality over the past century, it reads like a giant U, with the high ends in the 1920s and right now and the bottom curve in the '40s, '50s, and '60s. Not coincidentally, those low-inequality years were also the years when the wealthiest tier of the population was subject to the highest income, capital gains, and estate taxes. Such aggressive taxation was initially set in place as part of the New Deal, based on the idea that people should be taxed according to their ability to pay. As a result, the wealthiest portion of the population wound up paying as much as 94 percent of their income in taxes and, between 1939 and 1945, national tax revenues escalated from $1 billion to over $18 billion. Did the rich go broke during those years? Not many of them. Nor did they stop working hard, stop taking economic risks, or stop investing their money back into the economy, many of the arguments against progressive taxation that are offered up today. In many ways, those low-inequality years represented the American economy at its healthiest. The post–World War II era was characterized by some of the most rapid growth in the history of our country, much of it benefiting the swelling middle class.[9]

Progressive taxation began to dissolve with the tax reforms of the Reagan years and tax rates on the wealthy have been falling ever since. With the arrival of the Bush administration in 2000, taxes took another dramatic swing in favor of the top tier of the population and at the expense of everyone else. Today the richest .01 percent pays just 34 percent of taxes as opposed to the 60 percent they paid as recently as 1980. As a result of such tax cuts, in 2000 the government collected nearly 21 percent of the gross domestic product in taxes but by 2004 that had dropped to just over 16 percent. Surely it's no coincidence that, since 2000, we have also shifted from a $236 billion budget surplus to a $300 billion deficit.[10]

Where do those receding tax dollars not go? Sixty percent of the federal budget is automatically spoken for to cover things like Social Security, Medicare, and interest on our escalating national debt, leaving just 40 percent left over for what's called discretionary spending. Most of that discretionary spending is also spoken for, with 23 percent going toward defense, homeland security, and international affairs, the costs of which have risen considerably since 9/11 and the onset of the Iraq war. This means that when the coffers run low, which they inevitably do in a country that's spending more and taxing less, more money gets taken away from education, social services, conservation, community development, and all those other area where the majority of the population is currently starving for help.[11]

Instead of trying to remedy this taxation imbalance, the current administration is hightailing it in the opposite direction. Though it claims recent tax cuts benefit low- and middle-income families, in truth 53 percent of Bush tax cuts go to people in the top 10 percent of the population, with more than 15 percent going to the top .1 percent of taxpayers—145,000 people who earn at least $1.6 million a year. Those earning more than $10 million a year now pay a lesser share of their income in taxes than those earning $100,000. Surely, if we want more money for increased government support, this is one of the first places where we should begin demanding change.[12]

While we're stirring up that tax pot, we can also press toward curbing the generous tax breaks provided to the wealthiest portion of the population. For example, half the tax subsidies for IRAs, 401(k)s, and other retirement accounts go to the richest one-tenth of households. In addition, the Bush tax cuts enacted in 2003 rolled back rates on capital gains to just 15 percent, as opposed to the top rate of 35 percent. This means that taxpayers owe even less on income off investments, another arena in which the extremely rich primarily benefit. Instead, we could shift toward providing tax breaks that reward individuals and corporations for taking steps to even things out—for instance by providing health insurance and retirement plans for their workers or by making charitable donations.[13] In addition, we can look more closely at how those tax dollars are distributed. We can challenge the notion that a full 23 percent of government discretionary spending must go toward defense and homeland security, when so many citizens continue to struggle with domestic concerns like education, health care, and child care. As citizens and voters, we can let our priorities be known.

With the money freed up by new tax laws, politicians would have little reason not to confront touchy issues like health care, pensions, child care, and education reform in a bold and effective way. Already in 2007, despite the resistance of the current administration, we've seen lawmakers pressing for changes in areas where current policies have become untenable to their constituents. Congress has committed to pushing through a student-loan-reform package that would reduce interest rates, increase the size of Pell Grants, and provide loan relief to students who opted for public service careers. Facing threats of an administration veto, both the House and the Senate also passed bills that extended health insurance to uninsured children in low-income families. We can continue to press state and federal politicians to debate and act upon such vital issues. And when they do come forward with plans, we can make it clear that we'll settle for nothing less than concrete and fundamental change.[14]

Some politicians counter the demands for a more responsible social contract in America with the argument that, as the richest and most productive nation in the world, our economy is working so well we can't afford change. But we have plenty of ammunition to fight this one too. In many cases, the United States falls decidedly behind other nations that face similar conditions when it comes to trade, investment, technology, and the environment. In comparing the U.S. to the nineteen other advanced industrial countries that make up the Organization for Economic Cooperation and Development, the Economic Policy Institute found us lacking in a number of critical areas. There's no question that we can learn a great deal from countries that have adopted strong welfare states and labor protections about how to take care of both our citizens and our economic health.[15]

Income inequality in the U.S. is higher than in any of these nineteen other countries; though we may have more haves, we also have more have-nots. Other countries with equally high productivity levels have found room for government-subsidized health care, child care, and pensions. They've also found room for shorter workweeks and nearly twice the vacation time, much of it federally mandated, allowing citizens to achieve life balance and deepen family ties as opposed to just toeing the economic bottom line. The United States has the highest poverty rate and, even more shaming, the highest child poverty rate of any of the OECD countries. Poverty rates were lowest in Finland, Norway, and Sweden, all nations with extremely strong government-subsidized social safety nets.[16]

Throughout this book we've examined social programs in other industrialized nations that take care of their citizens far more effectively than we do in the U.S. today—education in Finland, family leave in Sweden, health care in Canada. Here are just a few more examples we might borrow from in forming a stronger social benefit system in our own country.

In France, new parents receive sixteen weeks of paid leave with the birth of their first and second children, and twenty-six weeks for each subsequent child. Parents are also entitled to share up to three years of job-protected leave at a lower, flat-rate pay scale, allowing either parent to take time off to raise young children without fear of permanent job loss. Single parents and those who have three or more children receive an additional government supplement, and there are means-tested benefits available to help low-income families with housing and schooling costs In contrast, in the U.S. new parents receive just twelve weeks unpaid leave under the Family and Medical Leave Act, and that only if they work for a company with more than fifty employees.

Under such circumstances, child care becomes a necessity, with 54 percent of American children under three in formal-care settings. Yet our limited government child care subsidies cover only the very poor. The French, however, continue to support working parents right up until their children reach school age. Starting at two months of age, French children can attend publicly run nurseries funded by government subsidies and means-tested parental fees. They remain open eleven hours a day and all staff members are strictly trained and hold diplomas in child care. Once they're two and a half to three years old, nearly all French children move on to free government-subsidized preschools. The teachers here also have graduate training in early education and earn wages above the average for all employed women. Such across-the-board government support not only eases the economic burden of child-rearing, it also encourages parents to maintain both a healthy work and family life, rather than being forced to choose between the two as so many working- and middle-class Americans feel they must do today.[17]

Not only does France boast one of the more generous family leave and child care policies in the world, it also excels in providing government-subsidized health care for all its citizens. In the World Health Organization's most recent global rankings on health care, France came out on top of the list. (The U.S was number 37, wedged in between Costa Rica and Slovenia.) What might we learn from their successful system? First, it emphasizes universal, comprehensive care rather than cost-cutting or corporate profits. For more than 96 percent of the population, medical care is free or fully reimbursed, with the exception of small co-pays. Care for chronic diseases ranging from diabetes to cancer and critical surgeries, like coronary bypass, are covered 100 percent. The kinds of high deductibles involved in many U.S insurance plans don't exist. Regardless of their income level, individuals can choose among health care providers and have access to a range of public, private, university, and general hospitals. Though doctors are reimbursed at a lower level than most in the U.S., their lower salaries are offset by nonexistent student loans —medical school is also paid for by the state—and minimal malpractice insurance. The country boasts three doctors for every one thousand citizens, considerably more than the United States' three for every twenty-seven hundred, further ensuring timely and thorough care. Up to 80 percent of the population also carries supplemental insurance provided by their employers, which covers expenses not paid for by the government, such as private hospital rooms and dental care.

Like family leave, health insurance is a branch of the French social security system. Health care costs are funded by a combination of general revenue (40 percent) and payroll taxes (60 percent), with the government picking up the tab for the unemployed. The system is not free of problems, most to do with managing costs. National insurance has run a deficit since the mid-'80s, swelling to a current level of $13.5 million. But overall the system bears numerous markers of success. France spends 10.7 percent of its GDP on health care, far less than the 16 percent we spend in the U.S. It also boasts a considerably lower infant death rate than we do, as well as low rates of preventable diseases like diabetes, heart disease, and respiratory disease. In addition, 65 percent of the French population reports satisfaction with the health care system, a far better showing than the 40 percent of Americans willing to make the same claim.[18]

Compared to many industrialized nations, the United States also falls short when it comes to ensuring a secure pension system for its elderly population. Aside from base-level Social Security payments, which are rarely enough to live on, Americans are increasingly reliant on voluntary contribution plans like 401(k)s that essentially require them to pay for their retirements themselves. Other nations run a gamut of pension programs that combine state and private funding to secure a far more stable old age for all citizens. For example, Switzerland's old-age insurance consists of a three-pillared system that combines basic state insurance, employer-provided plans, and individual investments to ensure that as few retirees as possible fall through the cracks.

The first of the three pillars in the Swiss system is a basic old age and survivor's insurance plan available to all citizens over the age of twenty, regardless of employment or income level. The plan is primarily funded by taxes equally split between employers and employees, with additional tax revenues covering roughly 20 percent of old age and 50 percent of disability payouts. The pensions drawn depend on an individual's income level and number of years in the workforce, with bonuses provided for child care and child rearing.

The second pillar consists of company pension funds provided to all employees, funded by employee contributions ranging from 7 to 18 percent of gross salary. Such pension schemes may be run by the employers themselves or by state or private funds, and employee contribution is obligatory. Self-employed workers can also voluntarily enroll in the system. In addition to these two sources of retirement income, Swiss retirees are boosted by a third pillar that provides tax breaks for money invested in voluntary private retirement accounts. Contributions to such accounts are taxed on payment, but not withdrawal, and there is no tax on any interest such accounts might accrue. In this way, the majority of Swiss citizens can turn to multiple sources—a mix of voluntary and obligatory contributions, funded by a combination of employers, employees, and the state—to generate enough income to ensure a comfortable retirement.[19]

The above are just a few of the numerous examples of social benefits provided by economically healthy industrialized nations throughout the world. Nearly all OECD countries provide more generous unemployment, health, education, and pension benefits than the U.S. They are not socialist countries, but rather countries whose governments harbor a sense of social responsibility. Nor is the impact purely financial. There are profound societal benefits in store for countries that help their citizens. Economic support engenders comfort and security and an empowered citizenry.

Not only do too many of our politicians and corporate denizens prefer to ignore what they might learn from other nations, they also seem to be doing their level best to export America's consumerist, money-based values. Alongside the full-scale invasion by McDonalds, Coca-Cola, and Starbucks, trends show an increasing prevalence of American-style executive pay packages in Europe, as demands made by corporate honchos overseas are now measured against the high net worth of CEOs in the United States.[20] The conservative wings in Canada and a number of European countries point to the U.S. model as successful and worthy of imitation. The U.S. does hold a position of considerable global power and the choices we make as a nation have profound worldwide implications. Do we want to export our societal trends in health care, education, retirement, personal debt, and lack of social safety nets? Do we want the world to begin adopting our current personal responsibility, "more is better" value system? Or do we want to offer another model, one based more in equality, collective responsibility, and the continual possibility of progressive social change?

THE CLASSLESS CLASS

The possibility of pressing for real, concrete change is invigorating. But even if we meet with terrific success, such change will not take place overnight. Legislation can require months and even years to work its way through Congress. Once passed, it's often enacted over a similarly extended period of time. In the meantime, we need to begin thinking about what we can do to ensure more stable and contented lives for ourselves. In part, this will be a question of taking every step we can to make sensible financial choices at a time when money truly is prohibitively tight. But, even more, it's a question of finding a way to grow comfortable in our current insecurity. To believe that identity equals more than money and to learn to stretch and fill our lives in nonmaterial ways.

In his 1983 treatise on class in America, Paul Fussell introduced the notion of a category X, one whose members have slipped free of class confines and whose goals and behavior don't cohere to any upper-, middle- or working-class conventions. X status is not earned by birthright or financial scrambling, but by "strenuous effort of discovery in which curiosity and originality are indispensable."[21] Members of category X serve a critical role in our society. They are the true pursuers of liberty. Though in the course of my research I spoke to plenty of people who were terrified about the future, there were others—the most inspiring group of all—who had defied every social or economic confinement laid upon them. It required redefining priorities and making sacrifices. But they confirmed that there is, gloriously and unashamedly, a way to bypass the financially trapped trap.

Five years ago, when Pilar left her fast-track job in the entertainment industry in New York to move to New Mexico, most people told her she was crazy. But despite the fact that she had lots of friends and a potentially high-earning career, Pilar saw something the others didn't. She saw that she was miserable.

"I guess I had changed," she explains. "I wasn't ambitious for the same things. In New York, and in that job, work was everything. I couldn't be free-spirited. I couldn't travel or devote time to family. And I realized that freedom is just too important to me."

Pilar had a very clear idea of what she wanted her new life to entail, including a dog, a pickup truck, and falling in love with a man who wasn't engaged in a single-minded charge to the top. She wanted to be in a city with trees, water, land for miles, and air she could actually breathe.

In abandoning her New York lifestyle, Pilar split with everything she'd once assumed she desired and would become. Though her parents divorced when she was young and her mother never had much money, Pilar graduated from one of the top East Coast liberal arts colleges, an education financed by a combination of grants and only recently paid off student loans. From there she went straight to Manhattan, nabbed a job as an assistant in a major entertainment company, and began working her way up the ladder. She was smart, focused, and outgoing, possessing all the ingredients for an educated professional middle-class success story. But about ten years in, Pilar went to New Mexico to visit her mother and when she returned to the city she realized she couldn't stay.

Once she'd moved to New Mexico, Pilar found a job at a local arts festival—earning a third of her New York salary—and waited tables on the weekends to make enough to put a down payment on that pickup truck and cover her rent. She got the dog. A year after moving, she met Eli, a photographer and elementary school teacher. They married two years later and, shortly after their wedding, Pilar got pregnant.

Today, Pilar earns $27,000 as the conference director for that same arts festival. Eli makes $25,000 teaching school, with the occasional small cash influx when he sells one of his photos. The family of three rents half of a small duplex for $950 a month in a neighborhood packed with $400,000 to $800,000 homes. They have one car, a ten-year-old Jeep Cherokee. Through living frugally, they have been able to save $10,000, with another $11,000 in their combined 401(k)s. And they have no debt.

"Sometimes I look at how much money we make and I really do

wonder how we scrape by," Pilar admits. "But we just forgo the luxuries and somehow it always manages to work out."

Even at age thirty-five, Pilar isn't overly concerned with their inability to afford bigger-ticket items like a home or a second car. She and Eli have set other priorities for themselves and how they want to raise their six-month-old son, Rowan.

"We're not buying a house any time soon. I see other people become such financial slaves to their homes. They're cash poor, time poor, energy poor. That's not what we want for ourselves right now. We're choosing freedom instead."

The arts festival has been exceedingly child friendly, something Pilar sees as a benefit of working for a small, creatively inclined nonprofit. Since she returned from her three-month maternity leave, she has pared her workweek down to four days. Two of those days she works from home and the other two she brings Rowan into the office with her, eliminating the need for child care. Even better, she gets to spend loads of time with her son.

"This works perfectly for now," she tells me, "though I know I won't be at the festival forever. It's small and, beyond what I'm doing now, there's really no place for me to grow. I have no idea what I'll ultimately do. Our larger plans have more to do with traveling, learning languages, and giving Rowan as broad and rich a range of life experiences as we can."

Pilar grew up in South America and, when Rowan is a year old, she and Eli plan to go back there. They're going to quit their jobs, collect their savings, and travel the continent for at least six months to a year, though Pilar could easily foresee staying much longer.

"We have no return date," she states emphatically. "We could be gone two, three, even five or six years. I grew up traveling. We spent lots of time on the road and I loved it. I want Rowan to experience that too. I want him to know that there are other cultures and other ways to be."

They plan to borrow some money from Pilar's mother to pad out their savings and just go as far as they can on what they have. They'll travel on the cheap, staying with family friends, perhaps renting a house on the beach in some small town for a few months. If they run low on money, Eli can always find work teaching English.

"Once you get out of America, things are cheaper and money stops being such an obstacle to quality of life. I have no doubt we'll figure out a way."

Pilar and Eli see their future as full of adventures and possibilities, no matter what their financial limitations. There's no question they've chosen category X, to step outside the conventional middle-class expectations, shed any former dreams for material possessions, and look for a life that's deeper in experience and meaning instead. Pilar admits she worries about their financial future, particularly how they would weather any sort of health crisis, but she refuses to accept that the only path to freedom is via cash in your pocket.

"I guess it's a question of deciding what's important to you," she tells me. "Sure there's money to think about. But there are so many more exciting and rewarding things out there too."

On some level, we all have the potential to become Pilar and Eli, to toss aside our ambitions, our suffering, and our angst. We can all upend our currents lives and reconfigure them according to what we truly aspire to and believe. I don't mean ten and twenty years down the line, if indeed financial realities have changed by then. I mean right now. Today.

If there's one thing we must keep in mind about our current economic situation it is this: We are not failures and we are not alone. We have it within us—every single one of us—to fight back if we so choose. Don't just tentatively poke at the boundaries of how life might be. Bust through them with all the power you can muster.

Be active. Be vocal. Be creative. Be radical. This is your life. Make it matter.

ACKNOWLEDGMENTS

First and foremost, I'm grateful to all those who were generous and open enough to share their stories, their fears, doubts, and dreams, and their intimate financial details with me, answering almost any question I dared to ask. Without them, this book would simply be a dry stack of numbers. Also to Heather Boushey, Matthieu Leimgruber, and Alexander von Hoffman for sharing their national and international economic expertise, and to Nick Von Hoffman, who served as a stellar compass for what's smart, accurate, and passionate.

As always, thanks to my parents for their unflagging support no matter what sort of curveball I've seen fit to throw them, and I've thrown a few.

My deepest appreciation to Gayatri Patnaik and Tracy Ahlquist at Beacon Press for their editorial insights, forwarded articles, and inevitably timely responses to even the smallest of queries. I'm thrilled that this book has found such an intelligent and welcoming home.

And above all to Tanya McKinnon, who first saw this as a book, who found it a home, who's been integral in helping me reshape my definitions of ambition, success, and values, and for whom the label of "agent" falls billions, perhaps even trillions, of miles short.

NOTES

1. THE NEW REALITY

1. Ehrenreich, *Fear of Falling*, 14.
2. Mishel, Bernstein, and Allegretto, *The State of Working America 2006/2007*, 26–27; Demos and Center for Responsible Lending, *The Plastic Safety Net*, 20.
3. U.S. Senate Committee on Health, Education, Labor, and Pensions and Senate Democratic Policy Committee, *The College Cost Crunch*, 2.
4. Mishel, Bernstein, and Allegretto, *The State of Working America 2006/2007*, 27.
5. Hacker, *The Great Risk Shift* (2006), 31.
6. Ibid., 101; National Association of Child Care Resource and Referral Agencies, *Breaking the Piggy Bank*, 10.
7. Joint Center for Housing Studies of Harvard University, *The State of the Nation's Housing 2006*, 9.
8. Silva, *A House of Cards*; Crustsinger, "Savings Tumble Poses Risk to Boomers."
9. Weller and Staub, *Middle Class in Turmoil*, 4.
10. Mishel, Bernstein, and Allegretto, *The State of Working America 2006/2007*, "Wealth," 23.
11. Kaiser Family Foundation, *Employer Health Benefits 2006*, 1, 4.
12. Day, "Retirement, Squeezed"; Hacker, *The Great Risk Shift* (2008), 122.
13. Samuelson, "What's the Biggest Threat to the U.S. Economy?"
14. U.S. PIRG Higher Education Project, *Paying Back, Not Giving Back*, 5–6, 10–11.
15. Newman and Chen, *The Missing Class*.
16. Warren and Tyagi, *The Two-Income Trap*, 230; DeNavas-Walt, Proctor, and Lee, *Income, Poverty, and Health Insurance Coverage in the United States, 2005*, 17.
17. Johnston, "Income Gap Is Widening, Data Shows"; Crustsinger, "Savings Tumble Poses Risk to Boomers."

2. FROM THE NEW DEAL TO THE NEW ECONOMY

1. Follansbee, "The Disappearing Middle Class," 105.
2. Correspondents of the *New York Times*, *Class Matters*, 24, 253.
3. Ibid., 24; White House Economics Statistics Briefing Room, "Income"; Weller and Staub, *Middle Class in Turmoil*, 4.
4. Correspondents of the *New York Times*, *Class Matters*, 25.
5. Ehrenreich, *Fear of Falling*, 15.
6. Kennedy, *Freedom from Fear*, 13.
7. Bernstein, *All Together Now*, 30.
8. Kennedy, *Freedom from Fear*, 163.
9. These programs included the Civil Works Administration, the Federal Deposit Insurance Corporation, the Federal Housing Administration, the Fair Labor Standards Act, the Public Works Administration, the Social Security Administration, the Securities and Exchange Commission, the Tennessee Valley Authority, and the Works Progress Administration.
10. Kennedy, *Freedom from Fear*, 365.
11. Ibid., 378.
12. Phillips, *Boiling Point*, 15.
13. Halberstam, *The Fifties*, 506; Coontz, *The Way We Never Were*, 171, 174.
14. Phillips, *Boiling Point*, 17–18.
15. Coontz, *The Way We Never Were*, 76–78.
16. Uchitelle, *The Disposable American*, 137.
17. McCall, *The Inequality Economy*, 19; Krugman, "Wages, Wealth and Politics."
18. Leicht and Fitzgerald, *Postindustrial Peasants*, 84; Phillips, *Boiling Point*, 42.
19. Phillips, *Boiling Point*, 50.
20. Ibid., 20.
21. Hacker, *The Great Risk Shift* (2006), 120.
22. Mishel, Bernstein, and Allegretto, *The State of Working America 2006/ 2007*, 23.
23. Florida, *The Rise of the Creative Class*, 48.
24. Uchitelle, *The Disposable American*, 145, 163.
25. Kornbluh and Bernstein, *Running Faster to Stay in Place*.
26. Gosselin, "If America Is Richer, Why Are Its Families So Much Less Secure?"
27. Aron-Dine and Shapiro, *New Data Show Extraordinary Jump in Income Concentration in 2004*.
28. Kennedy, *Freedom from Fear*, 163; U.S. Department of Labor, Bureau of Labor Statistics, "Annual Averages: Unemployment Rate"; Central Intelligence Agency, *The World Factbook*.

29. Greenhouse and Leonhardt, "Real Wages Fail to Match a Rise in Productivity."

30. Mishel, Bernstein, and Allegretto, *The State of Working America 2006/2007*, 12, 15, 24.

31. Economic Policy Institute, *The State of Working America 2006/2007*, "Facts and Figures: Income"; Krugman, "Wages, Wealth and Politics."

32. Ahrens, "The Super-Rich Get Richer"; Johnston, "Income Gap Is Widening, Data Shows."

33. Correspondents of the *New York Times*, *Class Matters*, 183, 185.

34. Wessell and Davis, "Pain from Free Trade Spurs Second Thoughts."

35. Appel, "More Uninsured Means More Healthcare Corporate Profits."

36. Correspondents of the *New York Times*, *Class Matters*, 12–14.

37. Coontz, *The Way We Never Were*, 168.

38. U.S. Department of Labor, Bureau of Labor Statistics, "Employment Status of the Civilian Population 16 Years and Over by Sex 1971 to Date"; U.S. Department of Labor, Women's Bureau, "Quick Facts."

39. Coontz, *The Way We Never Were*, 163, 168.

40. Selvin, "More Wives Becoming Primary Breadwinners."

41. U.S. Department of Labor, Women's Bureau, "Quick Facts."

42. Selvin, "More Wives Becoming Primary Breadwinners."

43. Warren and Tyagi, *The Two-Income Trap*, 13, 160; Hacker, *The Great Risk Shift* (2006), 7, 105.

44. Patillo-McCoy, *Black Picket Fences*, 17, 210.

45. DeNavas-Walt, Proctor, and Lee, *Income, Poverty, and Health Insurance Coverage in the United States, 2005*, 16. The population as a whole is 71.7 percent white, 12.2 percent black, 3.7 percent Asian, and 10.9 percent Hispanic.

46. Wheary, *Measuring the Middle*, 12.

47. Silva and Epstein, *Costly Credit*, 7.

48. Ibid.; Mishel, Bernstein, and Allegretto, *The State of Working America 2006/2007*, "Income," 13.

49. Hacker, *The Great Risk Shift* (2006), 27; Economic Policy Institute, *The State of Working America 2006/2007*, "Facts and Figures: Wealth."

3. COLLEGE PROMISES

1. Hennessy-Fiske, "That Raise Might Take 4 Years to Earn as Well"; Boushey, *Student Debt*, 7.

2. Wheary, *Measuring the Middle*, 18.

3. Correspondents of the *New York Times*, *Class Matters*, 25.

4. Mishel, Bernstein, and Allegretto, *The State of Working America 2006/2007*, table 3.17; Draut, *Strapped*, 54.

5. Correspondents of the *New York Times, Class Matters,* 21.

6. Hacker, *The Great Risk Shift* (2006), 74.

7. Nocera, "Sallie Mae Offers a Lesson on Cashing In."

8. Three-quarters of full-time college students hold down jobs to help pay for living expenses. Draut, *Strapped,* 45.

9. Sharkey, *Paying for Postsecondary Education,* 6.

10. Singletary, "College Costs."

11. Draut, *Strapped,* 55; Draut and Silva, *Generation Broke,* 7.

12. Draut, *Strapped,* 30; U.S. Senate Committee on Health, Education, Labor, and Pensions and Senate Democratic Policy Committee, *The College Cost Crunch,* 2–3.

13. Schemo, "Private Loans Deepen a Crisis in Student Debt"; Sturrock, "Private Loans Prove Costly for College Students"; Singletary, "College Costs."

14. Department of Education, "Repaying Your Student Loans"; Lederman, "Social Security and Defaulted Student Loans."

15. Draut, *Strapped,* 34; Berman, "Student Debt Crisis."

16. Draut and Silva, *Generation Broke,* 7.

17. Hacker, "The Rich and Everyone Else."

18. Draut and Silva, *Generation Broke,* 6; Mishel, Bernstein, and Allegretto, *The State of Working America 2006/2007,* 17.

19. Glater and Finder, "In Tuition Game, Popularity Rises with Price."

20. Glater, "Offering Perks, Lenders Court Colleges' Favor"; Glater, "College Officers Profited by Sale of Lender Stock"; Arenson and Schemo, "Report Details Deals in Student Loan Industry."

21. U.S. Department of Labor, Bureau of Labor Statistics, "May 2006 National and Occupational Employment and Wage Estimates United States"; "Editorial: The Decline and Fall of the Tenured Class," *Writer's Chronicle.*

22. Progress Report, "College Just Got a Lot Costlier."

23. Draut, *Strapped,* 33; Glater and Arenson, "Lenders Sought Edge against U.S. in Student Loans."

24. Sharkey, *Paying for Postsecondary Education,* 8; Glater and Arenson, "Lenders Sought Edge against U.S. in Student Loans"; Kunin, "A Math Lesson on College Loans."

25. Schemo, "Congress Passes Overhaul of Student Aid Programs."

26. Educational Policy Institute, *Global Higher Education Rankings,* 5.

27. Ibid., 54, 64; International Education Site, "Higher Education in Finland"; European Industrial Relations Observatory On-line, "Study Finds That 'Education Pays'"; College Board, "Education Pays," 10.

4. CAREER AND CONTRIBUTION

1. Eckstrom, "Student Debt Burdens New Pastors."
2. U.S Department of Labor, Bureau of Labor Statistics, "May 2006 National and Occupational Employment and Wage Estimates United States."
3. U.S. PIRG Higher Education Project, *Paying Back, Not Giving Back,* 5–6, 10–11.
4. U.S Department of Labor, Bureau of Labor Statistics, "Tomorrow's Jobs," 5.
5. Hacker, *The Great Risk Shift* (2008), 14, 27–28.
6. Bernhardt et al., *Divergent Paths,* 84–86.
7. Ibid., 65.
8. Bordoff, Deich, and Orszag, *A Growth-Enhancing Approach to Economic Security,* 6–7.
9. Hacker, *The Great Risk Shift* (2006), 63, 70, 72.
10. Draut, *Strapped,* 73.
11. Manning, *Credit Card Nation,* 234, 360.
12. Florida, *The Rise of the Creative Class.*
13. Osborne, "Marketplace of Ideas."
14. National Endowment for the Arts, "Financial Summary"; Pogrebin, "Arts Organizations Adjust to Decline in Funding"; White House Office of Management and Budget, "The Department of Defense"; Shah, "World Military Spending."
15. Pearce, *The Self-Sufficiency Standard for the City of New York 2004.*
16. Keegan et al., *Creative New York.*

5. TO HAVE OR TO HOLD

1. Armour, "High Costs of Child Care Can Lead to Lifestyle Changes, Adjustments"; Cassidy, "For the Best Child Care Start Looking Early."
2. Orenstein, *Flux,* 24.
3. Roberts, "To Be Married Means to Be Outnumbered."
4. Duggan and Kim, "Beyond Gay Marriage."
5. Warren and Tyagi, *The Two-Income Trap,* 51; Hacker, "False Positive," 4.
6. Warren and Tyagi, *The Two-Income Trap,* 7; Hacker, *The Great Risk Shift* (2006), 94, 101.
7. Draut, *Strapped,* 150–52.
8. Mishel, Bernstein, and Allegretto, *The State of Working America 2006/ 2007,* "International Comparisons," 12, "Family Income," 51; National Women's Law Center. "The Reality of the Workforce."

9. Martin et al., "Births: Final Data for 2004," 7.

10. Orenstein, *Flux,* 215.

11. Southern California Center for Reproductive Medicine, "IVF Cost Information."

12. Warren and Tyagi, *The Two-Income Trap,* 30; Armour, "High Costs of Child Care Can Lead to Lifestyle Changes, Adjustments."

13. Heymann et al., *The Work, Family and Equity Index,* 11.

14. Ibid., 7, 36. See full document for more detailed comparisons between nations.

15. Warren and Tyagi, *The Two-Income Trap,* 39.

16. Ibid., 13; McNally, "The Mommy Wage Gap."

17. U.S. Department of Labor, Bureau of Labor Statistics, "Time Spent in Primary Activities and Percent of the Civilian Population Engaging in Each Activity, Averages Per day by Sex, 2006 Annual Averages"; Ehrenreich, "A Grubby Business."

18. Boushey, "Mommies Opting Out of Work."

19. Ibid.

20. Coontz, *Marriage, a History,* 268.

21. Hacker, *The Great Risk Shift* (2006), 105.

22. Harden, "Numbers Drop for the Married with Children."

23. Coontz, *Marriage, a History,* 270–71.

24. Warren and Tyagi, *The Two-Income Trap,* 113.

25. Ibid., 6, 104.

26. Hacker, *The Great Risk Shift* (2006), 103.

27. United Nations Statistics Division, "Statistics and Indicators on Women and Men."

6. WHAT WERE THE BENEFITS?

1. Mattera, "Private Health Insurance Is Not the Answer."

2. Hacker, *The Great Risk Shift* (2006), 45.

3. Phillips, *Boiling Point,* 154.

4. Kaiser Family Foundation, *Employer Health Benefits 2006*; Lyman, "Census Reports Slight Increase in '05 Incomes."

5. Pear, "Without Health Benefits, a Good Life Turns Fragile"; Schoen et al., *Public Views on Shaping the Future of the U.S. Health System,* 15; Hacker, *The Great Risk Shift* (2006), 138.

6. Kaiser Family Foundation. *Employer Health Benefits 2006.*

7. Fuhrmans, "Citing Cost Concerns, More Workers Leave Firms' Health Plans."

8. Kaiser Family Foundation, *Employer Health Benefits 2006.*

9. Hacker, *The Great Risk Shift* (2006), 138–39.

10. Girion, "Study Says Individual Insurance Too Costly"; Pear, "Without Health Benefits, a Good Life Turns Fragile."

11. Draut, *Strapped,* 73.

12. Zedlin and Rukavina, *Borrowing to Stay Healthy,* 12; Warren and Tyagi, *The Two-Income Trap,* 84.

13. Mattera, "Private Health Insurance Is Not the Answer"; Appel, "More Uninsured Means More Healthcare Corporate Profits."

14. Mattera, "Private Health Insurance Is Not the Answer"; Bartlett and Steele, *Critical Condition,* 69, 199.

15. Mishel, Bernstein, and Allegretto, *The State of Working America 2006/ 2007,* "International Comparisons," 30. The countries surveyed were Australia, Austria, Belgium, Canada, Denmark, Finland, France, Germany, Ireland, Italy, Japan, the Netherlands, New Zealand, Norway, Spain, Sweden, Switzerland, and the United Kingdom.

16. Ibid., 32; "Canadian Health Care."

17. Saperstein, "Medicare for All"; Dressel, "Has Canada Got the Cure?"

18. Bartlett and Steele, *Critical Condition,* 4, 164, 184. See the full book for a more in-depth analysis of the state of the health-care industry.

19. Ibid., 15.

20. Ibid., 172.

21. Mishel, Bernstein, and Allegretto, *The State of Working America 2006/ 2007,* "International Comparisons," 31; Krugman, "Gold-Plated Indifference"; Bartlett and Steele, *Critical Condition,* 70.

22. Perez-Pena, "A Budget with a Breakthrough in Child Health Care"; Mass Care: The New Massachusetts Healthcare Law; State of California, "Governor's Health Care Proposal."

23. Freudenheim, "Company Clinics Cut Health Costs."

24. Gladwell, "The Moral-Hazard Myth."

25. Kaiser Family Foundation, *Employer Health Benefits 2006,* 5; Bernstein, *All Together Now,* 25; Hacker, *The Great Risk Shift* (2006), 152.

26. See Campaign for America's Future at http://home.ourfuture.org/; Citizens Healthcare Working Group at www.citizenshealthcare.gov/; The Commonwealth Fund at www.cmwf.org/; and Economic Policy Institute's "Agenda for Shared Prosperity" at www.sharedprosperity.org/.

27. Bernstein, *All Together Now,* 97; Schoen et al., *Public Views on Shaping the Future of the U.S. Health System,* 18.

28. Mishel, Bernstein, and Allegretto, *The State of Working America 2006/ 2007,* "International Comparisons," 34; National Coalition on Health Care, "Health Insurance Cost."

29. Gladwell, "The Moral-Hazard Myth"; Stark, "Medicare for All."

30. For a more detailed description of "Health Care for America" go to the Economic Policy Institute's "Agenda for Shared Prosperity" at www.sharedprosperity.org/bp180.html.

31. Schoen et al. *Public Views on Shaping the Future of the U.S. Health System,* 17.
32. Ruffenach, "Many Households Are at Risk in Their Retirement Finances."
33. Uchitelle, *The Disposable American,* 31.
34. Hacker, *The Great Risk Shift* (2006), 112.
35. Ibid.; Frontstin, *Savings Needed to Fund Health Insurance and Health Care Expenses in Retirement.*
36. For a more in-depth examination of the state of Social Security see Lowenstein, "A Question of Numbers."
37. Hacker, *The Great Risk Shift* (2006), 119.
38. Creswell, "Pay Packages Allow Executives to Jump Ship with Less Risk."
39. Mishel, Bernstein, and Allegretto, *The State of Working America 2006/ 2007,* "Wealth," 19; Day, "Retirement, Squeezed."
40. Singletary, "The Racing Savings Gap."
41. Hacker, *The Great Risk Shift* (2008), 122–23.
42. Draut and McGhee, *Retiring in the Red,* 4.
43. Frontstin, *Savings Needed to Fund Health Insurance and Health Care Expenses in Retirement.*
44. For more details on the universal 401(k) see Hacker, *The Great Risk Shift* (2006), 185–86.

7. BRIDGING THE GAPS

1. Warren and Tyagi, *The Two-Income Trap,* 15–54.
2. Weller and Staub, *Middle Class in Turmoil,* 14.
3. Treasury Direct, "The Debt to the Penny and Who Holds It."
4. Putnam, *Bowling Alone,* 272–73.
5. Economic Policy Institute, *The State of Working America 2006/2007,* "Facts and Figures: Wealth"; Mishel, Bernstein, and Allegretto, *The State of Working America 2006/2007,* 17; Bucks, Kennickell, and Moore, *Recent Changes in U.S. Family Finances*; Mishel, Bernstein, and Allegretto, *The State of Working America 2006/2007,* "Wealth," 24; Crustsinger, "Savings Tumble Poses Risk to Boomers."
6. Weller and Staub, *Middle Class in Turmoil,* 4.
7. Bahney, "The Bank of Mom and Dad."
8. Ehrenreich, *Fear of Falling,* 14–15.
9. Phillips, *Boiling Point,* 192; Porter, "Empty Nest Eggs."
10. Patillo-McCoy, *Black Picket Fences,* 2; Economic Policy Institute, *The State of Working America 2006/2007,* "Facts and Figures: Wealth."
11. Patillo-McCoy, *Black Picket Fences,* 53.

12. Manning, *Credit Card Nation,* 6; Demos and Center for Responsible Lending, *The Plastic Safety Net,* 4–5.

13. Demos and Center for Responsible Lending, *The Plastic Safety Net,* 8.

14. Ibid., 11.

15. Nellie Mae, *Undergraduate Students and Credit Cards in 2004,* 2; Manning, *Credit Card Nation,* 178.

16. Draut and Silva, *Generation Broke,* 1.

17. Demos and Center for Responsible Lending, *The Plastic Safety Net,* 7; Chu, "Retirees Up Against Debt"; Draut and McGhee, *Retiring in the Red,* 1–2.

18. Warren and Tyagi, *The Two-Income Trap,* 131.

19. *Frontline,* "Secret History of the Credit Card," interview with Christopher Dodd; Draut, *Strapped,* 104–5.

20. Manning, *Credit Card Nation,* 298. For those interested in a more detailed account of the inner workings of the credit card industry, Manning's book provides an excellent resource.

21. Ibid., 102.

22. Draut, *Strapped,* 104.

23. *Frontline,* "Secret History of the Credit Card," interviews with Edmund Mierzwinski and Julie Williams.

24. Speer, "Congress Takes Up Complaints on Credit Cards."

8. A QUESTION OF EQUITY

1. Joint Center for Housing Studies of Harvard University, *The State of the Nation's Housing 2006,* 33.

2. Saulny, "Rent's Bite Is Big in Kansas, Too."

3. Joint Center for Housing Studies of Harvard University, *The State of the Nation's Housing 2006,* 9.

4. Mishel, Bernstein, and Allegretto, *The State of Working America 2006/2007,* "Wealth," 12.

5. The online sources I consulted included Nationwide, Lending Tree, Bank of America, National Mortgage Alliance, Majestic Home Mortgage, and Sunset Mortgage.

6. Correspondents of *The New York Times, Class Matters,* 254.

7. Knox, "Apartment Rents Expected to Rise 5%."

8. Joint Center for Housing Studies of Harvard University, *The State of the Nation's Housing 2006,* 22; Knox, "Apartment Rents Expected to Rise 5%."

9. Scott, "The Apartment Atop the Garage Is Back in Vogue."

10. Rose, "The Most Expensive Rental Markets in America": Leonhardt,

"A Word of Advice during a Housing Slump"; MSN Real Estate, "The Most Expensive U.S. Cities for Renters."

11. Milchman, "The 40-Year-Old Roommate"; Scott, "Out of College, but Now Living in Urban Dorms."

12. U.S. Census Bureau, "Historical Census of Housing Tables"; Economic Policy Institute, *The State of Working America 2006/2007*, "Facts and Figures: Wealth."

13. Mishel, Bernstein, and Allegretto, *The State of Working America 2006/2007*, 23–25; Bucks, Kennickell, and Moore, *Recent Changes in U.S. Family Finances*, 28.

14. Bogardus Drew, *Buying for Themselves*, 17.

15. Bucks, Kennickell, and Moore, *Recent Changes in U.S. Family Finances*, 28; Masnick, Di, and Belsky, *Emerging Cohort Trends in Housing Debt and Home Equity*, 27.

16. Bucks, Kennickell, and Moore, *Recent Changes in U.S. Family Finances*, 28.

17. Perkins, "Nation Doomed to 2 Million Foreclosures"; Warren and Tyagi, *The Two-Income Trap*, 133.

18. Darlin, "Keep Eyes Fixed on Your Variable-Rate Mortgage"; Downey, "Mortgage-Trapped."

19. Lewis, *Liar's Poker*, 85, 108.

20. Apgar and Calder, *The Dual Mortgage Market*, 6, 7; Cho, "Housing Boom Tied to Sham Mortgages."

21. Apgar and Calder, *The Dual Mortgage Market*, 8; Cho, "Housing Boom Tied to Sham Mortgages"; Bajaj and Haughney, "Tremors at the Door."

22. Rothschild, "Attack of the Mortgage Vultures"; Perkins, "Nation Doomed to 2 Million Foreclosures."

23. Demos, *Building the American Dream*.

24. Nothaft and Change, *Refinance and the Accumulation of Home Equity Wealth*, 22.

25. Apgar and Calder, *The Dual Mortgage Market*, 12; Downey, "Report: High Cost Loans on the Rise"; Warren and Tyagi, *The Two-Income Trap*, 136.

26. Scott and Archibold, "Across Nation, Housing Costs Rise as Burden."

27. Warren and Tyagi, *The Two-Income Trap*, 231; Joint Center for Housing Studies of Harvard University, *The State of the Nation's Housing 2006*, 27.

28. Warren and Tyagi, *The Two-Income Trap*, 135–36.

29. Knox, "Buyers in More Markets Find Housing Out of Reach."

30. Karger, "America's Exploding Mortgage Crisis."

31. Goodnough, "Housing Slump Pinches States in Pocketbook."

32. Bajaj and Leonhardt, "Home for Sale, by Anxious Owner."

33. Silva, *A House of Cards.*

34. Bucks, Kennickell, and Moore, *Recent Changes in U.S. Family Finances,* 28: Kennickell and Shack-Marquez, *Changes in Family Finances from 1983 to 1989,* 12.

35. Booza, Cutsinger, and Galster, *Where Did They Go?* 1, 9, 19.

36. Personal interview.

37. Di, *"Million-Dollar" Homes and Wealth in the United States,* 11–13.

38. Shulman, "Middle Class Enclave in N.Y. Is Sold, and Tenants Worry"; Roberts, "In Surge in Manhattan Toddlers, Rich White Families Lead Way."

39. Follansbee, "The Disappearing Middle Class."

40. Correspondents of *The New York Times, Class Matters,* 22; Booza, Cutsinger, and Galster, *Where Did They Go?* 12.

41. Max, "Free Land in the Heartland."

42. Jacobs, *The Death and Life of Great American Cities,* 4.

43. Putnam, *Bowling Alone,* 193.

44. Bagli, "$5.4 Billion Bid Wins Complexes in New York Deal."

45. Sharoff, "A Bet That Urban and Affordable Can Coexist."

9. FROM RIPPLES TO REVOLUTION

1. For further reading and research on progressive activism and economic policy, see the following: the Center for Economic Policy Research, www.cepr.net/; Demos, www.demos.org/home.cfm; the Economic Policy Institute's "Agenda for Sharing Prosperity," www.shared prosperity.org/; the Freelancer's Union, www.freelancersunion.org/; the Hamilton Project at the Brookings Institution, www.brook.edu/es/ hamilton/hamilton_hp.htm; the Living Wage Campaign, www.living wagecampaign.org/; and United Professionals, www.unitedprofession als.org/.

2. Quoted in Kennedy, *Freedom from Fear.*

3. National Priorities Projects, "The War in Iraq Costs"; Bernstein, "There's Always Money for War."

4. Correspondents of *The New York Times, Class Matters,* 248.

5. Labaton, "Businesses Seek Protection on Legal Front."

6. Schwarz, "Politicians' Middle-Class Delusions."

7. Johnston, "Income Gap Is Widening, Data Shows."

8. Mallaby, "Attacking Inequality."

9. Piketty and Saez, *Income Inequality in the United States 1913–2002,* 10; Thorndike, "The Price of Civilization."

10. Krugman, "Whining over Discontent"; Lilly, *Should Advocates of Domestic Investment Worry about Tax Cuts?*

11. Lilly, *Should Advocates of Domestic Investment Worry about Tax Cuts?*

12. Correspondents of *The New York Times, Class Matters,* 182.

13. Mallaby, "Attacking Inequality"; Cohen, "The Filthy Rich Are Different from You and Me."

14. Palmer, "Student Loan Reform": Pear, "House Passes Children's Health Plan 225–204." See the Economic Policy Institute's *Agenda for Shared Prosperity* for further suggestions on how to improve the current social contract, at www.sharedprosperity.org/bp184.html.

15. Mishel, Bernstein, and Allegretto, *The State of Working America 2006/2007,* "International Comparisons."

16. Ibid., 12, 14, 27.

17. Heymann et al., *The Work, Family and Equity Index,* 33; Expatica, "A Guide to Daycare in France"; United Nations Statistics Division, "Statistics and Indicators on Women and Men"; Meyers and Gornik, "The European Model"; "Right Time for a Baby."

18. World Health Organization, *The World Health Report 2000,* 152; Embassy of France in the United States, "The French Health Care System"; Capell, "The French Lesson in Health Care."

19. U.S. Social Security Administration Office of Policy, "International Update: Recent Developments in Foreign Public and Private Pensions"; Just Landed, "Guide: Switzerland."

20. Fabrikant, "U.S.-Style Pay Packages Are All the Rage in Europe."

21. Fussell, *Class,* 212.

BIBLIOGRAPHY

Ahrens, Frank. "The Super-Rich Get Richer: Forbes 400 Are All Billionaires." *Washington Post,* September 22, 2006.

Apgar, William C., and Allegra Calder. *The Dual Mortgage Market: The Persistence of Discrimination in Mortgage Lending.* Cambridge, Mass.: Joint Center for Housing Studies of Harvard University, December 2005.

Appel, Adrianne. "More Uninsured Means More Healthcare Corporate Profits." *AlterNet,* April 10, 2007, www.alternet.org/healthwellness/50360/.

Arenson, Karen W., and Diana Jean Schemo. "Report Details Deals in Student Loan Industry." *New York Times,* June 15, 2007.

Armour, Stephanie. "High Costs of Child Care Can Lead to Lifestyle Changes, Adjustments." *USA Today,* April 18, 2006.

Aron-Dine, Aviva, and Isaac Shapiro. *New Data Show Extraordinary Jump in Income Concentration in 2004.* Washington, D.C.: Center on Budget and Policy Priorities, July 25, 2006.

Bagli, Charles V. "$5.4 Billion Bid Wins Complexes in New York Deal." *New York Times,* October 18, 2006.

Bahney, Anna. "The Bank of Mom and Dad." *New York Times,* April 20, 2006.

Bajaj, Vikas, and Christine Haughney. "Tremors at the Door." *New York Times,* January 26, 2007.

Bajaj, Vikas, and David Leonhardt. "Home for Sale, by Anxious Owner." *New York Times,* August 25, 2006.

Bartlett, Donald, and James Steele. *Critical Condition: How Healthcare in America Became Big Business—and Bad Medicine.* New York: Basic Books, 2004.

Berman, Talia. "Student Debt Crisis: Are There Any Solutions?" *AlterNet,* August 23, 2006, www.alternet.org/story/40187/.

Bernhardt, Annette, et al. *Divergent Paths: Economic Mobility in the New American Labor Market.* New York: Russell Sage Foundation, 2001.

Bernstein, Jared. *All Together Now: Common Sense for a Fair Economy.* San Francisco: Berrett-Koehler, 2006.

———. "There's Always Money for War." *AlterNet,* March 14, 2007, www.alternet.org/waroniraq/49194/.

Bogardus Drew, Rachel. *Buying for Themselves: An Analysis of Unmarried Female Home Buyers.* Cambridge, Mass.: Joint Center for Housing Studies of Harvard University, June 2006.

Booza, Jason C., Jackie Cutsinger, and George Galster. *Where Did They Go? The Decline of Middle-Income Neighborhoods in Metropolitan America.* Washington, D.C.: Brookings Institution, June 2006.

Bordoff, Jason E., Michael Deich, and Peter R. Orszag. *A Growth-Enhancing Approach to Economic Security.* Washington, D.C.: Brookings Institution, September 2006.

Boushey, Heather. "Mommies Opting Out of Work: A Myth That Won't Die." *AlterNet,* June 9, 2007, www.alternet.org/rights/53464/.

———. *Student Debt: Bigger and Bigger.* Washington, D.C.: Center for Economic and Policy Research, September 2005.

Bucks, Brian K., Arthur B. Kennickell, and Kevin B. Moore. *Recent Changes in U.S. Family Finances: Evidence from the 2001 and 2004 Survey of Consumer Finances.* Washington, D.C.: Federal Reserve Board, 2004.

Callahan, David, Tamara Draut, and Javier Silva. *Millions to the Middle: Three Strategies to Expand the Middle Class.* New York: Demos, August 30, 2004.

"Canadian Health Care." www.canadian-healthcare.org/.

Capell, Kerry. "The French Lesson in Health Care." *Business Week,* June 28, 2007.

Cassidy, Tina. "For the Best Child Care Start Looking Early." *Boston Globe,* September 17, 2006.

Central Intelligence Agency. *The World Factbook.* https://www.cia.gov/library/publications/the-world-factbook/.

Chambers, Veronica. *Having It All? Black Women and Success.* New York: Doubleday, 2003.

Cho, David. "Housing Boom Tied to Sham Mortgages." *Washington Post,* April 10, 2007.

Chu, Cathy. "Retirees Up Against Debt." *USA Today,* March 2, 2007.

Cohen, Roger. "The Filthy Rich Are Different From You and Me." *New York Times,* July 1, 2007.

College Board. "Education Pays: Second Update." *Trends in Higher Education Series 2006.* New York: College Board, 2006.

Coontz, Stephanie. *Marriage, a History: From Obedience to Intimacy or How Love Conquered Marriage.* New York: Viking. 2005.

———. *The Way We Never Were: American Families and the Nostalgia Trap.* New York: Basic Books. 1992.

Correspondents of *The New York Times. Class Matters.* New York: Times Books, 2005.

Creswell, Julie. "Pay Packages Allow Executives to Jump Ship with Less Risk." *New York Times,* December 29, 2006.

Crustsinger, Martin. "Savings Tumble Poses Risk to Boomers." *Washington Post,* February 1, 2007.

Darlin, Damon. "Keep Eyes Fixed on Your Variable-Rate Mortgage." *New York Times,* July 15, 2006.

Day, Kathleen. "Retirement, Squeezed." *Washington Post,* September 17, 2006.

Demos. *Building the American Dream: Asset-Building as a Foundation.* New York: Demos, August 3, 2004.

Demos and Center for Responsible Lending. *The Plastic Safety Net: The Reality Behind Debt in America.* New York: Demos, 2005.

DeNavas-Walt, Carmen, Bernadette D. Proctor, and Cheryl Hill Lee. *Income, Poverty, and Health Insurance Coverage in the United States, 2005.* Washington, D.C.: U.S. Census Bureau, August, 2006.

Di, Zhu Xiao. *"Million-Dollar" Homes and Wealth in the United States.* Cambridge, Mass.: Joint Center for Housing Studies of Harvard University, January 2004.

Downey, Kirstin. "Report: High Cost Loans on the Rise." *Washington Post,* September 9, 2006.

———. "Mortgage-Trapped." *Washington Post,* January 14, 2007.

Draut, Tamara. *Strapped: Why America's 20- and 30-Somethings Can't Get Ahead.* New York: Doubleday, 2006.

Draut, Tamara, and Heather C. McGhee. *Retiring in the Red: The Growth of Debt among Older Americans.* New York: Demos, February 2004.

Draut, Tamara, and Javier Silva. *Generation Broke: The Growth of Debt among Young Americans.* New York: Demos, October, 2004.

Dressel, Holly. "Has Canada Got the Cure?" *AlterNet,* August 29, 2006, www.alternet.org/story/40951/.

Duggan, Lisa, and Richard Kim. "Beyond Gay Marriage." *Nation,* July 18, 2005.

Eckstrom, Kevin. "Student Debt Burdens New Pastors." *Cleveland Plain Dealer,* November 5, 2005.

Economic Policy Institute. *The State of Working America 2006/2007,* "Facts and Figures: Income." Washington, D.C.: Economic Policy Institute, 2006. www.stateofworkingamerica.org/facts.html.

Economic Policy Institute. *The State of Working America 2006/2007,* "Facts and Figures: Wealth." Washington, D.C.: Economic Policy Institute, 2006. www.stateofworkingamerica.org/facts.html.

"Editorial: The Decline and Fall of the Tenured Class." *Writer's Chronicle* 39, no. 4 (February 2007).

Educational Policy Institute. *Global Higher Education Rankings: Affordability and Accessibility in Comparative Perspective 2005.* Washington, D.C.: Educational Policy Institute, 2005.

Ehrenreich, Barbara. *Bait and Switch: The (Futile) Pursuit of the American Dream.* New York: Metropolitan Books, 2005.

———. *Fear of Falling: The Inner Life of the Middle Class*. New York: Harper Perennial, 1990.

———. "A Grubby Business." *Guardian,* July 12, 2003.

———. *Nickel and Dimed: On (Not) Getting By in America*. New York: Henry Holt and Company, 2001.

European Industrial Relations Observatory On-line. "Study Finds That 'Education Pays,'" December 18, 2003, www.eurofound.europa.eu/eiro/2003/12/feature/fio312202f.html.

Expatica. "A Guide to Daycare in France," September 2006, www.expatica.com/actual/article.asp?subchannel_id=27&story_id=3479.

Fabrikant, Geraldine. "U.S.-Style Pay Packages Are All the Rage in Europe." *New York Times,* June 16, 2006.

Florida, Richard. *The Rise of the Creative Class ... And How It's Transforming Work, Leisure, Community and Everyday Life*. New York: Basic Books, 2002.

Follansbee, Joe. "The Disappearing Middle Class." *Seattle,* August 2006, 103–108.

Freudenheim, Milt. "Company Clinics Cut Health Costs." *New York Times,* January 14, 2007.

Frontline. "Secret History of the Credit Card." Originally aired November 23, 2004. www.pbs.org/wgbh/pages/frontline/shows/credit/.

Frontstin, Paul. *Savings Needed to Fund Health Insurance and Health Care Expenses in Retirement*. Washington, D.C.: Employment Benefit Research Institute, Issue Brief no. 295, July, 2006.

Fuhrmans, Vanessa. "Citing Cost Concerns, More Workers Leave Firms' Health Plans." *Wall Street Journal,* August 25, 2006.

Fussell, Paul. *Class: A Painfully Accurate Guide through the American Status System*. New York: Ballantine Books, 1983.

Galbraith, John Kenneth. *The Affluent Society: 40th Anniversary Edition*. New York: Mariner Books, 1998.

Girion, Lisa. "Study Says Individual Insurance Too Costly." *Los Angeles Times,* September 14, 2006.

Gladwell, Malcolm. "The Moral-Hazard Myth." *New Yorker,* August 29, 2005.

Glater, Jonathan D. "Offering Perks, Lenders Court Colleges' Favor." *New York Times,* October 24, 2006.

———. "College Officers Profited by Sale of Lender Stock." *New York Times,* April 5, 2007.

Glater, Jonathan D., and Karen W. Arenson, "Lenders Sought Edge against U.S. in Student Loans." *New York Times,* April 15, 2007.

Glater, Jonathan D., and Alan Finder. "In Tuition Game, Popularity Rises with Price." *New York Times,* December 12, 2006.

Goodnough, Abby. "Housing Slump Pinches States in Pocketbook." *New York Times,* April 8, 2007.

Gosselin, Peter G. "If America Is Richer, Why Are Its Families So Much Less Secure?" *Los Angeles Times,* October 10, 2004.

Greenhouse, Steven, and David Leonhardt. "Real Wages Fail to Match a Rise in Productivity." *New York Times,* August 28, 2006.

Hacker, Andrew. "The Rich and Everyone Else." *New York Review of Books,* May 25, 2006.

Hacker, Jacob S. *The Great Risk Shift: The Assault on American Jobs, Families, Health Care and Retirement and How You Can Fight Back.* New York: Oxford University Press, 2006.

———. *The Great Risk Shift: The New Economic Insecurity and the Decline of the American Dream.* New York: Oxford University Press, 2008.

———. "False Positive: The So-Called Good Economy." *New Republic,* August 16 and 23, 2004, 14–17.

Halberstam, David. *The Fifties.* New York: Villard Books, 1993.

Harden, Blaine. "Numbers Drop for the Married with Children." *Washington Post,* March 4, 2007.

Hennessy-Fiske, Molly. "That Raise Might Take 4 Years to Earn as Well." *Los Angeles Times,* July 24, 2006.

Heymann, Jody, et al. *The Work, Family and Equity Index: Where Does the United States Stand Globally?* Boston: Project on Global Working Families, 2007.

International Education Site. "Higher Education in Finland." www.intstudy.com/articles/nfineduc02.htm.

Jacobs, Jane. *The Death and Life of Great American Cities.* New York: Vintage, 1992.

Johnston, David Cay. "Income Gap Is Widening, Data Shows." *New York Times,* March 29, 2007.

Joint Center for Housing Studies of Harvard University. *The State of the Nation's Housing 2006.* Cambridge, Mass.: Joint Center for Housing Studies of Harvard University, 2006.

Just Landed. "Guide: Switzerland." www.justlanded.com/english/switzerland/tools/just_landed_guide/jobs/old_age_insurance.

Kaiser Family Foundation. *Employer Health Benefits 2006 Annual Survey,* "Summary of Findings." Menlo Park, Calif: Kaiser Family Foundation, 2006.

Kamenetz, Anya. *Generation Debt: Why Now Is a Terrible Time to Be Young.* New York: Riverhead Books, 2006.

Karger, Howard. "America's Exploding Mortgage Crisis Reveals That Home Ownership Isn't Paradise for Everyone." *AlterNet,* June 14, 2007, www.alternet.org/stories/53826/.

Keegan, Robin, et al. *Creative New York.* New York: Center for an Urban Future, December 2005.

Kennedy, David M. *Freedom from Fear: The American People in Depres-*

sion and War, 1929–1945. Oxford and New York: Oxford University Press, 2001.

Kennickell, Arthur, and Janice Shack-Marquez, *Changes in Family Finances from 1983 to 1989: Evidence from the Survey of Consumer Finances*. Washington, D.C.: Federal Reserve Board, 1992.

Knox, Noelle. "Apartment Rents Expected to Rise 5%." *USA Today,* May 29, 2006.

———. "Buyers in More Markets Find Housing Out of Reach." *USA Today,* June 27, 2006.

Kornbluh, Karen, and Jared Bernstein, *Running Faster to Stay in Place: The Growth of Family Work Hours and Incomes*. Washington, D.C.: New American Foundation, June 29, 2005.

Krugman, Paul. "Gold-Plated Indifference." *New York Times,* January 22, 2007.

———. "Wages, Wealth and Politics." *New York Times,* August 18, 2006.

———. "Whining over Discontent." *New York Times,* September 8, 2006.

Kunin, Madeleine May. "A Math Lesson on College Loans." *New York Times,* June 13, 2007.

Labaton, Stephen. "Businesses Seek Protection on Legal Front." *New York Times,* October 29, 2006.

Lederman, Doug. "Social Security and Defaulted Student Loans." *Inside Higher Ed,* December 5, 2005, http://insidehighered.com/news/2005/12/08/supreme.

Leicht, Kevin T., and Scott T. Fitzgerald,. *Postindustrial Peasants: The Illusion of Middle-Class Prosperity*. New York: Worth, 2007.

Leonhardt, David. "A Word of Advice during a Housing Slump: Rent." *New York Times,* April 11, 2007.

Lewis, Michael. *Liar's Poker: Rising through the Wreckage on Wall Street*. New York: Norton, 1989.

Lilly, Scott. *Should Advocates of Domestic Investment Worry about Tax Cuts?* Washington, D.C.: Center for American Progress, July 27, 2006.

Lowenstein, Roger. "A Question of Numbers." *New York Times,* January 16, 2005.

Lyman, Rick. "Census Reports Slight Increase in '05 Incomes." *New York Times,* August 30, 2006.

Mallaby, Sebastian. "Attacking Inequality." *Washington Post,* September 4, 2006.

Manning, Robert. *Credit Card Nation: The Consequences of America's Addiction to Credit*. New York: Basic Books, 2000.

Martin, Joyce A., et al. "Births: Final Data for 2004." *National Vital Statistics Reports* 55, no. 1, September 29, 2006.

Masnick, George S., Zhu Xiao Di, and Eric S. Belsky. *Emerging Cohort Trends in Housing Debt and Home Equity*. Cambridge, Mass.: Joint Center for Housing Studies of Harvard University, January 2005.

Mass Care: The New Massachusetts Healthcare Law. www.masscare.org/.

Mattera, Phil. "Private Health Insurance Is Not the Answer." *AlterNet,* February 23, 2007, www.alternet.org/story/48371/.

Max, Sarah. "Free Land in the Heartland: Small Towns in Kansas, North Dakota, and Other States Are Rolling Out the Red Carpet for Newcomers." *CNN/Money,* December 23, 2004, http://money.cnn.com/2004/ 12/22/real_estate/buying_selling/thursday_freeland/.

McCall, Leslie. *The Inequality Economy: How New Corporate Practices Redistribute Income to the Top.* New York: Demos, December 6, 2004.

McNally, Terrence. "The Mommy Wage Gap." *AlterNet,* June 12, 2006, www.alternet.org/story/36896/.

Meyers, Marcia, and Janet C. Gornik. "The European Model: What We Can Learn from How Other Nations Support Families That Work." *American Prospect,* November 2004. Available at www.thirdworld traveler.com/Europe/European_Model_Families.html.

Milchman, Kari. "The 40-Year-Old Roommate." *New York Press,* January 11, 2007.

Mishel, Lawrence, Jared Bernstein, and Sylvia Allegretto, *The State of Working America 2006/2007.* Ithaca, N.Y.: ILR, 2006.

MSN Real Estate. "The Most Expensive U.S. Cities for Renters." http:// realestate.msn.com/Rentals/Article.aspx?cp-documentid=262175 &vv=450.

National Association of Child Care Resource and Referral Agencies. *Breaking the Piggy Bank: Parents and the High Cost of Childcare.* Arlington, Va.: 2005.

National Coalition on Health Care. "Health Insurance Cost." www.nchc.org/facts/cost.shtml.

National Endowment for the Arts. "Financial Summary," 2005, www.nea.gov/about/05Annual/index.php.

National Priorities Projects. "The War in Iraq Costs." www.national priorities.org/Cost-of-War/Cost-of-War-3.html.

National Women's Law Center. *The Reality of the Workforce: Mothers Are Working Outside the Home.* Washington, D.C.: National Women's Law Center, March 2004.

Nellie Mae. *Undergraduate Students and Credit Cards in 2004: An Analysis of Usage Rates and Trends,* May 2005, www.nelliemae.com/library/ research_12.html.

Newman, Katherine S,, and Victor Tan Chen. *The Missing Class: Portraits of the Near Poor in America.* Boston: Beacon Press, 2007.

Nocera, Joe. "Sallie Mae Offers a Lesson on Cashing In." *New York Times,* April 21, 2007.

Nothaft, Frank E. , and Yan Change. *Refinance and the Accumulation of Home Equity Wealth.* Cambridge, Mass.: Joint Center for Housing Studies of Harvard University, March 2004.

Orenstein, Peggy. *Flux: Women on Sex, Work, Love, Kids, & Life in a Half-Changed World.* New York: Anchor Books, 2000.

Orman, Suze. *The Money Book for the Young, Fabulous, and Broke.* New York: Riverhead Books, 2005.

Osborne, William. "Marketplace of Ideas: But First, the Bill." *ArtsJournal.com,* March 11, 2004.

Palmer, Kimberly. "Student Loan Reform: What to Expect." *U.S. News & World Report,* June 22, 2007.

Patillo-McCoy, Mary. *Black Picket Fences: Privilege and Peril among the Black Middle Class.* Chicago: University of Chicago Press, 2000.

Pear, Robert. "House Passes Children's Health Plan 225–204." *New York Times,* August 2, 2007.

———. "Without Health Benefits, a Good Life Turns Fragile." *New York Times,* March 5, 2007.

Pearce, Diana. *The Self-Sufficiency Standard for the City of New York 2004.* New York: Women's Center for Education and Career Advancement, November 2004.

Perez-Pena, Richard. "A Budget with a Breakthrough in Child Health Care." *New York Times,* April 2, 2007.

Perkins, Broderick. "Nation Doomed to 2 Million Foreclosures." *Realty Times,* June 8, 2007.

Phillips, Kevin. *Boiling Point: Democrats, Republicans, and the Decline of Middle-Class Prosperity.* New York: Random House, 1993.

Piketty, Thomas, and Emmanuel Saez. *Income Inequality in the United States 1913–2002.* November 2004. Available at elsa.berkeley.edu/~saez/piketty-saezOUP04US.pdf.

Pogrebin, Robin. "Arts Organizations Adjust to Decline in Funding." *New York Times,* February 21, 2007.

Porter, Eduardo. "Empty Nest Eggs; Inherit the Wind; There's Little Else Left." *New York Times,* March 26, 2006.

Progress Report. "College Just Got a Lot Costlier." *Wiretap,* July 6, 2006, www.wiretapmag.org/stories/38539.

Putnam, David. *Bowling Alone: The Collapse and Revival of American Community.* New York: Simon & Schuster. 2001.

"Right Time for a Baby: UK vs. France." *Panorama.* Available at http://news.bbc.co.uk/1/hi/programmes/panorama/5079140.stm #france.

Roberts, Sam. "In Surge in Manhattan Toddlers, Rich White Families Lead Way." *New York Times,* March 23, 2007.

———. "To Be Married Means to Be Outnumbered." *New York Times,* October 15, 2006.

Rose, Lacey. "The Most Expensive Rental Markets in America." Forbes.com, August 25, 2006.

Rothschild, Matthew. "Attack of the Mortgage Vultures." AlterNet, April 5, 2007, www.alternet.org/story/50120/.

Ruffenach, Glenn. "Many Households Are at Risk in Their Retirement Finances." *Wall Street Journal,* June 6, 2006.

Samuelson, Robert J. "What's the Biggest Threat to the U.S. Economy?" *Newsweek,* July 9, 2007, 55.

Saulny, Susan. "Rent's Bite Is Big in Kansas, Too." *New York Times,* October 23, 2006.

Saperstein, Guy T. "Medicare for All: The Only Sound Solution to Our Healthcare Crisis." *Alternet,* January 16, 2007, www.alternet.org/story/46550/.

Schemo, Diana Jean. "Congress Passes Overhaul of Student Aid Programs." *New York Times,* September 7, 2007.

———. "Private Loans Deepen a Crisis in Student Debt." *New York Times,* June 10, 2007.

Schlosser, Eric. *Fast Food Nation: The Dark Side of the All-American Meal.* Boston: Houghton Mifflin, 2001.

Schoen, Cathy, et al. *Public Views on Shaping the Future of the U.S. Health System.* New York: Commonwealth Fund, August 2006.

Schwarz, Jonathan. "Politicians' Middle-Class Delusions." *TomPaine.com,* August 21, 2006.

Scott, Janny. "The Apartment Atop the Garage Is Back in Vogue." *New York Times,* December 2, 2006.

———. "Out of College, but Now Living in Urban Dorms." *New York Times,* July 13, 2006.

Scott, Janny, and Randall C. Archibold, "Across Nation, Housing Costs Rise as Burden." *New York Times,* October 3, 2006.

Selvin, Molly. "More Wives Becoming Primary Breadwinners." *Hartford Courant,* February 11, 2007.

Shah, Anup. "World Military Spending." Global Issues. www.globalissues.org/Geopolitics/ArmsTrade/Spending.asp.

Sharkey, Amanda. *Paying for Postsecondary Education: An Issue Brief on College Costs and Financial Aid.* Washington, D.C.: Center for American Progress, March 2005.

Sharoff, Robert. "A Bet That Urban and Affordable Can Coexist." *New York Times,* July 25, 2006.

Shipler, David. *The Working Poor: Invisible in America.* New York: Vintage, 2005.

Shulman, Robin. "Middle Class Enclave in N.Y. Is Sold, and Tenants Worry." *Washington Post,* November 12, 2006.

Silva, Javier. *A House of Cards: Refinancing the American Dream.* New York: Demos, January 2005.

Silva, Javier, and Rebecca Epstein. *Costly Credit: African Americans and Latinos in Debt.* New York: Demos, May 2005.

Singletary, Michelle. "College Costs: A Tough Equation." *Washington Post,* October 29, 2006.

————. "The Racing Savings Gap." *Washington Post,* July 16, 2006.

Southern California Center for Reproductive Medicine. "IVF Cost Information." Available at www.socalfertility.com/ivf-cost-information.html.

Speer, Jack. "Congress Takes Up Complaints on Credit Cards." National Public Radio, July 18, 2007, www.npr.org/templates/story/story.php? storyId=7761629.

Stark, Pete. "Medicare for All." *Nation,* February 6, 2006.

State of California. "Governor's Health Care Proposal." gov.ca.gov/ pdf/press/Governors_HC_Proposal.pdf.

Sturrock, Carrie. "Private Loans Prove Costly for College Students." *San Francisco Chronicle,* October 25, 2006.

Thorndike, Joseph J. "The Price of Civilization: Taxation in Depression and War, 1933–1945." Tax History Project, http://taxhistory.tax.org/ Articles/taxjustice.htm.

Treasury Direct. "The Debt to the Penny and Who Holds It." www.treasurydirect.gov/NP/BPDLogin?application=np.

Uchitelle, Louis. *The Disposable American: Layoffs and Their Consequences.* New York: Knopf, 2006.

United Nations Statistics Division. "Statistics and Indicators on Women and Men, Table 5c: Maternity Leave Benefits." New York: United Nations Statistics Division, 2005. http://unstats.un.org/unsd/ demographic/products/indwm/ww2005/tab5c.htm.

U.S. Census Bureau. "Historical Census of Housing Tables." www.census.gov/hhes/www/housing/census/historic/owner.html.

U.S. Department of Education. "Repaying Your Loans." http://studentaid.ed.gov/PORTALSWebApp/students/english/ repaying.jsp.

U.S. Department of Labor, Bureau of Labor Statistics. "Annual Averages: Unemployment Rate." Available at www.whitehouse.gov/fsbr/ employment.html.

————. Current Population Survey. "(Unadj) Civilian Labor Force Level— Women." http://data.bls.gov/PDQ/servlet/SurveyOutputServlet.

————. "May 2006 National and Occupational Employment and Wage Estimates United States." www.bls.gov/oes/current/oes_nat.htm# b00–0000.

————. "Time Spent in Primary Activities and Percent of the Civilian Population Engaging in Each Activity, Averages Per day by Sex, 2006 Annual Averages." www.bls.gov/news.release/atus.to1.htm.

————. "Tomorrow's Jobs." *Occupational Outlook Handbook.* Washington, D.C.: U.S. Bureau of Labor Statistics, December 20, 2005.

U.S. Department of Labor, Women's Bureau. "Quick Stats 2006." www.dol.gov/wb/stats/main.htm.

U.S. PIRG Higher Education Project. *Paying Back, Not Giving Back: Student Debt's Negative Impact on Public Service Career Opportunities.* Boston: U.S. PIRG Higher Education Project, April 2006.

U.S. Senate Committee on Health, Education, Labor, and Pensions and Senate Democratic Policy Committee. *The College Cost Crunch: A State-by-State Analysis of Rising Tuition and Student Debt.* Washington, D.C.: June 28, 2006.

U.S. Social Security Administration Office of Policy. *International Update: Recent Developments in Foreign Public and Private Pensions.* Baltimore, Md.: August 2005.

Warren, Elizabeth, and Amelia Warren Tyagi. *The Two-Income Trap: Why Middle Class Parents Are Going Broke.* New York: Basic Books, 2003.

Weller, Christian E., and Eli Staub. *Middle Class in Turmoil.* Washington, D.C.: Center for American Progress, 2006.

Wessell, David, and Bob Davis. "Pain From Free Trade Spurs Second Thoughts." *Wall Street Journal,* March 28, 2007.

Wheary, Jennifer. *Measuring the Middle: Assessing What It Takes to Be Middle Class.* New York: Demos, 2005.

White House Economics Statistics Briefing Room. "Income." www.whitehouse.gov/fsbr/income.html.

White House Office of Management and Budget. "The Department of Defense." www.whitehouse.gov/omb/budget/fy2005/defense.html.

World Health Organization. *The World Health Report 2000: Health Systems: Improving Performance.* Geneva, Switzerland: World Health Organization, June 2000.

Zedlin, Cindy, and Mark Rukavina. *Borrowing to Stay Healthy: How Credit Card Debt Is Related to Medical Expenses.* New York: Demos, January 2007.

INDEX